潘复琴◎编著

金融（风险管理方向）

术语英汉对照解读

FINANCIAL TERMS ON RISK MANAGEMENT

AN ENGLISH-CHINESE WORD BOOK

中国出版集团
世界图书出版公司
广州·上海·西安·北京

图书在版编目（CIP）数据

金融（风险管理方向）术语英汉对照解读：英汉对照 / 潘复琴编著 . — 广州：世界图书出版广东有限公司，2016.10（2025.1重印）
ISBN 978-7-5192-1983-3

Ⅰ . ①金… Ⅱ . ①潘… Ⅲ . ①金融风险—风险管理—名词术语—英、汉 Ⅳ . ① F830.9-61

中国版本图书馆 CIP 数据核字（2016）第 255560 号

金融（风险管理方向）术语英汉对照解读

策划编辑 宋 焱
责任编辑 张梦婕
出版发行 世界图书出版广东有限公司
地 址 广州市新港西路大江冲25号
http:// www. gdst. com. cn
印 刷 悦读天下（山东）印务有限公司
规 格 710mm × 1000mm 1/16
印 张 18.5
字 数 300 千
版 次 2016 年 10 月 第 1 版 2025 年 1 月 第 3 次印刷
ISBN 978-7-5192-1983-3/F・0234
定 价 88.00 元

前　　言

过去几年中我担任了学校金融（风险管理方向）专业硕士研究生的英语教学工作。从培养方案中可以清楚看到英语教学的目标不仅仅是培养学生交际型语言应用能力，更重要的是可以读懂金融专业核心英文文献，包括主干课程所使用的原版教材、在国际期刊上公开发表的金融专业论文、世界各大财经媒体推送的金融时事报道等。这些专业英语的应用能力帮助学生迅速了解在全球化背景下金融专业发展的动向、存在的问题和解决的办法，让学生第一时间掌握即时资讯，与同行交流意见，并参与到金融事件中去。在带领学生阅读并理解一些金融专业文献（如金融风险管理方向的核心纲领性文件《巴塞尔新资本协议》）的过程中，我们发现了一些需要面对的问题：a）如何分析结构复杂的长句子？ b）如何辨别一些高频出现的词汇在具体语境中的意义（如："position"在特定上下文中是"地位"的意思还是"头寸"的意思？ c）金融专业英语中常用的一些词汇搭配是什么？ d）了解了常用金融词汇，在口头表达和书面写作时使用这些词汇还是有困难怎么办？这些问题屡屡出现，使我萌生了一个想法：为什么不带领学生们在日常的学习中进行这些专业高频词汇的采集呢？为金融专业的学生和行业从业者提供一个金融术语的英汉指南，集中学习重难点词汇。

感谢中国人民大学国际学院 2014 级和 2015 级金融风险管理专业硕士研究生在过去的两年中积极参与到金融词汇采集的兴趣小组中来，是他们在平日的专业文献阅读和学习中发现并积累了本书中所选的词条，在小组协作中为每一个词条选择在金融领域常用的搭配词组；也要感谢中国人民大学文学院 2015 级汉语国际教育专业硕士研究生谢晶晶、陈圆两位同学，是她们完成了整本书的格式编排和校对工作，涉及每一个词条的音标、字体、字号、颜色等细微之处。本书共收集词条 1 276 个，书中的音标采用英式发音的国际音标（DJ），基于 Daniel Jones 主编的《英语发音字典》（*English Pronouncing Dictionary*, 1972）。

这本书得到了中国人民大学国际学院院级新开课程项目经费的资助，在此向支持本书编写工作的学院领导和同事们表示真诚的感谢。我也要感谢世界图书出版公司的宋焱编辑，她为该书的编辑出版做了大量细致入微的工作。最后感谢我的家人，在我埋头编写这本书的过程中，为我分担了我应尽的家庭责任。本书是教学实践中的一点积累，但学科进步日新月异，行业操作在不同国家和地区各不相同，语言表达也随之变化。读者在学习的过程中要注意这一点。加之编著者本人水平有限，错误与不妥之处在所难免，敬请读者匡谬指正。

潘复琴

2016 年 8 月 15 日

条目安排示例

[①]**admission**[②] [əd'mɪʃ(ə)n] [③]*n.* [④]承认；入场费；进入许可

[⑤]**Phrase(s):** ***admission of debt; admission of proof; admission tax***

◇ [⑥]*Any admission of analytical errors in the risk modeling would damage its reputation in the financial market* . 承认任何风险建模上的分析错误，都将损害其在金融市场的声誉。

◇ *You have to pass the Medical College Admission Test (MCAT) if you want to become a medical student in the USA*. 在美国如果你想上医学院，就必须通过医学院入学考试。

词条示例中每个上标编号的具体解释：

[①]词条按照 26 个英文字母的顺序排列，每一个新的词条从**粗体**单词开始；少量单词只有在与其他单词并存的情况下才能在金融专业中有特定意义，所以这些词条直接以词组的形式出现，如：back money（拖欠款）。

[②]音标基于 Daniel Jones 主编的《英语发音字典》（*English Pronouncing Dictionary*，1972），属于英式发音的国际音标。

[③]词性的描述采用英文缩略形式。*n.* 名词；*v.* 动词；*vt.* 及物动词；*vi.* 不及物动词；*adj.* 形容词；adv. 副词；*PHR.* 词组。

[④]词条中的单词或者词组的中文释义。同一词性下不同的意思使用分号间隔。不同的词性之间也使用分号隔开词性的英文缩略词。

[⑤]词条中出现的单词在金融领域常见的词组搭配，有多个词组时使用分号间隔。

如果词条中首次出现的就是词组，这部分将被省略。

⑧例句部分通常由1—2个中英文例句组成。先出现英文例句，再出现中文翻译。如果例句直接引自参考文献中的书籍，则在中文翻译后面标注上出处，如：7（158）指的是该词条下的该条英文例句出自参考书目中第七本书的第158页。

目　录

A

abatement [ə'beɪtm(ə)nt] *n.* 减少；消除；减轻

Phrase(s): ***abatement of tax; abatement measures***

◇ *Tax abatement program is usually adopted by governments to stimulate investment in new industries.* 政府通常采用纳税减免来刺激对新产业的投资。

above-the-line [ə'bʌvðəl'aɪn] *n.* 线上预算；（资产负债表或损益表上的）账上项目

Phrase(s): ***above-the-line expenditure; above-the-line receipt***

◇ *Teachers in both public and private schools are eligible for a certain amount of above-the-line deductions in the personal income taxing system of the USA. The deduction can be used to cover necessary teaching supplies and expenses.* 在美国的个人所得税征税系统中，公立和私立学校的教师都可以获得一定金额的税前扣减。这笔钱用于支付必要的教学用品和花费。

absolute ['æbsəluːt] *adj.* 绝对的；完全的

Phrase(s): ***absolute value; absolute necessity; absolute limit***

◇ *New college graduates have no absolute value to the employer; they're only worth what they can do for the employer in the future.* 刚毕业的大学生，其能力对雇主来说没有绝对价值，其价值只在于未来工作中可以发挥的能力。

accelerate [ək'seləreɪt] *vt.* 促进；加快

Phrase(s): ***accelerated depreciation***

◇ *Alibaba's new business mode has shaped and accelerated the growth in Chinese consumption*. 阿里巴巴公司新的业务模式塑造了中国消费行业并加速了其发展。

acceptance [ək'sept(ə)ns] *n.* 承兑

Phrase(s): ***acceptance commission; acceptance house***

◇ *Another example is an acceptance, whereby a bank agrees to pay the face value of a bill at maturity*. 另一个例子是承兑，银行同意支付票据到期的面值。

acceptor [ək'septə] *n.* 受票人；承兑人

Phrase(s): ***voucher acceptor***

◇ *The only acceptor of this draft is the Agricultural Bank of China, Shanghai Branch.* 这张汇票的唯一承兑人是中国农业银行上海分行。

accommodation [əkɒmə'deɪʃ(ə)n] *n.* 通融；贷款

Phrase(s): ***accommodation bill; accommodation party***

◇ *Accommodation bill is the bill of exchange where the drawee signing is helping another company (the drawer) to raise a loan.* 通融汇票的受票人签字是帮助另一个公司即出票人筹措贷款。

accounting [ə'kaʊntɪŋ] *n.* 会计学；*v.* 记述；报告

Phrase(s): ***cost accounting; accounting practices; mental accounting***

◇ *The debate revolves around specific accounting techniques*. 这场争论的焦点是具体的会计技术。

◇ *After learning this course, students will develop and enhance skills in financial management and financial accounting statement analysis*. 学完这门课程，学生们的财务管理和财务会计报表分析能力将会增强。

accredited [ə'kredɪtɪd] *v.* 公认的；授信的

Phrase(s): ***accredited investors***

◇ *Up to ten accredited financial institutions will work in partnership to provide student loans to college students from poor background.* 多达 10 家经认可的金融机构将合作为来自贫困家庭的大学生提供学生贷款。

accretion [ə'kri:ʃ(ə)n] *n.* 增值；增长

Phrase(s): ***asset accretion; accretion rate***

◇ *Accretion can occur through a company's internal development or by way of mergers and acquisitions*. 通过公司内部增长或者兼并与收购方式，公司价值可以增值。

◇ *Security and a steady accretion of job opportunities will help people in Europe walk out of the shadow of "Brexit"*. 安全保障和稳步增长的就业机会将会帮助欧洲人民走出英国“脱欧”的负面影响。

accrual [ə'kru:əl] *n.* 应计项目；权责发生制

Phrase(s): ***accrual basis; accrual basis accounting***

◇ *In order to know the financial health of a company, the correlation between the cash flow from operations and the accounting accruals must be closely watched.* 为了了解公司的财务健康状况，就必须密切关注经营活动中的现金流量和会计应计项目之间的相关性。

accrued [ə'krʊd] *adj.* [会计] 应计的；增值的；权责已发生的

Phrase(s): ***accrued wages; accrued taxes; accrued item***

◇ *The main current liabilities are accounts payable and accrued expenses*. 主要的流动负债是应付账款和应计费用。

◇ *The calculation of accrued interest differs slightly between Treasury bonds and corporate bonds*. 国债和公司债券在应计利息的计算上略有不同。

accumulated [ə'kjʊ:mjuˌleɪtɪd] *adj.* 累积的；累计的；达到

Phrase(s): ***accumulated profit; accumulated reserve***

◇ *The accumulated service years of a pension plan participant have an important relation with his(her) retirement income.* 退休计划参与者的累积服务年限与他（她）的退休收入有着重要的关系。

acquisition [ˌækwɪ'zɪʃ(ə)n] *n.* 收购；获得

Phrase(s): ***vertical acquisition; stock acquisition***

◇ *The acquisition helped BCCI make its initial entrance into the US market*. 那项并购帮助国际商业信贷银行首次跻身美国市场。

◇ *Firms that are poorly managed are more attractive as acquisitions than well-managed firms because a greater profit potential exists*. 由于更大的潜在收益的存在，管理不良的公司会比管理良好的公司有更大的收购吸引力。

active ['æktɪv] *adj.* 积极的；有效的

Phrase(s): ***active assets; active capital***

◇ Is that pledge still active? 这承诺仍然有效么？ 7（590）

adjustable [ə'dʒʌstəbl] *adj.* 可调整的

Phrase(s): *adjustable-rate mortgages(ARMs)*

◇ *Higher interest rates put payment pressure on homeowners who had taken out adjustable-rate mortgages.* 更高的利率给已经采用可调整利率抵押贷款的房主带来支付压力。7（19）

adjustment [ə'dʒʌs(t)m(ə)nt] *n.* 调整；修订；理算（保险）

Phrase(s): *adjustment of loss; adjustment mechanism*

◇ *The recent price adjustment of gold jewelry is due to the rise of the international gold price.* 近期黄金首饰的价格调整是由于国际黄金价格的上涨。

administration [ədmɪnɪ'streɪʃ(ə)n] *n.* 管理；实行

Phrase(s): *administration expenses; administration in bankruptcy*

◇ *Hedge fund administration is part of a burgeoning cottage industry that attempts to make funds more transparent to investors.* 对冲基金行政管理服务是一个正在蓬勃发展的作坊式行业的组成部分，目的是增加基金对投资者的透明度。

◇ *The new mayor entered office promising to run a clean administration and to regain the city government's reputation.* 新市长上任承诺廉洁管理，重建市政府声誉。

admission [əd'mɪʃ(ə)n] *n.* 承认；入场费；进入许可

Phrase(s): *admission of debt; admission of proof; admission tax*

◇ *Any admission of analytical errors in the risk modeling would damage its reputation in the financial market.* 承认任何风险建模上的分析错误，都将损害其在金融市场的声誉。

◇ *You have to pass the Medical College Admission Test (MCAT) if you want to become a medical student in the USA.* 在美国如果你想上医学院，就必须通过医学院入学考试。

advance [əd'vɑːns]] *vt.* 预付；前进；*n.* 增长；借款

Phrase(s): *advance account; advance compensation; advance from shareholder*

◇ *All the participants need to pay in advance before the seminar begins.* 所有研讨会参加者都必须提前付款。

adverse ['ædvɜːs] *adj.* 不利的；相反的；敌对的

Phrase(s): ***adverse balance; adverse exchange***

◇ *The decline of prime-age workforce in the job market has a long-term adverse effect on a country's economy.* 就业市场上壮年劳动力的下降对一个国家的经济产生了长期的不利影响。

◇ *Some investors complained that the current market structure caused the "adverse selection" problem, diverting trading to dark venues during stable period.* 一些投资者抱怨说，目前的市场结构带来“逆向选择”的问题，在市场平稳期使交易转向了“黑池”。

advice [əd'vaɪs] *n.* 建议；忠告；劝告；通知

Phrase(s): ***advice for collection; advice of drawing; advice of payment***

◇ *You might want some investment advice before putting money into a new project.* 在投资一个新的工程项目之前，你可能会想要一些投资建议。

advisory [æd'vaɪz(ə)rɪ] *adj.* 顾问的；提供咨询的

Phrase(s): ***Advisory Committee; Basel Committee***

◇ *Mr. Brown chairs an advisory board which serves a troubled investment firm.* 布朗先生担任一个咨询委员会主席，该委员会服务于一家陷入困境的投资公司。

◇ *Different advisory committees represent different interest groups.* 不同的咨询委员会代表不同的利益集团。

affiliate [ə'fɪlɪeɪt] *v.* 使紧密联系；*n.* 附属企业

Phrase(s): ***affiliate with; affiliate to***

◇ *Many small newspapers are affiliated with the principal Television stations.* 许多小型报纸隶属于主要的电视台。

◇ *All rights of this software are reserved by Oracle and/or its affiliates.* 甲骨文公司和 / 或其附属机构保留该软件的所有权利。

after-acquired ['ɑːftəə'kwaɪəd] *n.* 事后取得

Phrase(s): ***after-acquired property***

◇ *"After-acquired property" is property which is acquired by a borrower after a security agreement is signed or by a debtor after a bankruptcy case is commenced.* 事后取得财产是指借款人在签署安全协议后，或者债务人在破产程序开始后取得的财产。

after-tax ['ɑːftətæks] *adj.* 税后的

Phrase(s): *after-tax cost of debt*

◇ *The after-tax income can increase by enterprises income increase. It can also be caused by a tax reduction.* 税后收益的增加可以是由企业收入增加引起的，也可以是由企业税款减少带来的。

◇ *Our goal is to use the after-tax net profits to advance and support staff training and products' innovation.* 我们的目标是使用税后净利润推动和支持员工培训和产品创新。

agency ['eɪdʒ(ə)nsɪ] *n.* 代理；机构

Phrase(s): *agency agreement; agency expenses; agency fee*

◇ *The agency system is not working well.* 代理体制运营不佳。

◇ *The medicine which was prescribed to Ms Sharapova was banned by the World Anti-Doping Agency only at the start of the year.* 开给莎拉波娃女士的这个处方药是今年年初才被世界反兴奋剂组织列为禁药的。

agent ['eɪdʒ(ə)nt] *n.* 代理人；代理商；*adj.* 代理的

Phrase(s): *sales agent; sole agent; general agent*

◇ *Hedge fund managers act as agents for investors.* 对冲基金经理扮演投资者的代理人角色。

◇ *The best residential selling agent award went to Sweethome in LA this year.* 来自洛杉矶的"甜蜜之家"获得了本年度的最佳住宅销售代理奖。

aggregate ['ægrɪgət] *n.* 总计；总数；总体数字

Phrase(s): *aggregate assets and liabilities; aggregate gross position; aggregate performance*

◇ *This table shows the aggregate amounts of dividends and earnings of this company in the years from 1996 to 2000.* 此表显示该公司在 1996 年到 2000 年间分红和收益的总金额。

aggregation [ˌægrɪ'geɪʃən] *n.* 聚集；集聚

Phrase(s): *aggregation of property*

◇ *The use of growth as a basis for planning is just a reflection of the very high level of aggregation used in the planning process.* 将增长作为规划的基础是一种在规划过程中

聚集了很高水平的思考。

◇ *The future does not belong entirely to a world of data aggregation; it still needs human interactions and fictional stories.* 未来世界并不会完全被海量的数据所充斥，它依然需要人际交往和虚幻故事。

agreement [ə'griːm(ə)nt] *n.* 协议；协定；合同书

Phrase(s): ***repurchase agreements; swap agreement***

◇ *Many financial instruments and agreements have features that convey implicit or explicit options to one or more parties.* 许多金融工具和协议都有向一个或多个缔约方传递隐含或明确选择的功能。

◇ *The government may seek to delay payments due later this year, yet it will require the agreement of all creditors.* 该政府可能延迟支付今年晚些时候将到期的款项，但需要获得全部债权人的同意。

agricultural [ægrɪ'kʌltʃərəl] *adj.* 农业的

Phrase(s): ***Agricultural Bank of China***

◇ *Financial - services employees and seasonal agricultural workers coming from other European countries are welcomed by UK now.* 英国目前欢迎来自欧洲其他国家的金融服务从业人员和季节性农业工人。

algorithm ['ælgərɪð(ə)m] *n.* 算法；运算法则

Phrase(s): ***ranking algorithm; approximation algorithm; genetic algorithm***

◇ *Virtual keyboard (VK) uses sophisticated artificial intelligence algorithms that allow the user to format the document.* 虚拟键盘（VK）使用复杂的人工智能算法，允许用户设计文件版面。

alienation [eɪlɪə'neɪʃ(ə)n] *n.* 让渡；转让

Phrase(s): ***growing alienation***

◇ *In today's ever-changing technology, man and nature is in growing alienation, which is contrary to the human nature.* 在科技日新月异的今天，人与自然日益疏远，这违背了人的自然本性。

allocation [ælə'keɪʃ(ə)n] *n.* 配给；分配

Phrase(s): ***asset allocation; pricing and allocations***

◇ *The allocation of family resources triggered quarrels and fights.* 家产如何分配引发纷争。

◇ *What portfolio allocation would you choose?* 你会选择哪种资产组合配置？

allotment [ə'lɒtm(ə)nt] *n.* 分配；配股

Phrase(s): ***resource allotment; property allotment; allotment of shares***

◇ *Responsibility allotment has its foundation and rules to abide by.* 责任分配有其依据和原则。

◇ *The allotment of profits will be announced next Monday.* 利润分配将于下星期一公布。

allowable [ə'laʊəbl] *adj.* 可获宽免；免税的

Phrase(s): ***allowable business loss; allowable expenses***

◇ *Self-employed people in the USA usually have tax-allowable expenses, such as the cost of equipment and the rent of working place.* 美国的个体经营者通常有免税的费用，如设备的成本和工作地点的租金等。

allowance [ə'laʊəns] *n.* 津贴；零用；允许；限额

Phrase(s): ***allowance for debts; allowance for depreciation by wear and tear***

◇ *The benefits for the marketing director position in this company include a relocation allowance and three-week annual leave.* 该公司市场总监职位的福利包括搬迁津贴和三周的年休假。

alternate ['ɔːltəneɪt] *adj.* 代替的；交替的

Phrase(s): ***alternate trustee***

◇ *But let me offer up an alternate theory: VCs are trying to win deals by appealing to entrepreneurial ego.* 但我有不同的看法：风险投资人正在试图通过迎合创业虚荣心，赢得交易。

alternative [ɔːl'tɜːnətɪv] *adj.* 替代的；备选的

Phrase(s): ***alternative investment market (AIM); alternative method***

◇ *Effective advertisements aim to persuade consumers that their brands are the best alternative to other existing products in the market.* 效果好的广告旨在让消费者相信：它们的品牌是市场上现存同类产品最好的替代品。

◇ *Given that the interest rate in similar alternative investments is 10 percent.* 给定类似的替代投资的利率是 10%。

amalgamation [əmælgə'meɪʃ(ə)n] *n.* 合并；混合

Phrase(s): ***amalgamation and pagination; amalgamation of character***

◇ *As a business law practitioner, it's important to know the differences among amalgamations, mergers and consolidations.* 作为商法的从业人员，了解合并、兼并和整合的区别是至关重要的。

ambit ['æmbɪt] *n.* 范围；界限

Phrase(s): ***ambit of charges***

◇ *This fund specifically supports non-profit initiatives within the ambit of elementary education in Sub-Saharan countries.* 本基金特别支持在撒哈拉沙漠以南的国家开展非营利性质的基础教育方案

amortization [əˌmɔːtaɪ'zeɪʃən] *n.* 摊销

Phrase(s): ***depreciation and amortization; loan amortization***

◇ *Analysis by the sinking - fund procedure is also known as "amortization with interest on first cost".* 以偿债基金步骤进行分析，也就是"对初始成本进行带利息分期偿还"。

◇ *The reason is that depreciation and amortization and noncash expenses have been deducted out.* 原因是折旧摊销和非现金费用已经被扣除了。

amount [ə'maʊnt] *n.* 数量；总额；总数

Phrase(s): ***amount due from banks; amount payable; amount receivable***

◇ *It must be a huge amount of money needed to bring the poor in the world up to the poverty line every year.* 每年把世界贫困人口拉到贫困线以上一定需要巨大的资金量。

analysis [ə'nælɪsɪs] *n.* 分析；分解；验定

Phrase(s): ***factor analysis; discriminate analysis; survival analysis***

◇ *In addition, this analysis assumes that the quantity transacted is within normal market sizes.* 此外，这项分析假设交易数量在正常市场规模内。

ancillary [æn'sɪlərɪ] *adj.* 附属的；补充的

Phrase(s): ***ancillary risk; ancillary system***

◇ *Financial entities may also be involved in other similar activities that are ancillary to the business of banking*. 金融企业也可以从事其他与银行业相关的类似业务。

◇ *This high-margin business is crucial to banks' earnings and a vital source of direct and ancillary jobs*. 这个高利润业务对银行收益至关重要，同时也是直接和辅助岗位的重要来源。

annual ['ænjʊəl] *adj*. 年度的；每年的

Phrase(s): ***annual account; annual balance; annual growth rate; annual report***

◇ *The European Community started out with six members, four languages, 177million people and $1. 6 trillion in annual output*. 欧共体最初包括六个成员国、四种语言、1. 77 亿人口和 1. 6 兆美元的年产值。

◇ *As the world's largest auto market, China is predicted to have slower annual sales growth in coming years*. 作为全球最大的汽车市场，预计中国在未来几年年销售增长速度将放缓。

anticipated [æn'tɪsəˌpeɪtɪd] *adj*. 预期的；期望的

Phrase(s): ***anticipated expenditure; anticipated net profit; anticipated revenue***

◇ *The FAO attributed the anticipated cost hikes largely to frequent extreme weather*. 联合国粮农组织将预期的成本提升主要归因于频发极端气候的影响。

◇ *Economic recession and high inflation prompted economic reforms*. 经济衰退和高通货膨胀促使经济改革的发生。

antitrust [æntɪ'trʌst] *adj*. 反垄断的；反托拉斯的

Phrase(s): ***antitrust law***

◇ *The jury found that the oil company had violated antitrust laws*. 陪审团裁决这家石油公司触犯了反垄断法。7（68）

apparent [ə'pær(ə)nt] *adj*. 显然的；表面的

Phrase(s): ***apparent deficit; apparent financial solvency***

◇ *The apparent recklessness could encourage consumers to spend rather than save*. 这明显的轻率举措可能会鼓励消费者消费而不是储蓄。

◇ *It takes many years before the success or failure of a financial tip becomes apparent*. 一个理财建议是成功还是失败需要很多年才能看清。

appointed [ə'pɒɪntɪd] *adj.* 指定的；约定的

Phrase(s): ***appointed actuary; appointed auditor; appointed trustee***

◇ *The court-appointed mediator announced that the Argentina government had reached an agreement with the major creditors on the issue of loan payment.* 法庭指定的调解人宣布，阿根廷政府已与主要债权人在贷款支付问题上达成协议。

appraisal [ə'preɪz(ə)l] *n.* 评价；估量

Phrase(s): ***scientific appraisal; calm appraisal***

◇ *Shareholders of the acquired company have appraisal rights to ask the acquiring company to buy their shares at a fair value.* 被收购公司的股东有估量权，即要求收购公司以合理的价格购买他们持有的股票。

◇ *Based on a recent appraisal, the company believes it could sell the land for $900 000 on an aftertax basis.* 根据最近的一项评价，该公司确信它能以税后基础价格 90 万美元卖出这块土地。

appreciation [əpriːʃɪ'eɪʃ(ə)n] *n.* 增值；升值

Phrase(s): ***capital appreciation return; stock appreciation; capital appreciation***

◇ *You have to take capital appreciation of the property into account.* 你得将那个房产的资本增值考虑进来。

appropriation [əˌprəʊprɪ'eɪʃ(ə)n] *n.* 拨款；批准支出

Phrase(s): ***appropriation of land; congress for appropriation***

◇ *Special appropriation allocated by the government to an enterprise shall be accounted for as government investment unless otherwise stipulated.* 国家拨给企业的专项拨款，除另有规定者外，应当作为国家投资入账。

approved [ə'pruːvd] *adj.* 经核准的；被批准的

Phrase(s): ***approved assets; approved basket stock; approved charitable institution; approvedsubordinated loan***

◇ *Any rule has to be approved by the United States Securities and Exchange Commission.* 任何条例都必须经过美国证券交易委员会的审批。7（984）

arbitrage ['ɑːbɪtrɪʒ] *n.* 套利

Phrase(s): ***market arbitrage; triangular arbitrage***

◇ *Perhaps the most basic principle of capital market theory is that equilibrium market prices are rational in that they rule out arbitrage opportunities.* 资本市场的基本原则是，均衡市场价格是理性的，因为它们排除了套利机制。

◇ *If its risk premium were not zero, you could earn arbitrage profits.* 如果风险溢价不为零，就可以赚取套利利润。7（324）

arrangement [ə'reɪn(d)ʒm(ə)nt] *n.* 安排；约定

Phrase(s): ***arrangement fee***

◇ *Japanese digital wallets can be loaded with cash at stores or through an arrangement with a credit card company.* 日本的数字钱包可在商店或通过信用卡公司的安排进行充值。

◇ *There are many different kinds of sinking fund arrangements; some sinking funds start about 10 years after the initial issuance.* 偿债基金的约定有很多种，其中一些首次发行 10 年以后才启用。

arrears [ə'rɪəz] *n.* 欠款

Phrase(s): ***arrears of pay; arrears of revenue***

◇ *There are 300 000 households who are more than six months in arrears with their mortgages.* 拖欠抵押贷款超过 6 个月的家庭有 30 万户。7（469）

assessable [ə'sesəbl] *adj.* 可估价的；可征收的

Phrase(s): ***assessable income; assessable loss; assessable profit***

◇ *Assessable profit is an important measure used to determine an individual's taxable income in many countries.* 在很多国家，应课税利润都是评估个人应税收入的重要措施。

assessment [ə'sesmənt] *n.* 估价；评估

Phrase(s): ***dispassionate assessment; credit assessment***

◇ *Each company's annual report must have an assessment of the company's internal control structure and financial reporting.* 每个公司的年报都必须包含公司内部管控结构和财务报告的评估。

◇ *One alternative will be to measure credit risk in a standardized manner, supported by external credit assessments.* 一种方法是根据外部评级结果，以标准化处理方式计量信用风险。

asset ['æset] *n.* 资产

Phrase(s): ***asset allocation; asset management; financial asset***

◇ *Financial assets determine how the ownership of real assets is distributed among investors.* 金融资产决定如何在投资者之间分配资产的所有权。

◇ *Bankers'acceptances are considered very safe assets.* 银行承兑券被认为是非常安全的资产。7（31）

assignment [ə'saɪnm(ə)nt] *n.* 分配；任务

Phrase(s): ***assignment method***

◇ *Written rating definitions must be clear and detailed enough to allow third parties to understand the assignment of ratings.* 评级的书面定义必须足够清晰、详细，以便使第三方能理解如何评级。

associate [ə'səʊʃɪeɪt] *n.* 助理；合伙人；*v.* 联系；关联

Phrase(s): ***associate director***

◇ *Banks may associate or map their internal grades to the scale used by an external credit assessment institution or similar institution.* 银行可以将自己的内部评级与外部信用评估机构或类似机构的评级联系（或映射）起来。

◇ *In this case, an increase in inventory is associated with decreasing cash flow.* 在这种情况下，投资的增长总是伴随着现金流的减少。6（29）

assurance [ə'ʃʊər(ə)ns] *n.* 担保；保证

Phrase(s): ***assurance of interest***

◇ *Due diligence and legal liability for the proceeds give investors assurance.*（银行）对收益的尽职调查和法律责任让投资者放心。

asymmetric [ˌæsɪ'metrɪk] *adj.* 不对称的

Phrase(s): ***asymmetric information***

◇ *Asymmetric information leads to agency risk.* 信息不对称导致代理风险。

attributable [ə'trɪbjʊtəbl] *adj.* 可归因于的；由什么引起的

Phrase(s): ***attributable profit; attributable share value***

◇ *The bank must maintain a continuous monitoring process that is appropriate for the specific exposures (either immediate or contingent) attributable to the collateral to be utilised as a risk mitigant.* 对于抵押品用来作为风险缓释工具的特定贷款，银行必须建立连续的（及时的或者是偶然的）监控过程。

auction ['ɔːkʃ(ə)n] *vt.* 拍卖；竞卖；*n.* 拍卖

Phrase(s): ***auction hunters; foreclosure auction; auction fraud; open auction***

◇ *Cash settlement can be conducted through an auction, which defines the recovery rate.* 现金结算可以通过拍卖来进行，以此得出回收率。

◇ *The company is currently competing in an auction to win the right to drill for crude oil on a large piece of land in Russia.* 该公司目前正在一个拍卖会上参与竞争，以期获得在俄罗斯一块大面积土地上钻取原油的权利。

audit ['ɔːdɪt] *n.* 审计；查账

Phrase(s): ***audit trail; audit commission***

◇ *New audit guidelines and ethical standards should be established in response to corporate scandals at companies such as Enron.* 为应对诸如安然公司这样的丑闻，必须建立新的审计准则和道德标准。

◇ *This makes it critical that the company's audit committee, comprised of independent directors, take the lead on the current inquiry.* 这使得审计委员会（由独立董事组成）在当前调查中所起的主导作用变得很关键。7（667）

authorization [ɔːθəraɪ'zeɪʃ(ə)n] *n.* 授权；批准

Phrase(s): ***authorization by direction; authorization by instruction; authorization by warrant***

◇ *Authentication and authorization are two important security issues in the developing process of online payment system.* 在线支付系统开发过程中，认证和授权是两大安全要点。

authorized ['ɔːθəraɪzd] *adj.* 权威认可的；审定的；经授权的

Phrase(s): ***authorized capital; authorized fund; authorized representative***

◇ *The supervisory committee should be provided with a list of personnel authorized to trade, as well as a list of allowed transactions.* 监督委员会应得到授权交易的人员名单，以及允许交易的清单。

◇ *Dispute can happen if the contract is not properly authorized or executed.* 如果合同没有经过适当的授权或没有执行，则可能发生争议。

automated ['ɔːtəˌmeɪtɪd] *adj.* 自动化的

Phrase(s): *automated quotation system*

◇ *NASDAQ was originally an acronym for the National Association of Securities Dealers Automated Quotations system.* “纳斯达克”起初是美国“全国证券交易商协会自动报价系统”首字母的缩略式。

autoregressive [ɔːtəʊ'rɪgresɪv] *n.* 自回归

Phrase(s): *autoregressive process; autoregressive analysis*

◇*Evaluation could be carried out by means of Generalized Autoregressive Conditional Heteroscedasticity (GARCH), which could make hedge ratio vary with time.* 评估可采用广义自回归条件异方差（GARCH 模型），使套期保值率随时间变化。

◇ *The autoregressive model is applied to the monthly runoff probability forecast.* 把自回归模型用于月径流概率预报中。5（207）

average ['æv(ə)rɪdʒ] *n.* 平均的；平常的

Phrase(s): *average cost; average daily turnover; average propensity to save*

◇ *We are going to compare the average return on the stock market with the returns on other securities.* 我们打算将股票市场的平均收益和其他证券的收益进行比较。

B

backed [bækt] *adj.* 有背的；有财力支持的；*v.* 支持

Phrase(s): ***asset-backed security; mortgage-backed securities.***

◇ *Securitisation exposures can include but are not restricted to the following: asset-backed securities, mortgage-backed securities, credit enhancements, liquidity facilities, etc.* 资产证券化风险暴露包括（但不局限于）以下方面：资产支持型证券、住房抵押贷款支持型证券、信用提升和提供流动性等等。

backfire [bæk'faɪə] *v.* 适得其反；*n.* 回火

Phrase(s): ***operation backfire***

◇*Second, being too close to front office activities can backfire.* 其次，(风险管理部门)与前台联系过于紧密，可能会造成事与愿违的结果。7（33）

background ['bækgraʊnd] *n.* （画等的）背景；底色；背景资料；配乐

Phrase(s): ***accounting background; audit background***

◇ *Review monthly property manager financial reporting, which is done by in-house staff having accounting and audit backgrounds.* 复核月度资产管理财务报告，这是由具有会计和审计背景的内部工作人员所完成的。13（135）

back money [bæk 'mʌnɪ] *PHR.* 拖欠款

◇ *It is structured around the ability of the borrower to draw and pay back money based on its needs.* 这是基于借款者借款的需求和支付欠款的能力所设计的。

backstop ['bækstɒp] *n.* 挡球网；支撑物

Phrase(s): ***backstop tone***

◇ *The concept behind LoCs is that they provide a financial backstop.* 信用证的意义在于它可以提供融资支持。

backward shift operator ['bækwəd ʃɪft 'ɒpəreɪtə] *PHR.* 后向移位算子

◇ *The lag operator is also called backward shift operator and sometimes denoted by B.* 滞后算子也被称为后向移位算子，有时记为 B。5（202）

backward stepwise method ['bækwəd 'stepwaɪz 'meθəd] *PHR.* 向后逐步法

◇ *There are two different methodologies for stepwise regression, the backward stepwise method and backward removal method. Both methods start with a rich model that includes all regressors specified to be included in the design for the analysis.* 逐步回归有两种方法，即向后逐步法和向后剔除法。这两种方法都是从一个包含所有回归因子的模型开始，这些回归因子是在设计回归分析时确定的。5（114）

bad [bæd] *adj.* 坏的；不好的；不良的

Phrase(s): ***bad debt; bad year***

◇ *The bank must have the ability to assess the characteristics of the receivables pool, including history of the seller's arrears, bad debts, and bad debt allowances.* 银行必须有能力评估应收账款池的特征，包括销售方欠款、坏账和坏账拨备的历史。

bailout ['beɪlaʊt] *n.* 紧急救助；跳伞

Phrase(s): ***government bailout; bailout loans***

◇ *Greece's four big banks are in their best shape now, receiving their third bailout in as many years.* 希腊四大银行当前处于最佳状态，多年来第三次获得了紧急救助。

balance ['bæl(ə)ns] *n.* 平衡；余额

Phrase(s): ***balance sheet;balance of payments; balance of trade***

◇ *Revolving exposures are defined as those where customers' outstanding balances are permitted to fluctuate based on their decisions to borrow and repay, up to a limit established by the bank.* 循环贷款被定义为在银行建立的限额下，根据客户借款和偿还的情况，允许客户贷款余额上下波动。

◇ *It has a balance sheet consisting of assets and liabilities.* 它的资产负债表包括资

产和负债项目。13（65）

balance sheet ['bæl(ə)ns ʃiːt] *PHR.* 资产负债表

◇ *The balance sheet is an accountant's snapshot of a firm's accounting value on a particular date, as though the firm stood momentarily still.* 资产负债表是一张在特定日期内公司会计价值的快照，就好像公司暂时停止运作。6（20）

band [bænd] *n.* 带；价值；*vt.* （将价格、收入等）划分档次；把……联合起来；*vt. & vi.* 结合起来；伙同；*vi.* 聚集；联合（起来）（通常与 together 连用）

Phrase(s): *structuring band*

◇ *Measures of the exposure will be based on the replacement cost plus potential future exposure add-ons across the different product types and maturity bands.* 此类风险暴露将根据重置成本加上不同产品类别和不同期限潜在暴露附加值来计算。

bank [bæŋk] *n.* 银行

Phrase(s): *Bank of China; the Agricultural Bank of China*

◇ *The cost of insurance against bank default surges in economic recession times.* 对银行违约的保险成本在经济衰退时期呈现出激增态势。

banker ['bæŋkə] *n.* 银行家；庄家；银行主；银行经理

Phrase(s): *investment bankers*

◇ *The second way to maximize proceeds in an asset securitization is for the investment banker to create more cost-efficient structures.* 使资产证券化收益最大化的第二步，对于投资银行家而言，是创造更多具有成本效益的结构。

banking ['bæŋkɪŋ] *n.* 银行业；银行业务

Phrase(s): *union banking corporation*

◇ *Under the market-based approach, institutions are permitted to calculate the minimum capital requirements for their banking book equity holdings using a simple risk weight method or an internal models method.* 根据市场法规定，允许银行采用简单的风险权重法或内部模型法，对银行账户的股权持有计算最低资本要求。

banking system ['bæŋkɪŋ 'sɪstəm] *PHR.* 银行系统

◇ *Availability delay refers to the time required to clear a check through the banking system.* 可用性延迟指的是在一个银行系统中兑换支票所需要的时间。

Bank of America [bæŋk (ə)v ə'merɪkə] *n.* 美洲银行

◇ *In trade-intensive American industries, Bank of America Merrill Lynch estimates that output was growing at an annual rate of just 0. 1% by the end of 2015.* 美国银行——美林证券估计截至 2015 年末，美国贸易密集型产业的年产量增幅仅达到 0. 1%。

bank risk [bæŋk rɪsk] *PHR.* 银行风险

◇ *The case not only demonstrated the concern that bank risk could be masked, but it also highlighted the concerns with subprime lending.* 该案例不仅表明银行风险可能会被掩盖，同时也强调了次级贷款的风险。13（302）

bankruptcy ['bæŋkrʌptsɪ] *n.* 破产；倒闭；彻底失败

Phrase(s): ***corporate bankruptcy***

◇ *Credit risk is the risk that the obligor will default by either refusing to pay or declaring bankruptcy.* 信用风险指的是债务人会拒绝偿还贷款或者宣布破产（无力偿还）的风险。13（70）

bankruptcy proceeding ['bæŋkrʌptsɪ prəʊ'siːdɪŋ] *PHR.* 破产法律程序

◇ *When the firm defaults, only the clearinghouse is involved in the bankruptcy proceedings.* 当一家公司违约时，只有清算所可以参与到破产程序中。

barbell ['bɑːbel] *n.* 杠铃

Phrase(s): ***barbell portfolio; barbell bond***

◇ *Such portfolio consisting of very short and very long maturities is called a barbell portfolio.* 超短期和超长期证券组合被称为杠铃式投资组合。

Barclays [bɑː'kleɪz] *n.* 巴克莱银行（英国）

◇ *Barclays said itwould leave Africa and focus on its core banking activities in Britain and America aftera century's business on the continent.* 在非洲大陆开展业务一个多世纪后，巴克莱宣布将离开非洲，重点发展在英国和美国的核心银行业务。

bargain ['bɑːgɪn] *n.* 交易；契约；协定；特价商品；便宜货

Phrase(s): ***drive a hard bargain; keep one's side of the bargain***

◇ *Top managers in financial institutions are often given options to buy stock at a bargain price.* 金融机构的高层管理者通常享有以便宜的价格购买股票的权利。

base [beɪs] *n.* 基础；根据；基数；*vt.* 基于；把……建立在

Phrase(s): ***base on***

◇ *The seller's financial condition and the trend of its customer base should be taken into consideration when specifying all material elements of the receivables purchase programme.* 在规定购入应收账款方案中所有重要因素时，应当考虑销售方的财务状况和客户变化趋势。

Basel ['bɑːzəl] *n.* 巴塞尔

Phrase(s): ***the Basel Convention; Basel Capital Accord***

◇ *Internal Ratings-Based (IRB) approach is the core of the New Basel Accord.* 内部评级法是巴塞尔新资本协议的核心。

Basel Committee ['bɑːzəl kə'mɪtɪ] *n.* 巴塞尔委员会

◇ *Basel Committee on Banking Supervision develops policies and standards for multinational cooperation on banking supervisory matters.* 巴塞尔银行监管委员会为多国在银行监管事务方面的合作制定政策措施和标准。

baseline ['beɪslaɪn] *n.* 基线；网球场的底线；棒球场的垒线

Phrase(s): ***baseline expenditure***

◇ *The company's persistent efforts to reduce energy consumption and carbon footprint helped it regain its reputation as an environment-friendly leader.* 这家公司在节能减排方面持续不懈的努力帮助其重建环保领跑者的声誉。

base year [beɪs jɪə] *PHR.* 基年

◇ *Common-base year financial statements are constructed by dividing the current year account value by the base year account value.* 常用基年财务报表是用当年账户价值除以基年账户价值构建形成的。6（81）

basic ['beɪsɪk] *adj.* 基本的；首要的；*n.* 基础；基本；要素

Phrase(s): ***the basics of***

◇ *This chapter gives the basics about interest rate derivatives.* 这个章节介绍了利率衍生品的基本信息。

◇ *You can use the same basic formula for commercial banking.* 你可以使用相同的基本计算公式来处理商业银行业务。

basically ['beɪsɪk(ə)lɪ] adv. 主要地；从根本上说；基本；基本上；总的说来

◇ *The current solution to immigrant problem is basically not to allow anyone to come in, except for a few urgently needed professionals.* 当前解决移民问题的办法基本上就是不让任何人进来，除了少量急需的专业人员。

basis ['beɪsɪs] *n.* 基础；主要成分；基准；基本原则

Phrase(s): ***on the basis of***

◇ *The premium is normally settled on a quarterly basis but typically accrues on a daily basis.* 正常情况下，溢价是以季度为基础计算的，但通常会每日累积。13（318）

basket ['bɑːskɪt] *n.* 一篮子

Phrase(s): ***basket default swaps***

◇ *Basket default swaps,like all portfolio trades,are structured with the parties taking a view on the inherent correlation in the basket.* 正如所有的投资组合交易，一篮子违约互换是在篮子内部各方认同相互关联的基础上构造的。13（313）

◇ *A basket option is a type of financial derivative, where different assets are grouped together in a basket.* 一篮子期权是一种金融衍生工具，将不同的资产组合在一起。

Bayesian ['beɪzɪən] *adj.* 贝叶斯定理的；贝叶斯判决规则的

Phrase(s): ***Bayesian probability theory; Bayesian statistics; Bayesian modeling***

◇ *Bayesian statistics is a rigorous method for making decisions based on the subjectivistic interpretation of probability.* 贝叶斯统计是一种基于概率的主观解释来做出判断的严格方法。5（70）

Bayesian Information Criterion ['beɪzɪən ɪnfə'meɪʃ(ə)n kraɪ'tɪərɪən] *n.* 贝叶斯信息准则

◇ *Akaike's Information Criterion(AIC) and Bayesian Information Criterion (BIC) are two important parameters to evaluate the quality oflogistic regression models.* 评价逻辑回归模型优劣的两个重要参数是赤池信息准则和贝叶斯信息准则。

bear [beə] *n.* 熊；（在证券市场等）卖空的人；*vt.* 承担；忍受；支撑；生育；*vi.* 生（孩子）；结（果实）；与……有关；*adj.* 跌价的；股票行情下跌的；卖空者的

Phrase(s): ***bear market***

◇ *In the past years, the world stock markets were in bear territory.* 过去几年，全世

界股市处于熊市状态。

bearer ['beərə] *n.* 持票人

Phrase(s): ***bearer bill***

◇ *Tax heaven countries notoriously welcome anonymous bearer-share companies which are known for vehicles of criminals.* 避税天堂国家历来欢迎那些匿名的不记名股份公司，这类公司将罪犯带到各个地方。

bearer bond ['beərə bɒnd] *PHR.* 不记名债券

◇ *Bearer bonds were once the dominant type, but they are now much less common (in the United States) than registered bonds.* 不记名债券曾经是主要发行类型，但现在在美国，记名债券更为常见。6（523）

bearish ['beərɪʃ] *adj.* 行情看跌的

Phrase(s): ***ultra bearish***

◇ *The table shows the percentage of three types of investors who were bullish, bearish, or neutral during a four-week period.* 此表显示在四周时间内对行情看跌或看涨或者不在乎涨跌的三类投资者百分比。6（468）

behalf [bɪ'hɑːf] *n.* 代表；利益

Phrase(s): ***on behalf of***

◇ *Managers and the board of directors should all act on behalf of stockholders.* 经理和董事会都应该代表股东利益来行动。

behave [bɪ'heɪv] *v.* 表现

Phrase(s): ***behave well; behave oneself***

◇ *The rate of return on each stock behaves as a random variable.* 每只股票的收益率表现为随机形式。

behavior [bɪ'heɪvjə] *n.* 走势；表现；行为

◇ *Irreputable behavior of a financial institution damages its future development.* 金融机构有损声誉的行为损害其未来发展。

bell-shaped ['bel ʃeipt] *adj.* 钟形的

◇ *A credit loss distribution is not a normal bell-shaped distribution, instead, it is a heavily skewed curve.* 信用损失分布不是正态的钟形分布，恰恰相反，它是一种严重

倾斜的曲线。

below [bɪ'ləʊ] *adv.* 在下面；prep. 在……下面

Phrase(s): ***go below; below normal***

◇ *Small business exposures below €1 million may be treated as retail exposures if the bank treats such exposures in its internal risk management systems consistently over time and in the same manner as other retail exposures.* 如果长期以来银行在内部的风险管理系统对小企业贷款的处理方法一致，并且以和其他零售贷款相同的方式处理，100 万欧元以下的小企业贷款可以作为零售贷款处理。

benchmark ['ben(t)ʃmɑːk] *n.* 基准

Phrase(s): ***benchmark interest rate***

◇ *The benchmark for the deposit rate set by the central bank of this country has not been so low for many years.* 由该国央行设定的存款利率基准达到多年以来的新低。

beneficial [benɪ'fɪʃ(ə)l] *adj.* 有利的，有益的

Phrase(s): ***mutual beneficial; beneficial use***

◇ *The corporate structures released to the public didn't reveal who were the true beneficial owners.* 对外公布的公司结构图并没有透露出谁是真正的受益者。

benefit ['benɪfɪt] *n.* 利益，好处

Phrase(s): ***maximum benefit; economic benefit***

◇ *There are many benefits of opening the doors of community colleges to international students.* 社区大学向国际学生开放有很多好处。

best interest [best 'ɪnt(ə)rɪst] *PHR.* 最佳利益

◇ *The best interest of Apple's huge investment in ride-sharing software Didi could be the potential market of Apple's driverless cars in China.* 苹果公司巨额投资嘀嘀打车的最佳利益可能会是无人驾驶汽车未来在中国的巨大市场。

bet [bet] *n.* 打赌；*v.* 打赌

Phrase(s): ***make a bet***

◇ *I bet you have never seen a more successful IPO.* 我敢打赌你从来没有见过一个更成功的首次公开募股（IPO: Initial Public Offerings）。

beta ['bi:tə] *n.* 贝塔

Phrase(s): ***beta coefficient***

◇ *Covariance and correlation are essential to understand the beta coefficient, which is a measure of the risk arising in the stock market.* 协方差和相关性是理解贝塔系数的关键要素，而贝塔系数是股票市场的一种风险指数。6（376）

beyond [bɪ'jɒnd] *prep.* 超过；越过；那一边；在……较远的一边；*adv.* 在远处；在更远处；*n.* 远处

Phrase(s): ***go beyond***

◇ *Depending on the way the liquidity facility is drawn up, it may go beyond mere liquidity support and provide credit support to the transaction as well.* 根据流动性工具创造的方式，它可能不仅仅提供流动性支持，还可提供交易的信用支持。13（178）

bid [bɪd] *n.* 出价；投标；喊价；叫牌；*vt. & vi.* 出价；投标

Phrase(s): ***bid price;bid rate***

◇ *The highest bid for this oil painting at the auction was 200 pounds.* 这幅油画在拍卖会上的最高竞价是 200 英镑。

bilateral [baɪ'læt(ə)r(ə)l] *adj.* 两侧的；双边的；双方的；双向的；双系的

Phrase(s): ***bilateral meeting; bilateral agreement***

◇ *Bilateral transactions between parties or dealers are normally referred to as OTC deals.* 交易各方或交易商之间的双边交易通常被称为场外交易（OTC: Over-the-counter）。13（310）

bilateral agreement [baɪ'læt(ə)r(ə)l ə'gri:m(ə)nt] *PHR.* 双边协议

◇ *Turkey and Greece have signed a bilateral agreement to control the growing tension over the migration issue.* 土耳其和希腊签署了一项双边协议来控制移民问题引发的紧张局势。

bilateral deal [baɪ'læt(ə)r(ə)l di:l] *PHR.* 双边交易

◇ *A properly structured securitization would transform financial claims that have remained bilateral deals and been highly illiquid to tradable securities with better liquidity.* 一个结构合理的证券化将会把双边交易且流动性较差的金融债权转变成具有更高流动性的可供交易的证券。13（284）

bilinear [baɪ'lɪnɪə] *adj.* 双线性的

Phrase(s): *bilinear form; bilinear transformation*

◇ *Some other nonlinear processes include bilinear models, autoregressive models with random coefficients, and threshold models.* 其他一些非线性过程包括双线性模型、具有随机系数的自回归模型，以及门限模型。5（220）

bill [bɪl] *n.* 票据；钞票；清单；*v.* 开账单

Phrase(s): *bill of exchange; pay the bill; commercial bill*

◇ *The new tax proposal would help private-equity fund managers to cut their bills substantially.* 这项新的税收提议将有助于私募股权基金经理大幅削减他们的账单。

◇ *Securities issued with one year or less to maturity are called Treasury bills; they are issued as zero-coupon instruments.* 期限为一年或者少于一年的债券称为短期国库券，以零息票方式发行。5（113）

billion ['bɪljən] *n.* 十亿；数以十亿计；大量；一万亿；*adj.*（法美）十亿的；（英德）万亿的；无数的

◇ *The government needs to borrow 2 billion dollars abroad to meet its budget deficit plan.* 该政府需要向外国借款 20 亿美元来满足其预算赤字计划。

binary ['baɪnərɪ] *adj.* [数] 二进制的；二元的；二态的

Phrase(s): *binary tree; binary code*

◇ *The probit regression model is a nonlinear regression model where the dependent variable is a binary variable.* 概率回归模型是一个非线性回归模型，它的因变量是一个二元变量。13（149）

BIS (Bank for International Settlements) [bæŋk fɔ:(r) ɪntə'næʃ(ə)n(ə)l 'set(ə)lm(ə)nts] *abbr.* 国际清算银行

◇ *According to the New Basel Capital Accord, claims on the Bank for International Settlements, the International Monetary Fund, the European Central Bank and the European Community may receive a 0% risk weight.* 根据巴塞尔新资本协议规定，对国际清算银行、国际货币基金组织、欧洲中央银行和欧盟债权的风险权重可以为 0。

bivariate [baɪ'værɪɪt] *adj.* 二变量的

Phrase(s): *bivariate function; bivariate table; bivariate normal*

◇ *For instance,a bivariate normal distribution is characterized by two expected values, two variances and one covariance.* 比如一个二元正态分布具有两个期望值、两个方差和一个协方差。5（53）

bizarre [bɪ'zɑː] *adj.* 怪异的

Phrase(s): ***bizarre word***

◇ *Due to the decline of oil price this year, the government suffered a big loss in oil exports; thus it responded by a bizarre system of restricting imports which even led to a shortage of toilet paper.* 由于今年油价下跌，政府石油出口损失惨重，于是出台了限制进口的奇葩制度，甚至引发了卫生纸短缺。

block [blɒk] *n.* 块；街区；*vt.* 阻止；阻塞；限制

Phrase(s): ***a block of***

◇*Some large companies block or restrict access to LinkedIn on their internal networks for fear of the brain drain.* 一些大公司在公司内部网络阻止或者限制访问“领英”（一个全球职场人士沟通平台）以防止人才流失。

blockbuster ['blɒkbʌstə] *n.* 巨型炸弹；轰动

Phrase(s): ***blockbuster products***

◇ *Some Hollywood movies surprisingly became blockbusters in overseas markets, but lost much money at home.* 一些好莱坞出品的电影出人意料地在海外市场成为大片，却在国内市场赔钱。

board [bɔːd] *n.* 董事会；*v.* 登上（火车，轮船，飞机等）

Phrase(s): ***Financial Accounting Standards Board(FASB); Federal Reserve Board***

◇ *Public Relations Department spent a lot of time talking to investors, board directors, regulators and other stakeholders for a better external relation.* 为了建立更好的外联，公关部门花了很多时间与投资者、董事会成员、监管者以及其他利益相关者进行沟通。

body ['bɒdɪ] *n.* 团体；主体

Phrase(s): ***body corporate***

◇ *This research center, which is a government-funded body, works to assemble and analyse data on domestic environmental changes.* 这个政府资助的研究中心主要工作是采集和分析关于国内环境变化的数据。

bond [bɒnd] *n.* 债券

Phrase(s): *bond market; corporate bond; government bond*

◇ *Corporate bonds are classified by the type of issuer.* 公司债券可以按照发行者的类型进行分类。5（22）

◇ *European corporate-bond markets are about a third of the size of America's.* 欧洲企业债券市场约占美国的三分之一。

bondholder ['bɒndhəʊldə] *n.* 债券持有人；公债证书所有者；公司债所有者

◇ *Excess spread is the interest not paid to the bondholders nor used to pay fees.* 超额利差是不支付给债券持有人的利息，也不用于支付费用。13（98）

bond portfolio [bɒnd pɔːt'fəʊlɪəʊ] *PHR.* 债券组合

◇ *In bond portfolio management, a key measure of the interest rate exposure of a security or portfolio is duration.* 在债券组合管理中，久期是衡量单个证券或组合的利率风险的重要方法。5（173）

bond risk factors [bɒnd rɪsk 'fæktəz] *PHR.* 债券风险因子

◇ *When discussing bond risk factors, we usually agree that government bond markets have little credit risk.* 在讨论债券风险因子时，我们通常认为政府债券市场的信用风险是很低的。5（458）

bonus ['bəʊnəs] *n.* 奖金；红利

Phrase(s): *bonus issue*

◇ *It is always difficult for bosses to decide who to promote or how to divvy out bonuses.* 让老板决定提拔谁或者如何分配奖金总是很困难的。

book [bʊk] *adj.* 账簿上的

Phrase(s): *books of account; book value;book loss*

◇ *The accounting value of a company's assets is also called the book value of the assets.* 一个公司资产的会计价值也被称为其资产的账面价值。

◇ *Beta is not the only factor priced by the market. Other factors,such as a price-earnings factor, a dividend factor, a firm-size factor, can also explain stock returns.* 贝塔并不是市场定价的唯一影响因子。盈率因子、股息率因子、公司规模因子等其他因子也能够解释股票的收益率。5（179）

book-market factor [bʊk'mɑːkɪt 'fæktə] *PHR.* 账面市值比因子

book value [bʊk 'væljuː] *PHR.* 账面价值

◇ *Current assets and liabilities change rapidly, so the period when book values and market values look similar will not stay long.* 流动资产和负债变化很快，所以账面价值和市场价值相似的时间段不会太长。13（258）

boom [buːm] *vt.* 使繁荣；使迅速发展；*n.* 繁荣；激增

Phrase(s): ***boom year; baby boom***

◇ *The end of the commodity boom, corruption and people's longing for fresh faces resulted in the left-wing government's fall from grace.* 商品繁荣期的结束、腐败和人民对新鲜面孔的渴望导致了左翼政府的失宠。

boost [buːst] *vt.* 增加；提高；吹捧；向上推起

◇ *Many countries seek to boost domestic economy by curbing imports and boosting exports, however, this doesn't work all the time.* 许多国家寻求通过限制进口和促进出口来促进国内经济，然而这并不是总能奏效。

bootstrapping ['buːtstræpiŋ] *n.* 息票剥离法；*v.* 依靠自己的努力获得成功；自展

◇ *The simplest technique using on-the-run Treasury issues is called bootstrapping; this methodology is based purely on arbitrage arguments.* 最简单的方法是使用新发行的国债作为标准债券，称为息票剥离法，这种方法完全基于套利理论。5（152）

borrow ['bɒrəʊ] *vt. & vi.* 借入；借钱；借用；*n.* 借；借用；担保物；抵押

◇ *Making it easier to borrow, lend and invest across European internal borders will absolutely reduce funding cost for European firms.* 简化欧洲内部各国之间的借贷和投资无疑会降低欧洲企业的融资成本。

borrower ['bɔrəuə] *n.* 借钱人；借用人；剽窃者

Phrase(s): ***subprime borrower***

◇ *Due to easier and faster approvals, some borrowers with good credit were pushed into risky subprime loans which had been used as a penalty on people with poor credit.* 由于审批更加便捷，有一些信用良好的借款人也来申请为惩罚信用差的人而推出的高风险次级贷款。

borrowings ['bɒrəʊɪŋz] *n.* 借款；借用；借入

Phrase(s): ***direct borrowings***

◇ *Financing illiquid assets like real estate with short-term borrowings has long been a recipe for disaster,as the savings and loan crisis of the 1980s and early 1990s demonstrated.* 20 世纪 80 年代和 90 年代初的储贷危机已经证明，如房地产短期借款等非流动性资产的融资一直是灾难之源。14（78）

bottom ['bɒtəm] *n.* 底部；末端

Phrase(s): ***bottom up; bottom price***

◇ *The central government is determined to get to the bottom of all the corruption scandals.* 中央政府决心对所有的腐败丑闻一查到底。

bought [bɔːt] *v.* 购买；做出牺牲以获得；够支付；买通

Phrase(s): ***bought note; bought and sole note***

◇ Bought and sold note is needed when proceeding transfer of share in Hong Kong. 在香港进行股权转让时，需要出具股票买卖清单。

bound [baʊnd] *n.* 范围；约束

Phrase(s): ***upper bound; lower bound***

◇ *This approach also allows for the inclusion of constraints such as lower and upper bounds on particular assets or assets in particular industries or sectors.* 这一方法允许加入一些限制，比如对某些资产数量，某些行业或者市场设下限和上限。5（22）

Bowie bonds ['bəʊɪ bɒndz] *n.* 鲍伊债券

◇ *Bowie bonds were originated from British musician David Bowie whose albums were used as underlying collateral of the bond issued.* 鲍伊债券起源于英国音乐家戴维·鲍伊，他的唱片曾被作为发行债券的抵押品。

the Box-Jenkins approach [ðiː bɒks'dʒeŋkinz ə'prəʊtʃ] *PHR.* B-J 方法

◇ *The Box-Jenkins approach is named after two statisticians George Box and Gwilym Jenkins.* B-J 方法得名于两位统计学家乔治·鲍克斯和格威利姆·詹金斯。

◇ *The Box-Jenkins method consists of three steps: identification, estimation and diagnostic checking.* B-J 方法包括三步：识别、估计和诊断检验。5（242）

branch [brɑːn(t)ʃ] *n.* 树枝；支流；支店

Phrase(s): ***special branch***

◇ *Mobile banking, if attractive and secure enough to customers, can greatly reduce the cost of building expensive branches in different countries.* 如果手机银行足够安全，足够吸引顾客，将会大大降低在不同国家建立银行分支的昂贵成本。

breach [briːtʃ] *n.* 破坏；破裂；缺口；违背；*vt.* 攻破；破坏；违反

Phrase(s): ***breach of trust***

◇ *A security breach in a bank's networking system would cost a lot, including customers, earnings, even reputation.* 银行网络系统中的安全漏洞可能给银行带来巨大代价，包括客户、收益甚至名声。

break [breɪk] *vt.* （使）破；（将）划分为；*n.* 间断；终止

Phrase(s): ***breakdown; break-even point***

◇ *Asset securitization has the potential for reducing funding costs by breaking up a company into a set of various financial assets or cash flow streams.* 资产证券化有一种潜在能力，可以将一个公司分成一组不同的金融资产或现金流来降低融资成本。13（289）

breakdown bound ['breɪkdaʊn baʊnd] *PHR.* 崩溃界

◇ *The breakdown (BD) bound or point is the largest possible fraction of observations for which there is a bound on the change of the estimate when that fraction of the sample is altered without restrictions.* 当一部分样本发生无拘束的改变时，估计量的变化可能存在一个界限，崩溃界或者崩溃点指的就是这个界限中可能变化的最大样本部分。5（410）

break-even [breɪk'iːv(ə)n] *n.* 收支平衡点

◇ *When setting the bid price on a project, it should be known that the bid price represents a financial break-even level for the project.* 设置项目投标报价时，应该知道投标报价要体现该项目的财务收支平衡水平。

brief [briːf] *n.* 摘要；*adj.* 简短的

Phrase(s): ***brief talk; brief fee***

◇ *The magazine published a series of Brexit briefs to satisfy readers who were concerned about this topic.* 该杂志发表了一系列简短要文来满足关注“英国脱欧”话题的读者们。

broad [brɔ: d] *adj.* 广泛的；宽阔的；概括的；明显的

◇ *Within each business line, gross income is a broad indicator that serves as a proxy for the scale of business operations.* 在各产品线中，总收入是个广义的指标，代表业务经营规模。

Broad-based bond market indexes [brɔ:dbeɪst bɒnd 'mɑ:kɪt 'indeksis] *n.* 广义债券市场指数；宽基指数

◇ *Broad-based bond market indexes generally reflect the movement of the entire market; and two typical examples are the Dow Jones Industrial Average and the S&P 500.* 广义债券市场指数普遍反映整个市场的走势；两个典型的例子是道·琼斯工业平均指数和标准普尔 500 指数。

broker ['brəʊkə] *n.* （股票、外币等）经纪人；中间人；代理人

Phrase(s): *broker's firm; broker's representative*

◇ *Many American investors in equities are wondering whether they are receiving quality service from brokers in share trade.* 很多美国的股市投资者都想知道他们的股票交易经纪人是否为他们提供了高质量服务。

brokerage ['brəʊk(ə)rɪdʒ] *n.* 佣金；回扣；中间人业务

Phrase(s): *brokerage house; brokerage firm; brokerage charges*

◇ *Brokerage products which are not insured by Federal Deposit Insurance Corporation and have no bank guarantee may lose value easily.* 没有在美国联邦存款保险公司投保而且也没有银行担保的券商产品很容易失去价值。

Brownian motion [braunìən 'məʊʃ(ə)n] *PHR.* 布朗运动

◇ *A geometric Brownian motion (GBM) is a continuous-time stochastic process in which the logarithm of the randomly varying quantity follows a Brownian motion with drift. GBM is often used in mathematical finance to model stock prices.* 几何布朗运动是一种连续时间情况下的随机过程，其中随机变量的对数遵循布朗运动漂移。GBM 经常用于在金融数学中描述股票价格。

bucket ['bʌkɪt] *n.* 大量

Phrase(s): *buckets of*

◇ *This risk is quantified by dividing delinquencies of the pool of assets into time buckets such as 30 days, 60 days, 90 days, and so on.* 这种风险通过将资产池违约率划分为大量的时间间隔，如 30 天、60 天、90 天等等，从而进行量化风险。13（72）

budget ['bʌdʒɪt] *n.* 预算

Phrase(s): ***on a budget***

◇ *The presidential candidate has recently called for a balanced budget by cutting government spending; however, he didn't give a detailed plan.* 这位总统候选人最近呼吁通过削减政府开支来平衡预算，但是他没有给出一个详细的计划。

budgeting ['bʌdʒɪtɪŋ] *n.* 预定；预算

Phrase(s): ***capital budgeting***

◇ *The most important job of a financial manager is to create value from the firm's capital budgeting,financing, and net working capital activities.* 财务经理最重要的工作是，从公司的资本预算、融资以及净营运资本活动中创造价值。6（8）

bulk [bʌlk] *n.* 大多数；大部分；主体

Phrase(s): ***bulk buying; bulk transfer***

◇ *The energy giant released its restructuring plan, from which we can see the mining section is to sell part of its assets and the bulk of the jobs will be transferred to the new assets owners.* 能源巨头公布了其重组计划，从中我们可以看到，采矿公司将出售其部分资产，大量工作将转移给新的资产所有者。

bullet ['bʊlɪt] *n.* 子弹

Phrase(s): ***bullet portfolio; bullet bond***

◇ *A portfolio with maturities in the same range called a bullet portfolio.* 期限在相同范围内的投资组合被称为子弹式投资组合。

bull market [bʊl 'mɑːkɪt] *PHR.* 牛市

◇ *Commitments rose during the bull market years between 2003 and 2006, before dropping in tandem with the more recent economic crisis.* 委托业务在 2003 至 2006 年牛市时增加，然而随着近来的经济危机业务又开始下降了。6（625）

buoy [bɒɪ] *vt.* 使浮起；支持；鼓励

Phrase(s): ***buoy up; life buoy***

◇ *Buoyed by crude oil exports and booming tourism, this Middle East country's economy has grown at around 5% a year for a decade.* 在原油出口和旅游业蓬勃发展的推动下，这个中东国家的经济在过去十年一直以每年 5% 左右的速度在增长。

business ['bɪznɪs] *n.* 生意；业务；事情

Phrase(s): *business as usual; have no business; in business*

◇ *A poor credit record would affect the ability of Americans to get home loans, auto loans, and other consumer credit and business finance.* 不良信用记录将会影响美国人获取住房贷款、汽车贷款、其他消费信贷以及商业融资的资格。14（29）

business securitization ['bɪznɪs sɪkjʊərɪtʌɪ'zeɪʃ(ə)n] *PHR.* 企业资产证券化

◇ *Whole business securitization captures the residual value of a business (i. e. the valuation of the business) and creates securities that represent this residual value.* 整体企业资产证券化抓住企业的剩余价值（例如企业的估值）并且创造出代表这个剩余价值的证券。13（195）

buyer ['baɪə] *n.* 买方；买主；采购员

Phrase(s): *cap buyer; floor buyer*

◇ *In his term, the prime minister has made admirable progress; making it easier and faster for private buyers to acquire land, opening more sections to foreign investors and speeding up infrastructure construction are a just a few in the long list.* 总理在任期内取得了令人钦佩的进步，私人买家更加便捷地收购土地，对外商开放更多部门以及加快基础设施建设只是长长清单中的一小部分。

C

call [kɔːl] *n.* 提前赎回权；看涨（期权）

Phrase(s): ***call option; call price; call risk***

◇ *Some corporate bonds are issued with call provision,allowing the issuer to repurchase the bond at a specified call price before the maturity date.* 有些公司债券是和赎回条款一起发行的，这也就允许发行人在到期日之前按特定的赎回价格回购债券。4（295）

call protection [kɔːl prə'tekʃ(ə)n] *PHR.* 提前偿还保护

◇ *Callable bonds typically come with a period of call protection, an initial time during which the bonds are not callable.* 可赎回债券通常伴随着一段时间的提前偿还保护，也就是起初一段时间债券是不可提前偿还的。7（295）

canonical correlation analysis [kə'nɒnɪk(ə)l ˌkɒrə'leɪʃ(ə)n ə'næləsɪs] *PHR.* 典型相关分析

◇ *Cointegration tests based on canonical correlation analysis (CCA) are based on the idea that canonical correlations should discriminate those linear combinations of variables that are I(1) from those that are I(0).* 基于典型相关分析的协整检验是在这样一种想法上建立的，典型相关性应该从 I(0) 中区分出那些 I(1) 的变量线性组合。5（395）

cap [kæp] *n.* 帽子；顶；上限

Phrase(s): ***interest rate cap***

◇ *In order to tackle the refugee crisis, the country set a daily cap of 2 000 people migrants whom it allowed to cross its borders.* 为应对难民危机，该国设置了每日允许 2 000 移民跨国入境的上限。

capacity utilization [kə'pæsɪtɪ ˌjuːtɪlaɪ'zeɪʃən] *PHR.* 生产能力利用系数

◇ *Factories always need to look at their capacity utilization rate, which is the ratio of actual output produced with the installed equipment to potential output that could be produced.* 工厂必须经常关注它们的生产能力利用系数，即当前设备条件下的实际产量与潜在产量的比例。7（376）

capital ['kæpɪt(ə)l] *n.* 资本

Phrase(s): ***economic capital; capital adequacy***

◇ *Despite its sufficient capital, the bank will optimize its structure by reducing retail banking business and focusing on asset management and investment banking.* 尽管资本充足，银行还是将通过减少零售银行业务、专注于资产管理和投资银行来优化其结构。

capital allocation line ['kæpɪt(ə)l ˌælə'keɪʃ(ə)n laɪn] *PHR.* 资产分配线

◇ *Capital allocation line measures the risk of assets for investors by displaying the potential return on a certain level of risk.* 资本分配线通过显示在一定的风险水平上的潜在回报，来为投资者测量资本风险。

capital budgeting ['kæpɪt(ə)l 'bʌdʒɪtɪŋ] *PHR.* 资本预算

◇ *In real-life capital budgeting projects, most cash flows are not riskless, thus, the discount rate on the projects should be considered.* 现实生活中的资本预算项目中，大部分现金流是存在风险的，因此需要考虑这些项目的贴现率。

capital expenditure ['kæpɪt(ə)l ɪk'spendɪtʃə] *PHR.* 资本支出

◇ *A firm with excess cash can either pay a dividend or make a capital expenditure; the premise is that stockholders can get similar expected returns from either.* 拥有多余现金的公司可以支付股利或进行资本支出；前提是，股东可以从任一种形式中获得相似的预期收益。

capital market line ['kæpɪt(ə)l 'mɑːkɪt laɪn] *PHR.* 资本市场线

◇ *Bonds with warrants and convertible bonds have different effects on corporate cash flow and capital structure, yet both are involved in risks.* 附认购债券和可转换债券对公司的现金流和资本结构有不同的影响，但两者都涉及风险。

capital structure ['kæpɪt(ə)l 'strʌktʃə] *PHR.* 资本结构

◇ *The amount of leverage a firm uses is governed by its capital structure policy.* 一个公司使用的杠杆由该公司的资本结构决定。6（59）

cap volatility [kæp ˌvɒlə'tɪlətɪ] *PHR.* 帽式波动率

◇ *Cap volatility data is quite sensitive due to its asynchronous fashion, and far out-of-money or in-the-money data may not be updated often enough.* 帽式波动数据由于异步形态所以相当敏感，不能够经常更新远期价内和价外数据。

◇ *Our experiment consists of four types of data updated on a daily basis: a yield curve, a cap volatility matrix, a swaption volatility matrix, and Eurodollar future option (EDFO) prices or volatilities.* 我们的实验包括四种每天更新的数据类型，它们是：一个收益率曲线、一个帽式波动矩阵、一个利率交换选择权波动矩阵和欧洲美元期货期权价格或波动性。

carrying costs ['kærɪɪŋ kɔsts] *PHR.* 持有成本

◇ *Costs that rise with the level of investment in current assets are called carrying costs.* 伴随当前资产投资水平而产生的成本叫作持有成本。6（814）

carrying value ['kærɪɪŋ 'vælju:] *PHR.* 账面价值

◇ *The carrying value is the accounting value of a firm's assets, the accounting numbers of which are actually based on cost rather than true market values. To create value for the firm that exceeds its cost is universally expected.* 账面价值是企业资产的会计价值，其中会计数字实际上是基于成本而不是真正的市场价值。为公司创造超过成本的价值才是普遍预期的。

carve-out [kɑ:v'aʊt] *n.* 股权切离

◇ *In a carve-out, the firm turns a division into a separate entity and then sells shares in the division to the public.* 在股权分离中，公司把其中一部分分离出来成为一个单独的实体，然后将这部分的股份出售给公众。6（918）

cash [kæʃ] *n.* 现金； *v.* 将……兑现

Phrase(s): *cash basis; cash flows; cash discount*

◇ *The transaction will be immediately terminated if the counterparty fails to satisfy an obligation to deliver cash or securities or to deliver margin or otherwise defaults.* 一旦交

易对象不能按照规定给付现金、证券、保证金或违约，交易将立即终止。

cash asset [kæʃ 'æset] *PHR.* 现金资产

◇ *This frontier, combined with cash assets, generates the capital allocation line-the set of efficient complete portfolios.* 这条边界与现金资产结合，就生成了资本配置线——一系列有效完整投资组合。7（653）

cash distribution [kæʃ dɪstrɪ'bjuːʃ(ə)n] *PHR.* 现金分配

◇ *Dividend is a type of cash distribution of earnings; however, if the distribution is not made from current or accumulated retained earnings, then we can't use the term dividend.* 股息是一种利润的现金分配形式，但如果分配的不是当前或者累积的留存收益，则不能使用股息这个词。

cash equivalents [kæʃ ɪ'kwɪv(ə)l(ə)nts] *PHR.* 现金等价物

◇ *Four of the most important items found in the current asset section of a balance sheet are cash and cash equivalents, marketable securities, accounts receivable, and inventories.* 资产负债表中流动资产部分最重要的四项内容是现金和现金等价物、有价证券、应收账款和存货。6（832）

cash inflow [kæʃ 'ɪnfləʊ] *PHR.* 现金流入

◇ *Both cash inflows and cash outflows are unsynchronized and uncertain, because we can not predict precisely when the sales and costs happen.* 现金流入和现金流出既不同步也不确定，因为我们无法准确预测销售和成本发生的时间。

cash outlay [kæʃ 'aʊtleɪ] *PHR.* 现金支出

◇ *Firms often issue bonds and stocks in advance to prepare for the possibility of a large cash outlay to construct a new plant, for example.* 公司经常提前发行债券和股票，为可能出现的大量现金支出做准备，比如新建一个工厂。

cash settlement [kæʃ 'set(ə)lm(ə)nt] *PHR.* 现金结算

◇ *On a national basis, supervisors are expected to elaborate on some short-term exposures, such as exposures arising from cash settlements by wire transfer.* 根据各国情况，监管当局可以对一些短期贷款做出详细阐述，比如以电汇方式进行现金清算产生的风险暴露。

cash transaction [kæʃ træn'zækʃ(ə)n] *PHR.* 现金交易

◇ *In digital times, many young people prefer online payment like Alipay and WeChat Payment to cash transaction.* 在数字化时代，相对于现金交易，很多年轻人更喜欢支付宝、微信支付等在线付款方式。

cauchy distribution [kɒtʃɪ ˌdɪstrɪ'bjuːʃ(ə)n] *n.* 柯西分布

◇ *The Cauchy distribution is a continuous probability distribution which has a probability density function that can be expressed analytically.* 柯西分布是一种连续概率分布，其概率密度函数可以解析表达。

center limit theorem ['sentə(r) 'lɪmɪt 'θɪərəm] *PHR.* 中心极限定理

◇ *Center limit theorem tells us that if you flip a coin many times,the probability of getting a given number of heads should follow a normal curve, with mean equal to half the total number of flips.* 中心极限定理告诉我们，如果你多次投掷一枚硬币，正面朝上次数的概率会遵循正态分布，其平均值等于你投掷总次数的半数。

central counterparty ['sentr(ə)l 'kauntəˌpɑːti] *PHR.* 中央对手方

◇ *Systemic risks can actually increase because they concentrate risks on the central counterparty, the failure of which exposes all participants to risk.* 系统性风险事实上会增加，因为风险都被集中到中央对手方，而如果中央对手方一旦失败，所有参与者都将面临风险。

certificate [sə'tɪfɪkɪt] *n.* 证书；执照；证券

Phrase(s): ***certificate interest; birth certificate***

◇ *Excess spread is gross finance charge collections and other income received by the trust or special purpose entity minus certificate interest, servicing fees, charge-offs, etc.* 超额利差是信托机构和特别目的机构的总财务收入加上其他收入，再减去证券的利息、服务费用、注销金额等。

certificates of deposit [sə'tɪfɪkɪts (ə)v dɪ'pɒzɪt] *PHR.* 存款证明；定期存单

◇ *When cash on deposit with the lending bank, certificates of deposit or comparable instruments issued by the lending bank are held as collateral at a third-party bank.* 如在贷款银行有现金储蓄、存款证明或由贷款银行发行的其他类似工具，可以被第三方银行持有作为抵押品。

charge-offs [tʃɑːdʒɔfs] *n.* 坏账；销账

◇ *European Central Bank forecast loan loss provisions and net charge-offs of bad debt at Alpha Bank in Greece will continue to fall in the second quarter this year.* 欧洲中央银行预测，在今年第二季度希腊阿尔法银行贷款损失准备金和坏账冲销净额将继续下降。

chi-square distribution [tʃiskweə dɪstrɪ'bjuːʃ(ə)n] *PHR.* 卡方分布

◇ *The Chi-square distribution with k degrees of freedom is defined as the distribution of the sum of the squares of k independent standard normal variables.* 自由度为K的卡方分布被定义为K个独立标准正态变量平方和的分布。5（57）

chooser option ['tʃuzə 'ɒpʃ(ə)n] *PHR.* 任选期权

◇ *Chooser options allow the holder to choose whether the option is a call or aput.* 任选期权允许期权持有者选择该期权是看涨期权还是看跌期权。

chow test [tʃaʊ test] *PHR.* 邹检验

◇ *The Chow test was designed to test whether the coefficients in two linear regressions on different data sets are equal by a Chinese American Gregory Chow in 1960s.* 20世纪60年代，美籍华人邹至庄教授提出了"邹检验"，即在不同的数据集上的两个线性回归的系数是否相等。

clearinghouse ['klɪərɪŋ haʊs] *n.* 票据交换所；交易所

◇ *The prices of futures contracts are marked to the market daily; buyers turn over their daily losses to their brokers who will be subsequently compensated by the clearinghouse which must break even every day.* 期货合约的价格实行当日结算；买家把当日亏损转移给他们的经纪人，再由交易所补偿经纪人，交易所必须每天盈亏平衡。

clearing member ['klɪərɪŋ 'membə] *PHR.* 结算会员

◇ *Assuming the broker is a clearing member, the broker in turn deposits margins with the clearinghouse.* 假设交易商是结算会员，交易商反过来又在清算所存入保证金。

close-out ['kləuzˌaut] *n.* 结算；平仓

◇ *Close-out prices for concentrated positions and/or stale positions are more likely to be adverse to banks.* 如果市场持有的头寸和拟出售的头寸过于集中，平仓价可能对银行不利。

closed-end fund ['kləuzd'end fʌnd] *PHR.* 封闭型基金

◇ *Closed-end funds issue a fixed number of shares which are not redeemable from the fund.* 封闭式基金只发行固定数量的不可赎回的基金份额。

coefficient of determination [ˌkəʊɪ'fɪʃ(ə)nt (ə)v dɪˌtɜː mɪ'neɪʃ(ə)n] *PHR.* 决定系数

◇ *Coefficient of determination is a number that indicates the proportion of the variance in the dependent variable that is predictable from the independent variable.* 决定系数体现的是由独立变量预测而来的因变量中方差的比例。

cointegration [kəʊɪntɪg'reɪʃ(ə)n] *n.* 共整合现象

◇ *Cointegration analysis is a widely used econometric tool recently.* 协整分析是最近广泛使用的一种计量工具。5（373）

cointegrating vectors [kəʊ'ɪntɪgreɪtɪŋ 'vektəz] *PHR.* 协整向量

◇ *The r columns of the matrix β are the cointegrating vectors of the process.* 矩阵 β 的 r 列是过程的协整向量。5（385）

collateral [kə'læt(ə)r(ə)l] *n.* 抵押品；担保品；*adj.* 抵押的

Phrase(s): *collateral value; collateral security*

◇ *Thanks to the latest legal changes, major banks in Greece can repossess collateral and sell loans to third parties easier than before.* 得益于最新的法律调整，希腊的几大主要银行现在可以更加容易地收回抵押品或者将贷款出售给第三方。

collateralized bond obligations [kə'lætərəlaizd bɒnd ˌɒblɪ'geɪʃ(ə)ns] *PHR.* 担保债务凭证

◇ *Collateralized debt obligations, which include collateralized bond obligations and collateralized loan obligations, are the fastest-growing sectorin the bond area.* 债务抵押债券包括担保债务凭证和贷款抵押债券，是债券领域增长最快的部门。

collateralized debt obligations [kə'lætərəlaizd det ˌɒblɪ'geɪʃ(ə)n] *PHR.* 债务抵押债券

◇ *The basic difference between cash and synthetic CDOs is the amount of funding raised and the manner of its investment.* 现金和合成债务抵押债券的基本区别在于资金筹集的数量和投资方式。13（215）

collinearity [kəˌlɪniː'ærɪtɪ] *n.* 共线性；同线性

Phrase(s): ***collinear planes; collinear vectors***

◇ *Collinearity, also referred to as multicollinearity, occurs when two or more regressors have a linear deterministic relationship.* 共线性，也被称作多重共线性，是指两个或两个以上回归量有线性的确定性关系。5（124）

commercial [kə'mɜːʃ(ə)l] *adj.* 商业的；盈利的

Phrase(s): ***commercial invoice; commercial agreement; commercial loans***

◇ *Experience in many countries proves that commercial property lending has been a recurring cause of troubled assets in the banking industry over the past few decades.* 许多国家的经验证明，在过去几十年中，商业房地产贷款一直是造成银行业不良资产问题的原因。

commercial bank [kə'mɜːʃ(ə)l bæŋk] *PHR.* 商业银行

◇ *Commercial banks typically lend to real estate developers a fixed percentage of the appraised market value of a project.* 商业银行通常会借给房地产开发商项目市场估价的一定比例的贷款。6（561）

commercial draft [kə'mɜːʃ(ə)l drɑːft] *PHR.* 商业汇票

◇ *Commercial banks in the world today have no incentives to hold large quantities of safe and liquid assets because they know the central banks will provide liquidity if there is a panic.* 当今世界上的商业银行缺少动力去持有大量安全的流动性资产，因为它们知道一旦出现恐慌，中央银行就会为它们提供流动性资金。

commercial loans [kə'mɜːʃ(ə)l ləʊnz] *PHR.* 商业贷款

◇ *Commercial finance services include equipment leases, commercial loans, and SME (Small and medium enterprises) loans.* 商业金融服务包括设备租赁、商业贷款和中小企业贷款。8（130）

commercial paper [kə'mɜːʃ(ə)l 'peɪpə] *PHR.* 商业票据

◇ *Money market securities have low risks of default and they are in various forms, such as certificates of deposit, commercial paper, or Treasury bills issued by the US government.* 货币市场证券的违约风险较低，他们以各种形式存在，如存单、商业票据或者美国政府发行的国库券。

commission [kə'mɪʃ(ə)n] *n.* 佣金

◇ *Wages, salaries, and commissions are listed as priorities inliquidationprocess once a corporation decides to be bankrupt.* 一旦公司决定破产，在清算过程中工资、薪金和佣金被列为优先清算对象。

commitments [kə'mɪtm(ə)nt] *n.* 承诺条款

◇ *Commitments are off-balance sheet contracts whereby the bank commits to a future transaction that may result in creating a credit exposure at a future date.* 承诺条款是银行对未来可能导致信用风险暴露的交易做出承诺的表外合同。8（500）

common stock ['kɒmən stɒk] *PHR.* 普通股

◇ *The term common stock means different things to different people, but it is usually applied to stock that has no special preference either in receiving dividends or inbankruptcy.* 普通股对于不同的人来说有不同的意义，但是这一概念通常适用于在获取股利或者破产清偿时没有特殊优先权的股票。6（474）

common trends ['kɒmən trendz] *PHR.* 共同趋势

◇ *A property of cointegrated processes is the presence of integrated common trends.* 协整过程的性质是完整的共同趋势状态。5（374）

compensating balances ['kɔmpenseitiŋ 'bæl(ə)nsɪz] *PHR.* 补偿性余额

◇ *Compensating balances are deposits the firm keeps with the bank in low-interest or non-interest-bearing accounts.* 补偿性余额是公司留存在银行的低息或无付息账户的存款。

competitive offer [kəm'petɪtɪv 'ɒfə] *PHR.* 竞争性报价

◇ *In a competitive offer, the issuing firm sells its securities to the underwriter with the highest bid.* 在竞争性的报价中，发行公司以最高的出价出售其证券给承销商。

compound ['kɒmpaʊnd] *adj.* 复合的

Phrase(s): ***compound grow; compound interest; compound value***

◇ *If you invest your cash at compound interest, then each interest payment will be reinvested. Thus, the money that money makes will make you more money.* 如果你进行现金复利投资，那么每次支付的利息将再被投资；因此本金赚取的利息又会为你赚更多钱。

concentrated likelihood function ['kɒnsntreɪtɪd 'laɪklɪhʊd 'fʌŋ(k)ʃ(ə)n] *PHR.* 集中似然函数

◇ *Concentrated likelihood is a mathematical technique through which the original likelihood function (LF) is transformed into a function of a smaller number of variables, called the concentrated likelihood function (CLF).* 集中似然是一种数学技术，它将原似然函数转化为一个较小数量的变量，称为集中似然函数。5（387）

concentration limits [kɒns(ə)n'treɪʃ(ə)n 'lɪmɪts] *PHR.* 浓度限制；集中度限制

◇ *Transactions typically establish obligor concentration limits and industry concentration limits.* 交易通常建立债务人集中度限制和行业集中度的限制。8（182）

concession [kən'seʃ(ə)n] *n.* 让步；特许权

Phrase(s): ***make some concession***

◇ *In post-Brexit era, anti-EU sentiment suddenly grows all over the continent and Eurosceptic countries seeking concessions from the EU could also threaten to quit the club.* 英国脱欧后时代，整个欧洲大陆反欧盟情绪突然高涨，寻求欧盟让步的欧洲统一怀疑论国家也有可能威胁退出这个俱乐部。

conditional expectation [kən'dɪʃ(ə)n(ə)l ekspek'teɪʃ(ə)n] *PHR.* 条件期望

◇ *In the discrete case, the conditional expectation is a random variable that takes a constant value over the sets of finite partition associated.* 在离散的情况下，条件期望是一个在一组有限的相关分区拥有固定量的随机变量。

conditional distribution [kən'dɪʃ(ə)n(ə)l dɪstrɪ'bjuːʃ(ə)n] *PHR.* 条件分布

◇ *In an IID sequence all conditional distributions are identical to unconditional distributions.* 在独立同分布序列中，所有的条件分布与非条件分布相同。5（49）

conditional mean [kən'dɪʃ(ə)n(ə)l miːn] *PHR.* 条件均值

◇ *If the conditional mean is not specified adequately, then the construction of consistent estimates of the true conditional variance process would not be possible and statistical inference and empirical analysis might be wrong.* 如果条件均值没有充分给定，那么对真条件方差过程的一致估计的结构将不可能产生，而且统计推断和实证分析都将可能是错误的。5（293）

conditional prepayment rate [kən'dɪʃ(ə)n(ə)l ˌpriː'peimənt reɪt] *PHR.* 有条件的提前偿付率

◇ *The benchmarks used today are the conditional prepayment rate and the Public Securities Association (PSA) prepayment benchmark.* 今天所使用的基准是有条件的提前偿付率以及公共证券协会提前偿付基准。13（32）

conduit ['kɒndjʊɪt] *n.* 管道

◇ *If a bank serves as a sponsor of an asset-backed commercial paper (ABCP) conduit or similar programme that acquires exposures from third-party entities, then it can be considered as an originating bank of a certain securitization.* 如果银行作为资产支持型商业票据过手过程中的承销人，或者以类似方式从第三方购买资产，就可以认定其为资产证券化的发起行。

confidence level ['kɒnfɪd(ə)ns 'lev(ə)l] *PHR.* 置信水平

◇ *The t-statistics show that at a 99% confidence level we cannot reject the null hypothesis of zero coefficient for variable y.* t 值显示在 99% 的置信水平下我们不能拒绝变量 *y* 的系数为 0 的原假设。5（368）

conforming mortgages [kən'fɔːmiŋ 'mɔːgɪdʒs] *PHR.* 合规抵押贷款

◇ *These were low-risk conforming mortgages, meaning that eligible loans for agency securitization couldn't be too big and homeowners had to meet underwriting criteria establishing their ability to repay the loan.* 这些低风险的合规抵押贷款，意味着机构证券化的合格贷款不能太多，并且房屋所有者必须符合承保标准，证明自身偿还贷款的能力。7（18）

conservative investor [kən'sɜːvətɪv ɪn'vestə] *PHR.* 保守投资者

◇ *A conservative investor usually does not invest his account entirely on one project; on the contrary, he wants diversified products to lower risks.* 保守投资者通常不把所有账户资产完全投资在一个项目上；相反，他希望通过产品多样化来降低风险。7（151）

consistent [kən'sɪst(ə)nt] *adj.* 一致的

Phrase(s): *consistent with*

◇ *An estimator is called consistent if the limit in probability of the estimator equals the true parameter.* 一个估计量被称为具有一致性如果它的概率极限值等于它的真实值。5（60）

constant growth ['kɒnst(ə)nt grəʊθ] *PHR.* 固定增长

Phrase(s): ***constant growth dividends***

◇ *The company has an expectation to maintain a constant growth rate in its dividend in the coming 10 years.* 公司期望在未来 10 年保持一个股利固定增长率。

constant parameters ['kɒnst(ə)nt pə'ræmɪtə(r)z] *PHR.* 常量参数

◇ *Suppose that a distribution f is given and that μ is a constant parameter or a vector of constant parameters of the distribution f.* 假设一个分布 f 已给定，并且 μ 是一个常量参数或是分布 f 的一个常量参数的向量。5（59）

consumer credit [kən'sjuːmə 'kredɪt] *PHR.* 消费信贷；消费者信用

◇ *Many organizations sell information about the credit history of various companies; while some of them are also known as suppliers of consumer credit information.* 许多组织出售各种企业信用历史信息；而它们中的一些也同时是消费者信用信息供应商。

contango [kən'tæŋgəʊ] *n.* 期货溢价；交易延期费

◇ *When the market turned to contango, however, the long positions started to lose money as they got closer to maturity.* 然而，当市场转为期货溢价状态时，多头在接近到期日时开始赔钱。8（240）

contingency [kən'tɪndʒ(ə)nsɪ] *n.* 应急费用；意外开支准备金

Phrase(s): ***contingency plan***

◇ *Firms are suggested to set aside cash surpluses against contingencies like a large scale product recall or a lasting legal case.* 建议公司预留出意外开支准备金来应对突发事件，比如一个大规模的产品召回或一桩持久的法律案件等。

contingent deferred sales charges [kən'tɪndʒ(ə)nt dɪ'fɜːd seɪlz tʃɑːdʒs] *PHR.* 递延销售费用

◇ *The trusts issuing the notes are collateralized by a portion of future fees, expense charges, and contingent deferred sales charges (CDSC) expected to be realized on the annuity policies.* 信托公司发行的票据是由一部分未来的费用、开支费用以及预期在年金政策中实现的递延销售费来作为抵押的。13（205）

contract ['kɒntrækt] *n.* 合同；合约

Phrase(s): ***Futures Contract***

◇ *Derivatives are financial contracts traded in private over-the-counter (OTC) markets, or on organized exchanges.* 衍生产品是在私人场外市场或是有组织的交易所内交易的金融合约。

contraction [kən'trækʃ(ə)n] *n.* 收缩

◇ *Some companies follow the cyclicality of revenues, which means they do well in the expansion phase of the business cycle and do poorly in the contraction phase.* 一些公司有着收入的周期性，这意味着他们在商业周期的扩张阶段经营良好，但在收缩阶段却做得不好。

contraction risk [kən'trækʃ(ə)n rɪsk] *PHR.* 减期风险

◇ *Contraction risk happens to banks when the mortgage loan interest rate declines and the borrowers may accelerate payments in order to reduce the number of years to pay the interest.* 如果按揭贷款利率下降，借款人可能会加速还款以减少支付利息的年数，这对银行来说会产生减期风险。

contribution to risk [kɒntrɪ'bjuːʃ(ə)n tə rɪsk] *PHR.* 风险贡献度

◇ *The marginal contribution to risk can also be used to analyze the incremental effect of a proposed trade on the total portfolio risk.* 边际风险贡献度也能被用来分析某项交易对总的组合风险的增加效应。

convergence [kən'vɜːdʒəns] *n.* 会聚；集收敛

Phrase(s): ***convergence point***

◇ *5G technology may bring about the convergence of the makers of computers and telecoms equipment because they are forced by standardization and low margins in the market.* 受迫于市场的标准化和低利润，5G 技术可能会带来计算机和电信设备制造商的大整合。

convergence property [kən'vɜːdʒəns 'prɒpətɪ] *PHR.* 收敛性

◇ *The convergence property implies that the price of silver in the spot market must equal the futures price on the delivery day.* 收敛性意味着白银在到期日的现货价格必须等于它的期货价格。7（570）

conversion ratio [kən'vɜːʃ(ə)n 'reɪʃɪəʊ] *PHR.* 调换比率；转换比率

◇ *The face value of the bond divided by the conversion ratio is the conversion price of the bond*. 债券的票面价值除以转换比率得到债券的转换价格。

convexity [kən'veksɪtɪ] *n.* 凸性

Phrase(s): *logarithmic convexity; effective convexity*

◇ *This property of bond prices is called convexity because the shape of the bond price curve is convex*. 债券价格的这种性质被称为凸性，因为债券价格曲线呈现凸形。4(301)

convolution [ˌkɒnvə'luːʃ(ə)n] *n.* 卷积

◇ *Convolution is a mathematical operation on two functions which can be implemented through tabulation.* 卷积是有关两个函数的数学运算，它可以通过列表的形式得到。8（595）

copula function ['kɒpjʊlə 'fʌŋ(k)ʃ(ə)n] *PHR.* 连接函数

◇ *Copula is a Latin word meaning a link or a bond. Some derivations of copula functions begin with a relationship between marginals based on independence*. Copula 是一个拉丁词，意为连接或联系。Copula 函数的一些推导基于独立性的边际关系。

core capital [kɔː 'kæpɪt(ə)l] *PHR.* 核心资本

◇ *After the financial crisis of 2008, regulators in many countries began to emphasize on bank's supplement of their core capital so that customers' interest could be protected in case of another crisis*. 2008 年金融危机后，许多国家的监管机构开始重视银行核心资本的补充，以确保下一场危机来临时，客户利益得到保护。

corporate bonds ['kɔːp(ə)rət bɒndz] *PHR.* 公司债券

◇ *Corporate bonds are important means by which private firms borrow money directly from the public*. 企业债券是私人企业直接向公众借钱的重要手段。4（36）

corporate credit environment ['kɔːp(ə)rət 'kredɪt ɪn'vaɪrənm(ə)nt] *PHR.* 公司信用环境

◇ *The advantage of index trades is that they allow the carrying out of structured trades in a generalized portfolio so capital market participants may take views on the general corporate credit environment in a specific country or region or sector*. 指数交易的优势在于它们允许用一般化组合进行结构化交易，因此资本市场参与者可能会考虑某个具体国家、地区或行业内的一般化公司信用环境。13（314）

corporate charters ['kɔːp(ə)rət 'tʃɑːtəs] *PHR.* 公司章程

◇ *Corporate charters determine the percentage of voting shares needed to approve important transactions such as mergers and acquisitions.* 公司章程确定了批准重大交易如合并和兼并事项所需的投票权份额比例。

corporate governance ['kɔːp(ə)rət 'gʌv(ə)nəns] *PHR.* 公司治理

◇ *The minimum requirements to apply IRB approach are concerning several aspects including corporate governance and oversight, disclosure requirements and so on.* 采用 IRB 法的最低要求涉及几个方面，包括公司治理和监督、披露要求等。

corporate financial distress ['kɔːp(ə)rət faɪ'nænʃ(ə)l dɪ'stres] *PHR.* 公司财务困境

◇ *During economic recession period, corporate financial distress of private and public entities throughout the world was a frequent occurrence with important implications for their many stakeholders.* 在经济萧条时期，世界各地的私人和公共企业的公司财务困境频发，并且对他们众多的利益相关者产生重要影响。

corporate risk management ['kɔːp(ə)rət rɪsk 'mænɪdʒm(ə)nt] *PHR.* 公司风险管理

◇ *Securitization can be used as a corporate risk management tool because it removes the credit risk and the interest rate risk associated with the assets sold to the SPV.* 证券化能够作为一个公司风险管理工具是因为它把卖给特殊目的机构的资产所具有的信用风险和利率风险移除了。13（25）

correlation matrix [ˌkɒrə'leɪʃ(ə)n 'meɪtrɪks] *PHR.* 相关矩阵

◇ *A correlation matrix is a table of all possible correlation coefficients between a set of variables. The correlation matrix can be calculated by using statistical software SPSS or SAS.* 相关矩阵是一组变量之间所有可能的相关系数图表。相关矩阵可以通过使用统计软件 SPSS 和 SAS 来计算。

correlation [ˌkɒrə'leɪʃ(ə)n] *n.* 相关性

Phrase(s): ***correlation analysis; correlation coefficient***

◇ *We can assess the magnitude of exchange rate risk by examination of historical rates of change in various exchange rates and their correlations.* 我们可以通过检测不同汇率

及其相关性的历史变化率来评估汇率风险的大小。7（636）

cost [kɒst] *n.* 成本

Phrase(s): ***cost of capital; agency costs***

◇ *Such slow increases in revenue and big increases in cost point to an obvious conclusion: the company is over.* 利润增加如此缓慢而成本却大幅上升指向一个显而易见的结论：这家公司完蛋了。

cost effects [kɒst ɪ'fekts] *PHR.* 成本效应

◇ *The Net Present Value (NPV) of granting credit depends on five elements: revenue effects, cost effects, the cost of debt, the probability of nonpayment, and the cash discount.* 授予信用净现值（NPV）取决于五个要素：收入效应、成本效应、债务成本、拖欠的概率和现金折扣。

countercyclical [ˌkauntə'saiklikəl] *n.* 逆周期的

◇ *Countercyclical usually refers to the opposite direction of movement of the overall economic cycle in the stock market.* 逆周期通常指的是股票市场上与整体经济周期呈相反方向运行的现象。

counterparty ['kauntəˌpɑːti] *n.* 对手方；合约对方

Phrase(s): ***counterparty risk***

◇ *Banks will be required by the supervisory authorities to calculate the counterparty credit risk charge for OTC derivatives, repo-style and other transactions booked in the trading book, separate from the capital charge for general market risk and specific risk.* 监管当局要求银行除了计算一般市场风险和特定风险的资本要求外，还要对交易账户上反映的交易方场外衍生工具、回购协议类产品和其他交易工具等计算信用风险资本。1（134）

counterparty risk ['kauntər 'pɑːtɪ rɪsk] *PHR.* 交易对手风险

◇ *Counterparty risk weightings for OTC derivative transactions will not be subject to any specific ceiling.* 对衍生产品场外交易的交易对手风险权重将不设定最高限额。1（13）

coupon ['kuːpɒn] *n.* 息票；通票

Phrase(s): ***coupon bond; coupon date; coupon rate***

◇ *The coupon rate of the bond determines the interest payment: the annual payment equals the coupon rate times the bond's par value.* 债券的票息利率决定了利息支付：每年利息支付等于票息利率乘以债券的面值。4（293）

coupon leverage ['ku:pɒn 'li:v(ə)rɪdʒ] *PHR.* 息票杠杆

◇ *Inverse floaters with a wide variety of coupon leverages are available in the CMO (Collateralized Mortgage Obligation)market.* 在抵押担保债券市场，具有多种形式息票杠杆的反向浮动债券是可以流通的。8（58）

covariance [kəʊ'veərɪəns] *n.* 协方差

Phrase(s): ***covariance matrix; covariance analysis***

◇ *Homogeneous expectations assume that all investors have the same beliefs concerning returns, variances, and covariances. However, this doesn't mean all investors have the same aversion to risk.* 同质期望假定所有投资者对收益、方差和协方差信念一致。然而，这并不意味着所有的投资者都能同样地规避风险。

covariance matrix [kəʊ'veərɪəns 'meɪtrɪks] *PHR.* 协方差矩阵

◇ *The covariance matrix plays a key role in financial economics, especially in portfolio theory; the matrix of covariances among various assets' returns can help investors decide which assets to hold in diversified choices.* 协方差矩阵在金融经济学中起到关键作用，特别是在投资组合理论中；各种资产收益之间的协方差矩阵可以帮助投资者决定在多样化资产中选择持有哪些资产。

coverage ratio ['kʌv(ə)rɪdʒ 'reɪʃɪəʊ] *PHR.* 偿债备付率

◇ *A coverage ratio is a measure of a company's ability to satisfy fixed obligations, such as interest, principal repayment, or lease payments.* 偿债备付率用来衡量一个公司偿还固定债务的能力，比如利息、本金偿还或者租赁付款。5（133）

covered interest arbitrage ['kʌvəd 'ɪnt(ə)rɪst 'ɑ:bɪtrɪdʒ] *PHR.* 无风险套利

◇ *One typical application of covered interest arbitrage strategy is to exchange domestic currency for foreign currency at the current spot exchange rate, then invest the foreign currency at the foreign interest rate.* 无风险套利策略的一个典型应用是将本国货币以即期汇率兑换外国货币，然后以国外利率投资外汇。

CPI(consumer price index) [kən'sju:mə praɪs 'ɪndeks] *abbr.* 消费者物价指数

◇ *CPI is one of the most closely watched national economic statistics in many countries to measure inflation and reflect the real value of salaries and pensions.* 消费者物价指数是多国密切关注的国民经济数据之一，它被用来衡量通货膨胀以及反映工资和养老金的实际价值。

cramer's rule ['kreɪmərs ru:l] *PHR.* 克莱姆法则

◇ *Cramer's rule applies to the case where the coefficient determinant is nonzero, otherwise the system will be incompatible.* 克莱姆法则适用于系数行列式非零的情况，否则方程组无解。

credit ['kredɪt] *n.* 信用；贷款；信誉

Phrase(s): ***credit rating; credit card***

◇ *For short-term self-liquidating trade letters of credit arising from the movement of goods, a 20% CCF (credit conversion factor) will be applied to both issuing and confirming banks.* 对于与货物贸易有关的短期自偿性信用证，无论对开证行，还是对保兑行，信用风险换算系数均为20%。1（14）

credit conversion factor ['kredɪt kən'vɜ:ʃ(ə)n 'fæktə] *PHR.* 信用换算因子

◇ *A CCF of 75% will be applied to commitments, NIFs (note issuance facilities) and RUFs (revolving underwriting facilities) regardless of the maturity of the underlying facility.* 无论这些工具的期限如何，承诺、票据发行便利、循环授信便利的信用风险转换系数是75%。

credit crisis ['kredɪt 'kraɪsɪs] *PHR.* 信用危机

◇ *During the credit crisis that started in 2007, risk management systems collapsed in many financial institutions.* 在2007年开始的信用危机中，许多金融机构的风险管理系统崩溃了。

credit default swap ['kredɪt dɪ'fɔ:lt swɒp] *PHR.* 信用违约互换

◇ *Credit default swap is considered as a type of unfunded credit derivative which serves to hedge the credit risk of the portfolio.* 信用违约互换被视为一种资金来源非预置型信用衍生工具，它可以用来规避自产组合的信用风险。

credit derivatives ['kredɪt di'rivətivz] *PHR.* 信用衍生品

◇ *The development of credit derivatives has contributed to the stability of the banking system by allowing banks, especially the largest, systemically important banks, to measure and manage their credit risks more effectively.* 信用衍生产品的发展已为银行体系的稳定做出了贡献，特别是规模最大、具有系统重要性的银行，帮助他们更有效地度量和管理信用风险。8（224）

credit enhancement ['kredɪt ɪn'hɑːnsm(ə)nt] *PHR.* 信用增级

◇ *The securitization of subprime loans requires a larger amount of credit enhancement in order to create senior bond classes.* 次级贷款的证券化要求大量的信用增级从而创造高级层次的债券。13（23）

credit event ['kredɪt ɪ'vent] *PHR.* 信用事件

◇ *Banks should have the right to liquidate or take legal possession of the collateral timely in occurrence of credit events like the default, insolvency or bankruptcy of the counterparty.* 在发生违约、无力偿还或者破产等信用事件时，银行应该有权及时对交易对象的抵押品进行清算或者收为己有。

credit exposure ['kredɪt ɪk'spəʊʒə] *PHR.* 信用风险敞口

◇ *By altering settlement costs and credit exposures, multilateral netting systems for foreign exchange contracts could alter the structure of credit relations and affect competition in the foreign exchange markets.* 通过改变结算成本和信用风险敞口，外汇交易合约的多边净额结算能够改变信用关系的结构并且影响外汇交易市场的竞争。

credit period ['kredɪt 'pɪərɪəd] *PHR.* 信贷期限；付款期限

◇ *If a firm decides to grant credit to its customers, then the terms of sale will clearly state the credit period, the cash discount and discount period, and the type of credit instrument.* 如果一个公司允许客户赊欠，那么销售条款需要写清楚付款期限、现金折扣和折扣期限，以及信用工具的类型。

credit scoring ['kredɪt 'skɔːrɪŋ] *PHR.* 信用评分

◇ *Although credit scoring models and other mechanical rating methods use plenty of available information to avoid errors, sufficient human judgement is still a nessential supplement.* 尽管信用评分模型和其他评级技术方法使用大量现有信息来避免错误，

但足够的主观判断依然是重要补充。

credit spread ['kredɪt spred] *PHR.* 信用价差

◇ *A credit spread can be used as an options strategy where a high premium option is sold and a low premium option is bought on the same underlying security.* 信用价差可以作为一种期权策略，即对同一种标的证券出售高溢价期权，买入低溢价期权。

creditworthiness ['kredɪtˌwɜːiθnis] *PHR.* 好信誉；有资格接受信用贷款

◇ *Prime borrowers are entitled are entitled to high credit quality because they have strong employment and credit histories, income sufficient to pay the loans without compromising their creditworthiness, and substantial equity in the underlying property.* 优质借款人拥有高的信用质量，因为他们有强势的就业和信用记录，收入足以支付贷款，而不损害自己的信誉，并且他们的财产净值丰厚。8（21）

critical values ['krɪtɪk(ə)l 'væljuz] *PHR.* 临界值

◇ *In medical field, critical values are laboratory results which indicate a condition likely to require prompt clinical intervention; thus the lab should inform certain hospitals immediately.* 在医学领域，临界值是实验室提供的、需要及时进行临床干预的检验结果；因此，实验室应立即通知医院。

cross-currency risk [krɒs 'kʌr(ə)nsɪ rɪsk] *PHR.* 交叉货币风险

◇ *When a CDO (Collateralized Debt Obligation)transaction is comprised of debt or loans from various countries, particularly emerging markets, there is cross currency risk.* 当一个担保业务凭证交易是由来自各个国家的债务或贷款组成时，特别是新兴市场国家，就会存在交叉货币风险。8（268）

cross-hedging [krɒs'hedʒɪŋ] *n.* 交叉套期保值

◇ *In cross-hedging practice, investors can not hedge a long-term security with a short-term security, the two should be positively correlated and have the same maturity.* 在实施交叉套期保值时，投资者不能以短期证券对冲长期证券，两者应该是正相关，而且有相同的期限。

cross-sectional regression [krɒs'sekʃənəl rɪ'greʃn] *PHR.* 截面回归

◇ *Unlike the estimation of the characteristic line which uses time series data, the second-pass regression is a cross-sectional regression.* 不同于使用时间序列数据的特征

线估计，二次回归是一个横截面回归。5（178）

crown jewels [kraʊn 'dʒuːəls] *PHR.* 皇冠之珠（意指核心业务单元）

◇ *Many colorful metaphorical terms can be used to describe defensive tactics when the target managers don't support the merger business, such as crown jewels, golden parachutes and poison pills.* 当目标公司的管理层不支持合并时，有很多丰富多彩的隐喻词语来形容他们的防守战术，比如：皇冠之珠、黄金保护伞和毒丸计划等。

cumulative default rate ['kjuːmjʊlətɪv dɪ'fɔːlt reɪt] *PHR.* 累计违约率

◇ *Because these are cumulative default rates, the number must increase with the time horizon.* 由于这些属于累计违约率，因此数值一定会随着时间而增加。

cumulative probability ['kjuːmjʊlətɪv prɒbə'bɪlɪtɪ] *PHR.* 累计概率

◇ *Calculate the probability of the first event occurring,then the second event occurring, continue this process until you have calculated the individual probabilities for each independent event,finally you will get the cumulative probability by multiply the probabilities together.* 计算第一个事件发生的概率，接着计算第二个，继续这个过程直到你计算好每个独立的个体事件的概率，最后将得到的概率相乘就是累积概率。

currency ['kʌr(ə)nsɪ] *n.* 货币；通货

Phrase(s): ***currency option; currency futures***

◇ *The struggling government couldn't give clear responses to a sharp slowdown in the economy and to a falling currency, which worried foreign investors a lot.* 困境中的政府不能对急剧放缓的经济和货币的贬值做出明确回应，这让外国投资者非常担忧。

currency swap ['kʌr(ə)nsɪ swɒp] *PHR.* 货币互换

◇ *Currency swaps are agreements by two parties to exchange a stream of cash flows in different currencies according to a prearranged formula.* 货币互换是指双方根据预先确定的规则交换一系列不同类型货币的现金流的协议。

current assets ['kʌr(ə)nt 'æsets] *PHR.* 流动资产

◇ *Net working capital is defined as current assets minus current liabilities. It displays as positive when current assets are greater than current liabilities.* 净营运资本被定义为流动资产减去流动负债。当流动资产大于流动负债时，净营运资本为正。

current liabilities ['kʌr(ə)nt ˌlaiə'bilitis] *PHR.* 流动负债

◇ *A firm's liquidity can be measured by current assets compared to current liabilities; and the two items should be written on the balance sheets.* 公司的流动性可以通过比较流动资产与流动负债来得出；而这两项都应该写在资产负债表上。

current yield ['kʌr(ə)nt ji:ld] *PHR.* 当期收益率

◇ *Current yield is a bond's annual coupon divided by its price; and it should not be confused with a bond's yield to maturity.* 当期收益率是债券的价格除以年利息；不应把它与债券的到期收益率混淆。

cycle ['saɪk(ə)l] *n.* 周期

Phrase(s): ***economic cycle***

◇ *Facing temporary funding difficulty and a fall in credit rating, an executive of the company said with confidence that "We have to be patient. Cycles are an inherent part of oil business."* 面对暂时的资金困难和信用评级下降，公司一位高层自信地说道："我们要有耐心。石油企业经历周期是必然的。"

cyclical industry ['sɪklɪk(ə)l 'ɪndəstrɪ] *PHR.* 周期性行业

◇ *Cyclical industries gain much higher revenues in prosperous times and endure more losses in recession period; thus they are sensitive to economic cycles. Typical examples are steel, shipping and housing industries.* 周期性行业在繁荣时期获得更高收入，在经济衰退时期承受更大的损失；因此它们对经济周期敏感。典型的例子是钢铁、船舶和住宅产业。

D

daily interest ['deɪlɪ 'ɪnt(ə)rɪst] *PHR.* 日息；每日利息

Phrase(s): ***with daily compound interest; daily interest rate; computing Daily Interest***

◇ *Know how to calculate daily interest can help you determine the total amount of interest you earn from or you owe to the bank.* 知道如何计算每日利息可以帮助你确定从银行赚取的或者你欠银行的利息总额。

◇ *U. S. Dollar Daily Interest Chequing Account advertised itself to be competitive in foreign exchange rates and secure in funds transfer between different accounts when traveling abroad.* 美元日息支票账户在广告中声称自己具有竞争性的汇率，而且确保客户到国外旅行时在不同账户之间转移资金的安全。

daily margin call ['deɪlɪ 'mɑːdʒɪn kɔːl] *PHR.* 每日按金要求

◇ *Due to the swinging market or internal factors of a brokerage, a margin call is usually done on a daily basis, however, in times of high volatility a broker can make a margin call or calls intra-day.* 由于市场的摇摆性和券商的内部因素，保证金追缴通常是以一个交易日为单位的。但是，在价格大幅波动时，经纪人可以在一天之内要求一次甚至几次保证金追缴。

date [deɪt] *n.* 日期

Phrase(s): ***date of delivery; expected date of delivery***

◇ *Where the call is at the discretion of the protection seller, the maturity will always be at the first call date.* 如果期权由信用保护的出售者自行选择，期限应从第一个买入期权日开始计算。

◇ *To date, The OPEC Fund for International Development (OFID)has made financial commitments of more than US$ 19 billion to over 3 500 operations across 134 countries worldwide.* 迄今为止，欧佩克国际发展基金（OFID）已经横跨全球134个国家，为超过3 500个业务项目提供了超过190亿美元的资金支持。

DAX [dɑːks] *n.* 德国综合指数 5（15）

Phrase(s): ***DAX index; Frankfurtdax index***

◇ *The DAX index in Germany fell 5. 7 percent and the CAC-40 index in France lost 4. 7 percent.* 德国的DAX指数下跌5. 7个百分点，法国的CAC-40指数下跌4. 7个百分点。

◇ *The DAX, transated as German Stock Index in English, is a blue chip stock market index consisting of the 30 major German companies trading on the Frankfurt Stock Exchange.* DAX指数在英文中翻译为德国股票指数，反映30家德国主要公司的蓝筹股在法兰克福证券交易所的交易情况。

day count [deɪ kaʊnt] *PHR.* 日算

Phrase(s): ***day count basis; day count conventions;***

◇ *The floating payments will differ owing to day counts as well as movements in the reference rate.* 浮动利率会随着日息和参考利率的不同而变动。10（33）

dead account [ded əˈkaʊnt] *PHR.* 呆账；坏账

Phrase(s): ***dead account preparation; loss of dead account;***

◇ *Banks should be equipped with the ability to assess the credit quality of their borrowers; for example, whether they had a history of bad debts and whether they made timely adjustment to their dead account preparation.* 银行应配备评估借款人信用质量的能力，例如，他们是否有坏账历史以及他们是否及时调整他们的坏账准备。

deal [diːl] *n.* 交易

Phrase(s): ***package deal; forward deal; credit deal***

◇ *In post-Brexit era, Britain will face endless negotiations with other EU members on the terms of new trade deals, especially when Germany, France and Italy are not willing to let Britain leave unscathed.* 后脱欧时代，英国将面临与其他欧盟成员国对新贸易协定

条款无休止的谈判，特别是在德国、法国和意大利都不愿意让英国毫发无损地离开这样的情况下。

dealer ['diːlə] *n.* 经销商；商人

Phrase(s): *registered dealer; bond dealer; the dealer*

◇ *This securities firm is a registered broker-dealer, and a registered investment advisor registered with the U. S. Securities and Exchange Commission (SEC).* 这家证券公司是一个注册的经纪交易商，也是在美国证券交易委员会注册的注册投资顾问。

◇ *American shares are traded on several exchanges; Besides, there are also dozens of "alternative trading systems"and"single-dealer platforms".* 美国股票在多家交易所进行交易，除此之外还有众多另类交易系统和单一经销商平台。

dealing ['diːlɪŋ] *n.* 交易；行为

Phrase(s): *insider dealing*

◇ *While daily marking-to-market may be performed by dealers, verification of market prices or model inputs should be performed at least monthly by a unit independent of the dealing room.* 逐日按市场价值计价可由交易员完成，但对市场价格或模型参数的验证却需至少每月一次由交易室内一个独立的部门完成。

death duty [deθ 'djuːtɪ] *PHR.* 遗产税

◇ *Death duty is an old legal term used in some commonwealth countries; nowadays, it has been replaced by inherence tax or estate tax.* 遗产税（death duty）是曾经在一些英联邦国家使用过的旧的法律术语；如今，它已经被继承税或地产税（estate tax）取代。

debenture [dɪ'bentʃə] *n.* （英）[金融] 公司债券；信用债券；[税收] 退税证明书

Phrase(s): *debenture paper; debenture holder; securing debenture; capital debenture*

◇ *Debenture is an unsecured debt backed only by the credit worthiness and reputation of the borrower. Treasury bill issued by a government is a typical example because it is unlikely to default on the repayment.* 公司债券是一种无抵押债务，只依赖借方信用质量和声誉作为支持。政府发行的国债就是一个典型例子，因为政府不太可能拖欠还款。

◇ *To issuing firms, debentures have two advantages over other bonds; one is a fixed and low interest rate, and the other is a repayment date far in the future.* 对发行方来说，

信用债券在两个方面优于其他债券，一是固定低利率，还有一个是还款间隔时间长。

debit ['debɪt] *vt.* 记入借方；登入借方；*n.* 借方

Phrase(s): ***debit side; cash debit***

◇ *Generally speaking, the restaurant industry has the shortest cash cycles, because most customers pay bills in cash or use their debit/credit cards.* 一般来说，餐饮业的现金周期最短，因为大多数顾客用现金或使用他们的借记卡 / 信用卡付账。

◇ *The small bank abolished a scheme to charge a $5 monthly fee for debit-card purchase, as it discouraged customers from depositing in the bank.* 这家小银行取消了对借记卡每月收取 5 美元费用的方案，因为它打击了顾客在该银行存款的积极性。

debit balance ['debɪt 'bæl(ə)ns] *PHR.* 借方余额；借方差额

Phrase(s): ***debit ending balance; equity investment debit balance; adjusted debit balance***

◇ *If the income summary account has adebit balance, then the company has suffered a loss for the current perio*d. 如果收益汇总账户有借方余额，那么公司当期的经营为亏损。

◇ *When the number of debit entries is larger than the number of credit entries in an account, the account has a debit balance.* 当一个账户出现借方账目数量大于贷方账目数量时，该账户有借方差额。

debit card ['debɪt kɑ:d] *PHR.* 借记卡

◇ *The Bank of China customers can make withdrawals from more than a million ATMs worldwide, and of course you'll receive a debit card within a few days of opening your account.* 中国客户的银行可以在世界上超过一百万台自动取款机上取款，当然你会在开户几天之内收到借记卡。

debit entry ['debɪt 'entrɪ] *PHR.* 借方分录

Phrase(s): ***debit reverse entry account; bank debit entry***

◇ *In the double entry bookkeeping method, the left side of the account represents the debit entry and the right side represents the credit entry.* 在复式记账法中，账户左边代表借方分录，右边则代表贷方分录。

debt [det] *n.* 债务，借款

Phrase(s): ***external debt; floating debt; funded debt; debt capital***

◇ *The default of this state-owned enterprise warned the banks that they should lend to promising industries, not to hopeless ones which wait for the government to write off their bad debts.* 国有企业违约事件警告银行要贷款给有前途的产业，而不是那些等待政府勾销坏账的烂摊子国企。

◇ *Tax cut could stimulate economic growth, yet the growth could also be offset by higher debt-servicing costs.* 减税可以刺激经济增长，但增长也会被较高的偿债成本抵消。

debt equity ratio [det 'ekwɪtɪ 'reɪʃɪəʊ] *PHR.* 债资比率；负债权益比率

Phrase(s): ***total debt to equity ratio; Net Debt to Equity Ratio***

◇ *Traditional opinion holds that owing to tax shield effect of debt financing, market value is positively related to debt equity ratio.* 传统理论认为：由于债务融资具有税盾效应，因而公司的市场价值与债务权益比率正相关。6（92）

◇ *A high debt equity ratio indicates a company chooses to take higher risk by financing its growth with heavy debt.* 高负债权益比率表明公司选择承担更高的风险，使用高额债务扩大融资。

debt-equity swap [det'ekwɪtɪ swɒp] *PHR.* 债转股

Phrase(s): ***debt-equity swap enterprise; political debt-for-equity swap***

◇ *In debt-equity swap transactions, borrowers with financial difficulties transform loans into stock shares to delay debt repayment or to keep the company running.* 在债转股交易中，经济困难的借款人将贷款转换成股票来延迟偿还债务或维持公司的运转。

◇ *Under the circumstance of bankruptcy, the declaring company may conduct debt-equity swap to pay off its previous debt with equity with the permission of the bankruptcy court.* 破产的情况下，申请破产的公司在破产法庭准许下，可以通过债转股用股权偿还以前债务。

debtor ['detə] *n.* 债务人

Phrase(s): ***principal debtor; debtor nation; debtor country***

◇ *Actually in EU, some problems are more serious and urgent than Brexit; the fight going on between debtors and creditors on austerity issue is one of them.* 其实在欧盟，一些问题比脱欧更严重和紧迫; 债务国和债权国之间关于紧缩问题的矛盾就是其中之一。

◇ *Large state-owned enterprises in China should be responsible for the rapid growth in Chinese debt, for they are the biggest debtors in the country.* 大型国有企业应该对中国债务的快速增长负责，因为他们是国家最大的债务人。

debt service coverage ratio [det 'sɜːvɪs kʌv(ə)rɪdʒ 'reɪʃɪəʊ] *PHR.* 债务偿还比率

Phrase(s): ***percentage of loan paid off debt service coverage ratio; debt-to-service coverage ratio***

◇ *Debt service coverage ratio (DSCR) enables creditors to know how much debt a company currently owes and how much cash it has to pay the current and potential debts.* 债务偿还比率让债权人知道公司目前欠多少债务和它有多少现金可以支付现有的和潜在的债务。

◇ *Compared to debt ratio, debt service coverage ratio is more comprehensive in telling a company's debt-related expenses, such as interest, pension and sinking fund.* 相比负债率，债务偿还比率更全面地覆盖与债务相关的费用，如利息、养老金和偿债基金等。

debt-servicing [det'sɜːvisiŋ] *n.* 债务还本付息；债务偿还事务

◇ *It is essential for banks to assess financial conditions and debt-servicing capacities before granting any loan.* 银行在发放任何贷款之前评估贷款人的财务状况和偿债能力是必不可少的。

debt-to-income ratio [dettə'ɪnkʌm 'reɪʃɪəʊ] *n.* 负债收入比率

◇ *If you pay 3 000 rmb each month for your housing mortgage which is your only debt; and your monthly income totals at 10 000rmb, then your debt-to-income (DTI) ratio is 3 000÷10 000=0. 3(30%).* 如果你唯一的债务就是每月 3 000 元的住房抵押还款，而你的月收入总计是 10 000 元人民币，那么你的负债收入比率（DTI）就是 3 000÷10 000 = 0. 3（或者 30%）。

decision [dɪ'sɪʒ(ə)n] *n.* 决策；决定

Phrase(s): ***decision-making under risk; decision - makers***

◇ *Customers'outstanding balances may fluctuate based on their decisions to borrow and repay, up to a limit established by the bank.* 在银行建立的限额下，根据客户借款和偿还的情况，客户贷款余额会出现上下波动。

◇ *In most Global 500 companies, the decision-makers are predominantly white males, which indicates an existing of gender and racial discrimination.* 大多数全球 500 强企业里

决策者主要还是白人男性，这表明性别和种族歧视的存在。

declaration date [deklə'reɪʃ(ə)n deɪt] *n.* 董事会宣布授权支付股息日

Phrase(s): ***dividend declaration date***

◇ *On the declaration date, the directing board of a company announces its next dividend payment date and size; thus the declared dividend formally becomes the company's legal liability.* 在董事会宣布授权支付股息日，公司的董事会宣布其未来最近一次股息支付的日期和规模；由此这批股息正式成为公司的法律责任。

decline [dɪ'klaɪn] *n.* 下降；衰退；斜面

Phrase(s): ***in decline; decline period***

◇ *When the value of the currency in a country or region declines, exports increases and in turn helps put idle capacity to work and compensate for the shortfall in domestic spending.* 当货币的价值在一个国家或地区下降，出口增加反过来有助于启动闲置生产能力，弥补国内消费不足的问题。

deduct [dɪ'dʌkt] *vt.* 扣除；减去

Phrase(s): ***deduct verb; deduct chi; deduct illegally***

◇ *When a bank is required to deduct a securitisation exposure from regulatory capital, the deduction will be taken 50% from Tier 1 and 50% from Tier 2 with one exception.* 当要求银行从监管资本中扣除资产证券化风险暴露时，扣减数额应当是在一级资本中扣除 50%，二级资本中扣除 50%（一种情况除外）。

◇ *Materiality thresholds on payments are equivalent to retained first loss positions and must be deducted in full from the capital of the bank purchasing the credit protection.* 付款的临界值标准等于银行自己保留的第一损失头寸，因此必须全额从购买该项信用保护银行的资本中扣除。

deed [diːd] *n.* 契据

Phrase(s): ***trust deed; deed tax***

◇ *A deed is a legal instrument in written form which passes, affirms or confirms an interest, right, or property; and it is commonly used in real estate transfer to convey ownership from the old owner to the new owner.* 契约是书面的法律文书，用来通过、承认或确认利益、权利或财产；它常用于房地产转让中将所有权从老业主更替到新业主。

◇ *There are transfer taxes (7% to 8% depending on whether it is new), notary fees and deed fees, all of which add up to a total of about 10% of the purchase price of the property.* 另外还要缴纳房地产转让税（根据房屋的新旧，税率分 7% 和 8% 两档）、公证费和证书费，所有费用加起来大约相当于购房价格的 10%。13（163）

default [dɪ'fɔːlt] *n.* 违约 10（25）

Phrase(s): *default risk; loss given default(LGD); probability of default(PD); exposure at default(EAD)*

◇ *Facing low oil price at the beginning of this year, some oil companies postponed paying interest on its debt because it puts pressure on creditors to exchange debt for equity in order to avoid a default.* 面对今年初的低油价，一些石油公司推迟了偿还债务的利息，因为它会迫使债权人债转股以避免违约。

◇ *China's banks are risk due to a rash of defaults；luckily, compared to American Congress, Chinese government is more generous to recapitalize banks.* 中国的各家银行由于一连串的违约面临风险；幸运的是相比于美国国会，中国政府会更加慷慨地给这些银行注资。

defaulting [dɪ'fɔltɪŋ] *n.* 违约（default 的现在分词）

Phrase(s): *defaulting party; defaulting state; indenture defaulting*

◇ *There would be no one to bail out their creditors if America or Britain showed signs of defaulting.* 如果英美两国显示出违约迹象，将没有一个人有能力援救他们的债权人。

◇ *A firm defaulting on a required payment probably will reorganize its financial structure, otherwise it may be forced to liquidate its assets.* 公司如果不能按规定付款构成违约，很可能将重组其金融结构，否则可能被迫清算资产。

default interest [dɪ'fɔːlt 'ɪnt(ə)rɪst] *PHR.* 拖欠利息

Phrase(s): *Default Interest Rate; default on interest*

◇ *Default interest and late-charge provisions in mortgage loan documents should be carefully negotiated and written down to avoid future court cases.* 应该在抵押贷款文件中谨慎协商并明确写下拖欠利息和滞纳金条款，来避免未来的法庭案件。

◇ *Since default interest serves to encourage compliance with the borrowers'obligation, then it should not exceed the potential damage caused by default.* 既然违约利息是用来鼓

励借款人履行付款义务的，则其数目不应超过违约所造成的潜在损失。

default risk [dɪ'fɔːlt rɪsk] *PHR.* 违约风险；拖欠风险

Phrase(s): *default-risk structure; credit default risk*

◇ *For purchased corporate receivables, banks are expected to assess the default risk of individual obligors.* 对购入的公司应收账款，银行要评估单个债务人的违约风险。10（25）

◇ *The precise calculation of risk weights for default risk will depend on the bank's ability to decompose EL into its PD and LGD components in a reliable manner.* 违约风险权重的精确计算，将取决于银行以可靠的方式，将预期损失分解为违约概率和违约损失率的能力。1（66）

defensive [dɪ'fensɪv] *n.* 防守性；具抗跌力

Phrase(s): *defensive stocks; defensive actions*

◇ *A defensive stock is a stock that provides a constant dividend and stable earnings during various phases of the business cycle.* 防御性股票是一种在经济周期不同阶段提供恒定股息和稳定收益的股票。

◇ *Many active investors will only choose defensive stocks when the economic recession sign is shown; yet, in booming times, they will turn to stocks with higher betas to increase returns.* 许多活跃的投资者只会在经济衰退迹象显现时选择防御型股票；然而在经济蓬勃发展的时候，他们就会转向贝塔系数高的股票来增加收益。

deferral [dɪ'fɜːrəl] *n.* 延期；迟延；缓役

Phrase(s): *deferral method; deferral taxes; upgrade deferral*

◇ *The bank must have clearly articulated and documented policies in respect of the granting of extensions, deferrals, renewals and rewrites to existing accounts.* 对于逾期天数的计算，特别是对于授权展期、延期偿付、修改和沿用现有账户来说，银行必须有明确的规章制度。

◇ *Banking regulators globally have encouraged banks to make their pay deferral periods longer, at least a year or more.* 全球银行监管者曾鼓励银行延长薪酬的延期兑现时间，至少要在一年或一年以上。

deferred [dɪ'fɜːd] *adj.* 递延

Phrase(s): *deferred savings; deferred payments*

◇ *Deferred taxes result from differences between accounting income and true taxable income.* 会计收益和实际应税收入之间的差异导致递延税款。

◇ *On the balance sheet, deferred tax liability refers to taxes that are not paid today but have to be paid in the future.* 在资产负债表上，递延所得税负债是指今天没有支付，但必须在未来支付的税金。

deferred annuity [dɪ'fɜːd ə'njuːɪtɪ] *PHR.* 递延年金

Phrase(s): *deferred life annuity; deferred payment annuity; Tax-deferred Annuity*

◇ *A deferred annuity mainly has two phases, the savings phase in which you invest money into the account, and the income phase in whichyou receive payments.* 递延年金主要有两个阶段，首先是储蓄阶段，你必须把钱投资到储蓄账户，随后才是年金领取阶段。

◇ *Many people in the US buy deferred annuities as a retirement strategy, so they can accumulate their savings as well as earnings when they are young and receive rich returns when they are old.* 许多美国人购买递延年金作为退休的策略，他们可以在年轻的时候积累自己的储蓄和收益，在年老时获得丰厚的回报。

deferred charges [dɪ'fɜːd tʃɑːdʒs] *PHR.* 递延费用

Phrase(s): *deferred tax charges; deferred overhead charges; deferred insurance charges*

◇ *Deferred charges on the balance sheet refer to making prepayments for goods or services which have not been received, such as insurance premium or rent.* 递延费用在资产负债表上指在收到商品或服务之前预付款，如保险费或租金。

◇ *Deferred charges happen when a company pays for land rent for one year in advance in order to receive some favorable discount or a good location.* 公司为了得到一些优惠折扣或一个很好的位置提前一年支付土地租金时，递延费用就发生了。

deferred credit [dɪ'fɜːd 'kredɪt] *PHR.* 递延款项

Phrase(s): *deferred taxes credit; deferred sight credit*

◇ *Deferred credit on the balance sheet refers to income whose payment will be delayed because it can not be earned fully and timely with the expenses.* 资产负债表上的递延款项指的是延迟付款的收入，因为它不能在费用发生时及时而全面地取得。

◇ *Deferred credit is viewed asa long-term liability if it will take more than one year to provide services or merchandise to the customer that provided the payment.* 如果为已付费顾客提供服务或者商品的周期超过一年，递延款项将被视为长期负债。

deferred debit [dɪ'fɜːd 'debɪt] *PHR.* 递延借项

◇ *With a deferred debit card in hand, the merchant doesn't not charge the buyer's account immediately when the transaction happens ; the buyer just needs to sign the receipt and the charge will occur a few days later.* 递延贷记卡的功能就是买卖发生时，卖家不立即从买家账户里扣款，买家只需要在收据上签字，扣款几天以后才实际发生。

deferred income [dɪ'fɜːd 'ɪnkʌm] *PHR.* [会计] 递延收益

◇ *Deferred income refers to money a company receives when the services or products have not been delivered; it is reviewed as a liability until the delivery finishes.* 递延收益是指公司没有交付服务或产品时就收到了货款；它被视为一种负债直至交付结束。

deferred payment [dɪ'fɜːd 'peɪm(ə)nt] *PHR.* 延期付款

◇ *If a deferred payment is granted, the borrower is permitted to make payments at a fixed date inn the future. It often happens in retail business.* 如允许延期付款，借款人可以在未来某个固定日期完成付款。它经常出现在零售业务中。

◇ *As a small retail businessman, I often accept deferred payment from those who are bound to pay with their next month's wages.* 作为一个小的零售商人，我经常接受那些一定会用下一个月工资付款的人提出的延期付款要求。

deferred settlement [dɪ'fɜːd 'set(ə)lm(ə)nt] *PHR.* 递延结算

Phrase(s): ***Deferred Net Settlement System; Deferred Net Settlement***

◇ *A deferred net settlement system refers to final settlements occurring between participating banks at the end of a predefined settlement cycle when the net obligations between participants are calculated and presented to the settlement agent for settlement.* 延迟净额结算系统是指在一个预定义的结算周期结束时参与银行之间的最后结算，此时需要向代理结算人提交计算好的参与行之间的净债务。

deferred tax [dɪ'fɜːd tæks] *PHR.* 递延税款

Phrase(s): ***deferred income tax liabilities; deferred income tax payable***

◇ *In accounting context, when the tax value exceeds the accounting value, the company should recognise a deferred tax asset.* 在会计领域，当征税价值超过账面价值时，公司应确认一笔递延所得税资产。

◇ *Tax authorities may recognize revenue or expenses at different times than that of an accounting standard, which will cause a deferred tax asset.* 税务机关与会计准则确认收入或费用的时间可能不同，这将导致递延所得税资产的产生。

deficiency [dɪ'fɪʃ(ə)nsɪ] *n.* 不足

Phrase(s): ***deficiency account; clearing deficiency account; deficiency account statement***

◇ *There is a serious deficiency in traditional capital budgeting: the flexibility of real-world companies is often neglected when calculating net present value.* 传统资本预算有个严重不足：在计算净现值时往往忽略现实世界里公司的灵活性。

deficit ['defɪsɪt] *n.* 赤字；不足额

Phrase(s): ***budget deficit; trade deficit; deficit covering; deficit-covering finance***

◇ *Due to the global slump in energy prices, exports declined and economic growth slowed down in this country; the government has run deficits for the first time in five years' time.* 由于全球能源价格下滑，导致该国出口下降，经济增长放缓；政府运行也在五年内首次出现赤字。

◇ *Portugal was chastised by the European Commission because it had submitted a budget that missed the 3% of GDP deficit limit the euro zone imposes on its members.* 葡萄牙政府由于提交了一份预算，超过了欧元区成员国 GDP 3% 的赤字限制而受到了欧盟委员会的严惩。

define [dɪ'faɪn] *n.* 定义；规定；*v.* 下定义；使明确

Phrase(s): ***define name; define dates; define objectives***

◇ *A guarantee/credit derivative must represent a direct claim on the protection provider and must be explicitly referenced to specific exposures, so that the extent of the cover is clearly defined and incontrovertible.* 担保和信用衍生工具必须是信用保护提供

者的直接负债，而且必须明确对应具体的风险暴露，因此抵补的程度是定义清楚和不可撤消的。

◇ *In general, a corporate exposure is defined as a debt obligation of a corporation, partnership, or proprietorship*. 通常，公司贷款被定义为公司、合伙制企业或者独资企业的债务义务。

defined [dɪ'faɪnd] *adj.* 有定义的；定级的

Phrase(s): ***defined contribution plan; defined contribution pension plan***

◇ *A defined contribution plan gives participants flexibility to decide how their money will be invested depending on your risk bearing ability*. 养老金固定缴款计划给参与者提供灵活性，让他们根据自己的风险承受能力来决定如何投资这笔资金。

defined-benefit [dɪ'faɪnd'benɪfɪt] *n.* 收益确定型

◇ *Under a defined-benefit plan, you get a fixed amount of money per month when you are eligible for retirement benefits; the amount depends on your working length and your salaries during your working years*. 养老金固定收益计划下，等你到了享受退休福利的年龄就可以每月领取固定收益；收益数量取决于你的工龄和当时的工资水平。

defined-contribution [dɪ'faɪnd kɒntrɪ'bjuːʃ(ə)n] *n.* 固定缴款计划

◇ *Usually it is employers who contribute to a defined benefit plan; however, a defined contribution plan should be contributed by both employers and employees*. 养老金固定收益计划通常由雇主来定期支付；但养老金固定缴纳计划则需要雇主和员工共同参与来缴纳。

defined contribution plan [dɪ'faɪnd kɒntrɪ'bjuːʃ(ə)n plæn] *PHR.* 养老金固定缴款计划

◇ *Most employers in the southeast region of the country contribute to either a defined benefit or a defined contribution pension plan for their employees*. 这个国家东南部地区的大部分企业老板都为员工提供养老金固定收益或养老金固定缴纳计划。

deflation [dɪ'fleɪʃ(ə)n] *n.* 通货紧缩；放气贴现

Phrase(s): ***deflation gap; monetary deflation; inflation deflation***

◇ *In 1930s, President Roosevelt was determined to raise prices in the deflation-stricken economy. The choice to leave the gold standard-the centre of monetary orthodoxy at that time-indicated a complete departure from the past system.* 在 20 世纪 30 年代，罗斯福总统决定在受到通货紧缩严重冲击的经济体里提高资本价格。脱离当时货币政策的核心——金本位制表明完全背离过去的经济制度。

◇ *With the rapid growth of online grocery market, physical supermarkets are under great pressure; however, customers are enjoying shop-price deflation.* 网络食品市场的快速增长，给实体超市带来很大压力，但消费者却很享受商店的价格通缩。

deflationary [diː'fleiʃəˌnəri] *adj.* 通货紧缩的

Phrase(s): *deflationary force; deflationary spiral*

◇ *It is criticized by the western world that China's huge exports of industrial goods are flooding global markets, contributing to deflationary pressures and threatening producers worldwide.* 西方世界批判性地认为：中国庞大的工业商品出口充斥全球市场，带来通货紧缩的压力并威胁世界各地的生产商。

◇ *The disappointing prediction is that,for the next year and a half, deflationary pressures will dominate in the mature economies as goods and labor markets remain very slack.* 令人失望的预测是，由于商品和劳工市场仍然极为萧条，因此在接下来的一年半时间里，通缩紧缩的压力将在成熟经济体中成为主导。

defraud [dɪ'frɔːd] *vt.* 欺骗

Phrase(s): *defraud revenue; defraud refund*

◇ *The report said carrying out fraud with letters of credit and issuing fraudulent invoices to defraud export tax refunds may also be removed from the death penalty list.* 信用证诈骗和为骗取出口退税而虚开增值税专用发票等经济诈骗的死刑罪名也在取消之列。

deleverage [di'leɪvərɪdʒd] *v.* 削减头寸；减债

◇ *The government is planning to use low interest rates to encourage hourseholds to borrow more; however, it is also possible that they will take this opportunity to deleverage simultaneously.* 政府正计划利用低利率来鼓励家庭扩大贷款；然而他们也有可能利用这个机会去削减债务。

◇ *While the economy deleverages, it is difficult to prop up the currency in a country.* 在经济杠杆化过程中，维持一国货币的地位很艰难。

delist [diːˈlɪst] *vt.* 停牌

Phrase(s): *delist a company*

◇ *The company's stock was delisted from NYSE(The New York Stock Exchange) in September*, 2010. 2010 年 9 月，这家公司的股票被纽约证券交易所摘牌。

◇ *If a small group of people bought all the equity shares of a public firm, then the shares would be delisted from stock exchanges and could no longer be bought in the open market.* 如果一小群人买了一个上市公司所有的股票，那么这支股票将从证券交易所退市，不能再公开购买。

deliverable obligation [dɪˈlɪvərəblˌɒblɪˈgeɪʃ(ə)n] *PHR.* 交割的债项

◇ *The obligation used for purposes of determining cash settlement value or the deliverable obligation belong to the reference obligation under the credit derivative.* 用于确定现金结算价值或交割的债项属于信用衍生工具的参照债项。

delta [ˈdeltə] *n.* 避险比率；变动量；对冲值

Phrase(s): *delta-normal; delta hedging;*

◇ *When the equity has a delta significantly smaller than 1. 0, any value created will go partially to the bondholders.* 当股票的避险比率明显小于 1，任何创造出的价值都将部分地被债券持有人获得。

◇ *The delta of an option refers to the rate of change of the option prices, with respect to the change in price of the underlying asset.* 期权的对冲值指的是当标的资产价格变化时，期权价格的变化幅度。

demand [dɪˈmɑːnd] *n.* 需求

Phrase(s): *demand -pull inflation; supply demand*

◇ *It is estimated that the oil industry is producing almost 1m barrels a day more than the world is consuming and the demand will not match supply until next year.* 据估计，石油工业每天生产出的石油比世界实际消耗的多出 100 万桶，石油供应与需求要到明年才会匹配。

◇ *Demand-pull inflation is caused by increases in aggregate demand due to increased private and government spending, etc.* 需求拖动通货膨胀是由因个人及政府等支出上涨而导致的总需求量上涨引起的。

denominate [dɪ'nɒmɪneɪt] *n.* 以……（货币）计价

Phrase(s): *denominate quantity; dollar-denominate*

◇ *Brazil pays much higher interest on its debt, the vast majority of which is denominated in reais and of relatively short maturity.* 巴西为它的债务支付更高的利息，绝大部分债务以巴西雷亚尔计价，并且到期日相当短。

denomination [dɪˌnɒmɪ'neɪʃ(ə)n] *n.* 面额

Phrase(s): *new denomination; high denomination*

◇ *Banknotes come in denominations of 5, 10, 20, 50, 100 and 500 euros.* 欧元纸币有 5、10、20、50、100 和 500 不等的面额。

denominator [dɪ'nɒmɪneɪtə] *n.* 分母

Phrase(s): *specific denominator; denominator prefix; denominator values*

◇ *Using the U. S. dollar as the common denominator in quoting exchange rates greatly reduces the number of possible cross-currency quotes.* 在汇率报价时使用美元作为分母，大幅度减少了可能出现的交叉汇率报价数量。

◇ *In calculating the capital ratio, the denominator or total risk weighted assets will be determined by multiplying the capital requirements for market risk and operational risk by 12. 5 and adding the resulting figures to the sum of risk-weighted assets compiled for credit risk.* 在计算资本比率时，市场风险和操作风险的资本要求乘以 12. 5，再加上针对信用风险的风险加权资产，就得到分母，即总的风险加权资产。

deposits [dɪ'pɒzɪts] *n.* 存款；定金；储备

Phrase(s): *bank deposits; private deposits*

◇ *Many small islands in the Pacific Ocean are rich in natural gas deposits, which have triggered territory conflicts among surrounding countries in this region.* 许多太平洋小岛屿天然气储量丰富，引发了该地区周边国家的领土纠纷。

◇ *Under current banking system, large deposits sit on private banks' balance-sheets, which could not be used by the banks to make loans.* 现行的金融体制下，银行的资产负债表上拥有大量的存款，但不能被银行用于发放贷款。

depositor [dɪ'pɒzɪtə] *n.* 存款人；储户

Phrase(s): *small depositor; negative depositor; alternate depositor*

◇ *If interest rates continue going down, depositors would switch to cash, which pays no interest but doesn't charge any either.* 如果利率持续下降，储户就会把存款换成现金，虽然没有利息但也没有费用产生。

◇ *Concerned about investor and depositor panic, government comforted the public by saying banks needing more capital should not be viewed as being at risk of bankruptcy.* 考虑到投资者和储户恐慌，政府安慰民众，声称银行需要更多的资金不能被看作面临崩溃的风险。

depreciation [dɪˌpriːʃɪ'eɪʃ(ə)n] *n.* 折旧；贬值

Phrase(s): ***accelerated depreciation; depreciation reserves; currency depreciation; depreciation of fixed assets; depreciation cost***

◇ *The difference between the rate of depreciation of the physical asset and the rate of amortisation of the lease payments must not be so large as to overstate the CRM (credit risk mitigant) attributed to the leased assets.* 实物资产折旧率和租赁款摊还率之间的差异不能过大，否则将导致租赁资产风险缓释工具被高估。

◇ *Generally speaking, the yearly lease payment is less than the sum of yearly depreciation and yearly interest in the early part of the asset's life.* 一般来说，在资产生命的早期，每年的租赁费用少于每年折旧费用和年度利息之和。

◇ *The Leave camp of Brexit should not be too optimistic, because foreign orders do not respond instantly to sterling depreciation-which also raises the cost of imported inputs.* “脱欧”支持阵营不应过于乐观，因为国外订单不会对英镑贬值立即做出反应，贬值也加大了英国国内进口成本投入。

deregulation [diːˌregjʊ'leɪʃən] *n.* 放松管制

◇ *Raising economic growth through export-oriented manufacturing in a short period of time would be a challenge to the new Prime Minister, because the former government did poorly in deregulation and infrastructure which takes time to make up.* 想在较短的时间内通过出口为导向的制造业提高经济增长对新总理是一个挑战，因为前任政府在放松管制和基础设施建设方面表现很糟糕，这两项都需要时间来弥补。

derivative [dɪ'rɪvətɪv] *n.* 衍生物；派生物；*adj.* 派生的

Phrase(s): ***equity derivative; credit derivatives; derivative warrant; derivative securities***

◇ *Credit risk mitigants include guarantees, credit derivatives, collateral and on-balance sheet netting.* 信用风险缓释包括保证、信用衍生工具、抵押和表内净扣。

◇ *Maturity mismatches may arise when a bank uses credit derivatives to transfer the credit risk of a specified pool of assets to third parties.* 一家银行使用信用衍生工具将特定资产池的信用风险转移给第三方时，期限的错配可能会产生。

derived [dɪ'raɪvd] *n.* 派生的；衍生的

Phrase(s): ***derived deposit; derived demand deposit***

◇ *Gross income is defined as net interest income plus net non-interest income, yet, extraordinary or irregular items as well as income derived from insurance should be excluded.* 总收入定义为：净利息收入加上非利息收入，但不包括特殊项目以及保险派生收入。

description [dɪ'skrɪpʃ(ə)n] *n.* 描述；介绍

Phrase(s): ***beyond description; service description; detailed description***

◇ *This section provides a description of the risk components to be used by banks by asset class.* 这部分内容描述了银行按照资产类别使用的风险要素。

desirability [dɪˌzaɪərə'bɪlɪtɪ] *n.* 必要性；愿望；合意

Phrase(s): ***desirability study; desirability function; overall desirability***

◇ *It should encompass other value considerations, including customer demand, desirability of entering into new markets or expanding existing ones, and operational or mandatory initiatives.* 同时还应当包括其他的价值考虑，包括客户需求、进军新市场或者开拓原有市场的愿望，以及运作需要的或者强制性措施。

detachable warrant [dɪ'tætʃəbl 'wɒr(ə)nt] *PHR.* 可分割认股权证

◇ *Many American companies choose detachable warrants when issuing bonds because they are often actively traded on the American Stock Exchange, thus can be an effective method of raising new capital.* 美国许多公司发行债券时选择可分割认股权证，因为其在美国证券交易所交易活跃，因此可以作为筹集新资金的一种有效方法。

deteriorate [dɪ'tɪərɪəreɪt] *vt.* 恶化

◇ *A bond's credit rating can change as the issuer's financial strength improves or deteriorates; and you can get the information timely from major rating agencies.* 债券的信

用评级会随着发行公司的财务实力增强或恶化而变化；你可以从主要的评级机构及时得到信息。

◇ *Analysts and even some insiders from Chinese banks claimed that this kind of financial credit expansion would deteriorate the inflation and result in growing non-performing loans.* 分析师甚至中国一些银行业界人士也表示，这种信贷狂潮加剧了通胀，导致不良贷款增加。

devaluation [ˌdiːvæljʊ'eɪʃən] *n.* 货币贬值

Phrase(s): ***devaluation surcharge; assets devaluation***

◇ *The finance minister vowed to foreign counterparts that the country would not adopt a policy of competitive devaluation to boost the competitiveness of their exports in the world market.* 财政部长向国外同行发出誓言，该国将不采取竞争性货币贬值的政策来提高在世界市场上的出口竞争力。

◇ *In 1930s, in order to take American out of economic depression, President Franklin Roosevelt adopted many measures including a departure from the gold standard, devaluation of the dollar, and a boost to government spending.* 在20世纪30年代，为了使美国走出经济萧条，罗斯福总统采取了许多措施，包括放弃金本位制、美元的贬值和扩大政府开支。

developed [dɪ'veləpt] *adj.* 发达的

Phrase(s): ***developed countries***

◇ *Manufacturing is a much smaller part of most developed economies than services, however, its recent weakness still makes them nervous.* 相对于服务业，制造业在大多数发达经济体中只占一小部分，然而，最近的制造业疲软还是让这些国家感到紧张。

developer [dɪ'veləpə(r)] *n.* 发展商

Phrase(s): ***risk managersofdevelopers; real estate developers***

◇ *Real estate developers, small businesses and other borrowers have complained strenuously in recent weeks of weakening sales and scarce credit.* 房地产开发商、小型企业和其他贷款者近几周不断抱怨销售的疲软和信贷的缺乏。

◇ *Starbucks announced a deal with Percassi, a retail developer in Italy to open the chain's first location in the country where coffer culture was rooted.* 星巴克宣布与意大利

零售开发商 Percassi 合作，即将在这个咖啡文化深植其根的国家开设第一家连锁店。

Development Bank [dɪ'veləpm(ə)nt bæŋk] *n.* 开发银行；发展银行

Phrase(s): ***development financing bank; Development of Bank Products***

◇ *Their father had spent much of his working life abroad as an official at the Inter-American Development Bank, thus the sisters tasted all kinds of chocolate in the world.* 这对姐妹的父亲曾是美洲开发银行的官员，大部分工作时间在国外度过，因此她们品尝过世界上各种各样的巧克力。

◇ *That has restricted the growth of this particular market, where the only issuers have been the International Finance Corporation and the Asian Development Bank.* 这些要求限制了这一特殊市场的增长，仅国际金融公司和亚洲开发银行作为发行人在此发行过债券。

devise [dɪ'vaɪz] *v.* 发明；设计；*n.* 遗赠（pl. devises）

Phrase(s): ***devise services; specific devise***

◇ *Theories in Finance and mathematical theories can lead us to devise financial structures, which are complicated devices just like engines or nuclear reactors.* 金融学中的理论，数学理论，能帮助我们构造金融工具，金融工具就像发动机，或者核反应堆一样，都是复杂的工具。

◇ *If devise is used as a legal term, it refers to a gift in a will. It applies only to real property and takes effect after the testator's death.* 作为法律术语，遗赠指的是遗嘱中的一个礼物。它只适用于房地产，而且在立遗嘱人去世后生效。

dilution [daɪ'luːʃn] *n.* 摊薄；稀释

Phrase(s): ***Anti-dilution Provisions; dilution effect***

◇ *Dilution refers to the possibility that the receivable amount is reduced through cash or non-cash credits to the receivable's obligor.* 稀释指应收账款的债务人现金或非现金贷款减少应收账款数量的可能性。

◇ *An appropriate maturity treatment will apply when determining the capital requirement for dilution risk.* 确定稀释风险的资本要求时将进行适当的期限处理。

dime [daɪm] *n.* 一角硬币

◇ *In the USA, "quarters" (worth 25 cents each) and "dimes" (worth 10 cents each) are types of coin.* 在美国，“四分之一”（25 分）和“一角硬币”（10 分）是硬币的两种。

dimension [dɪ'menʃ(ə)n] *n.* 维度

Phrase(s): ***linear dimension; single dimension***

◇ *A qualifying IRB rating system must have two separate and distinct dimensions: (a) the risk of borrower default, and (b) transaction specific factors.* IRB 法下合格的评级体系有独立的、性质截然不同的两个维度：（a）借款人违约风险，（b）特定的交易风险。

◇ *A video game called "Quake" took us to the world of three dimensions for the first time, which was really innovative 20 years ago.* 视频游戏“雷神之锤”第一次把我们带进了三维世界，这在 20 年前实在是一种创新。

direct exchange [dɪ'rekt ɪks'tʃeɪndʒ] *PHR.* 直接汇兑

Phrase(s): ***direct exchange contract; direct exchange rate***

◇ *In other cases, goods are "indivisible" and cannot be chopped up into small parts to be used in direct exchange.* 在其他情况下，商品可能会无法分割，无法被切成一个个小部分用于直接交换。

◇ *If a direct exchange system is open to public, it would be extremely difficult for regulators to crack down on tax evasion and money-laundering.* 如果直接交换系统对公众开放，监管机构打击逃税和洗钱将非常困难。

direct investment [dɪ'rekt ɪn'ves(t)m(ə)nt] *PHR.* 直接投资

Phrase(s): ***private direct foreign investment; direct external investment***

◇ *Buying European bonds would be one of the available options for China to help Europe, an economist said, adding that China could boost trade with the region and spur direct investment.* 一位经济学家表示购买欧洲债券将是中国援助欧洲的有效选择之一，中国可以加强同这一地区的贸易往来，促进直接投资。

◇ *Modi's government, aiming at creating opportunities for investment, partnerships and growth, successfully turned India to be the world's top foreign direct investment destination.* 莫迪政府，旨在创造投资机会、建立伙伴关系和促进发展，成功地使印度成为世界领先的外国直接投资目的地。

direct labor cost [dɪ'rekt 'leɪbə(r) kɒst] *PHR.* 直接人工成本

Phrase(s): ***direct labor cost variance; direct labor cost budget; standard direct labor cost***

◇ *Good handing may account for only 50% of the direct labor cost in warehouse and 70% in distribution center.* 在仓库，货物搬运成本只占直接人工成本的 50%，而在配送中心占 70%。

◇ *This study especially discusses the transformation of WIP's（work in process）quantities and amounts, which then serves as the basis of defining the apportionment of direct labor cost and factory overhead.* 本研究特别探讨在制品数量与金额的转换，以作为分摊直接人工费用与制造费用之基础。

direct leases [dɪ'rekt li:sis] *n.* 直接租赁

Phrase(s): ***Direct Financing Leases***

◇ *If the lessor is an independent leasing company that purchases the asset from a manufacturer, these lessors need to finance their direct leases.* 如果出租人是一个独立的租赁公司，从制造商那里购买资产，这类出租人需要进行直接租赁融资。

direct sovereign guarantee [dɪ'rekt 'sɒvrɪn ˌgær(ə)n'ti:] *PHR.* 直接主权担保

◇ *If the supervisor is satisfied that the cover is robust and that nothing in the historical evidence suggests that the coverage of the counter guarantee is less than effectively equivalent to that of a direct sovereign guarantee, such a claim may be treated as covered by a sovereign guarantee.* 如果监管当局认为担保是严格的，而且无历史事实证明反担保不如直接的主权担保有效，该债项则可认为是主权担保。

dirt-cheap ['dɜ:t'tʃi:p] *adj.* 非常便宜的；adv. 非常便宜地

◇ *This small Pacific island country has an educated workforce, fertile farmland, plentiful gas reserves and a dirt-cheap currency.* 这个小的太平洋岛国有受教育的劳动力、良田、大量的天然气储量和一个非常便宜的货币。

dirty price ['dɜ:tɪ praɪs] *n.* 脏价（指债券包括应计利息的现金流现值）

Phrase(s): ***current dirty price; the dirty price of the cash bond***

◇ *In bond market, investors pay dirty price to acquire bonds.* 在债券市场上，投资者支付脏价来收购债券。

◇ *Dirty price is also known as the "full"or "invoice"price.* 脏价也被称为“全价”或“发票价格”。

discipline ['dɪsɪplɪn] *n.* 纪律

Phrase(s): ***market discipline; financial discipline; monetary discipline; price discipline***

◇ *Many urban spaces in Rio are beyond public control; people there know what to do to keep their communities clean, but they don't have the discipline to do it on a regular basis.* 里约热内卢许多城市区域无法进行公共管制；那里的人们知道怎么去保持社区清洁，但他们没有定期保持清洁的纪律。

◇ *The New Basel Capital Accord consists of three pillars. The purpose of Pillar 3 - market discipline is to complement the minimum capital requirements (Pillar 1) and the supervisory review process (Pillar 2).* 巴塞尔新资本协议由三大支柱组成。第三支柱市场纪律的目的是对最低资本要求（第一支柱）和监督检查（第二支柱）的补充。

disclose [dɪs'kləʊz] *v.* & *n.* 公开；揭露

Phrase(s): ***disclose act; authentication disclose***

◇ *Banks must disclose ECAIs（external credit assessment institutions）that they use for the risk weighting of their assets by type of claims.* 银行必须披露按每一债权种类确定其资产风险权重时所选用的外部评级机构。

◇ *Federal regulation requires that companies should disclose all relevant information to investors and potential investors.* 联邦法规要求，公司应对投资者和潜在的投资者披露所有的相关信息。

disclosure [dɪs'kləʊʒə] *n.* 信息披露

Phrase(s): ***full disclosure; voluntary disclosure; disclosure items; disclosure package; selective disclosure; disclosure management; fair disclosure***

◇ *Disclosure allows risk monitoring of the hedge fund, which is especially useful with active trading.* 披露允许对冲基金的风险监控，对活跃的贸易尤其有用。

◇ *Before the United States adopted insider trading and disclosure laws, many managers were alleged to have unfairly trumpeted their firm's prospects prior to equity issuance.* 美国采用内幕交易和信息披露法律以前，许多管理者涉嫌在公司股票发行前不公平地鼓吹自己公司的前景。

discount ['dɪskaʊnt] *vt. & n.* 贴现；折扣；折现

Phrase(s): ***time discount; discount rate; at a discount***

◇ *When measuring economic loss, all relevant factors should be taken into account. This must include material discount effects and material direct and indirect costs associated with collecting on the exposure.* 在计量经济损失时，应该考虑所有的相关因素。这包括重要的折扣效应，以及贷款清收过程中较大的直接和间接成本。

◇ *Domestic banks are certainly at risk from a rash of defaults. Markets now price the big lenders at a discount of about 30% on their book value.* 从一系列的违约情况看，国内的银行肯定存在风险。市场现在给出借方按账面价值约为30%的折扣。

discretion [dɪ'skreʃ(ə)n] *n.* 自由裁量权；谨慎；判断力

Phrase(s): ***administrative discretion; price discretion; absolute discretion; bounded discretion***

◇ *Where the call is at the discretion of the protection seller, the maturity will always be at the first call date.* 如果期权由信用保护的出售者自行选择，期限应从第一个买入期权开始计算。

◇ *The central bank announced that it would start intervening at its discretion in the currency market to prevent currency depreciations from deteriorating.* 央行宣布将开始行使对外汇市场干预的自由裁量权，防止货币贬值恶化。

dishonour [dɪs'ɔnə] *v. & n.* 拒绝兑付

◇ *The risks are that the importer does not accept the bill even though the goods have arrived, or dishonours an accepted bill when it matures.* 风险是即使货物已经到达，进口商也不接受账单，或者拒绝支付到期的账单。

dishonoured cheque [dis'ɔnəd tʃek] *PHR.* 空头支票

◇ *His Internet was disconnected by the telecommunication company because he gave it a dishonoured cheque caused by a wrong spelling.* 他的网络被电信公司断开，由于拼写错误他给对方开了一张拒付支票。

◇ *Dishonoured cheques could be caused by many reasons, such as post-dating, lack of funds in the drawings account, stop cheque requests or insufficient or incorrect signatories.* 拒付支票可由多种原因引起，如逾期、提款账户资金不足、止付支票的请求或者是

不完整或不正确的签名。

disintermediation [ˌdɪsɪntəmiːdɪ'eɪʃ(ə)n] *n.* 脱媒；从银行提款进行证券投资

Phrase(s): ***disintermediation room; financial disintermediation***

◇ *As interest rates are increasingly determined by the market and financial disintermediation that develops in China, the traditional loan-led banking model is bound to change.* 随着利率逐渐市场化和中国金融非中介化的发展，传统的以贷款为主导的银行模式必然改变。

◇ *In the process of disintermediation, companies have to put more internal resources to cover services and management of the funds, thus it is also involved with risks.* 脱媒的过程中，企业必须投入更多的内部资源，包括服务和对资金的管理，因此它也涉及风险。

dispenser [dɪ'spensə] *n.* 自动取款机

◇ *A secure money dispenser usually has two detectors to check whether an amount of money actually dispensed is coincident with an amount of money registered to be dispensed.* 安全取款机通常有两个探测器来检查吐出的金额和要求取出的金额是否一致。

disposable [dɪ'spəʊzəb(ə)l] *n.* 可任意处理的；可自由使用的

Phrase(s): ***disposable age; disposable income***

◇ *There is a very advanced technology on smartphone security, using disposable, one-time encryption keys to ensure that old messages stay scrambled even if hackers manage to get hold of the phone's permanent keys.* 智能手机现在有了一项高端安全技术，即使黑客能够获得该手机的永久密钥，也可使用任意的、一次性的加密密钥来确保旧信息杂乱排列。

◇ *When thinking of stimulating consumer spending, the government should firstly make sure there is a rise in disposable household income.* 政府在思考如何刺激消费时，首先要确保家庭可支配收入的提高。

distant ['dɪst(ə)nt] *adj.* 远期的；远距离的

Phrase(s): ***distant futures; distant payments***

◇ *The current market value of this swap is zero, which implies that all the near-term positive values must be offset by distant negative values.* 这个掉期交易的当前市场价值为零，这意味着所有近期正值必须抵消远期的负值。

distinct [dɪ'stɪŋ(k)t] *adj.* 有区别的；明显的；不同的

Phrase(s): ***distinct options; distinct characteristics; distinct level***

◇ *Under the market-based approach, institutions are permitted to calculate the minimum capital requirements for their banking book equity holdings using one or both of two separate and distinct methods: a simple risk weight method or an internal models method.* 根据市场法规定，允许银行采用一种或两种方法，即简单的风险权重法或内部模型法，对银行账户的股权持有计算最低资本要求。

◇ *A major innovation of the proposed New Accord is the introduction of three distinct options for the calculation of credit risk and three others for operational risk.* 新协议的主要创新表现是分别为计算信用风险和操作风险各规定了三种不同方法。

diversification [daɪˌvɜːsɪfɪ'keɪʃən] *n.* 分散投资

Phrase(s): ***market diversification; product diversification; portfolio diversification;***

◇ *The housing prices bubbles at domestic market and the depreciation of the currency have driven wealthy people in this country to pursue investment diversification.* 国内市场的房价泡沫的和货币贬值推动这个国家的有钱人追求投资多元化。

◇ *We believe there are many smaller developed markets and emerging markets that offer good diversification benefits.* 我们认为有许多较小的发达市场和新兴市场提供良好的分散投资收益。

dividend ['dɪvɪdend] *n.* 股息

Phrase(s): ***dividend receivable; dividend tax; dividend policy***

◇ *Some examples of a company's insider information could be a coming date of dividend payment, a breakthrough in product research & development or a major debt default.* 公司的一些内幕信息可能是未来一次股利支付的日期、一项产品研发的突破或一次重大债务违约。

◇ *Most banks in euro areas are still paying dividends to build up more capital by themselves.* 大多数欧元区银行还在通过支付红利来逐步建立更多资本。

document ['dɒkjʊm(ə)nt] *n.* 单据；文件

Phrase(s): ***internal documents; shipping document***

◇ *Leaked documents exposed that this development bank had worked with three different audit firms in the past five years.* 泄露的文件暴露出这个发展银行曾在过去五年中与三个不同的审计事务所合作。

◇ *A bank must follow all minimum requirements for assigning borrower ratings set out in this document, including the regular monitoring of the guarantor's condition and ability and willingness to honour its obligations.* 银行必须遵守新资本协议中给借款人评级的全部最低标准，包括对保证人状况、兑付债务能力及愿望的常规监控。

documentary credit [dɒkju'ment(ə)rɪ 'kredɪt] *PHR.* 押汇信用证；跟单信用证

Phrase(s): ***irrevocable documentary acceptance credit; documentary clean credit***

◇ *For short-term self-liquidating trade letters of credit arising from the movement of goods (e. g. documentary credits collateralised by the underlying shipment), a 20% CCF will be applied to both issuing and confirming banks.* 对于与货物贸易有关的短期自偿性信用证（如以相应的货运单为抵押的跟单信用证），无论对开证行，还是对保兑行，信用风险换算系数均为 20%。

◇ *Documentary credit arrangement is commonly used in international trade, where a bank in the importer's country undertakes to pay for a shipment, provided the exporter submits the required documents, such as a clean bill of lading,certificate of insurance, certificate of origin) within a specified period.* 跟单信用证广泛用于国际贸易中，具体做法是出口商在指定时间内提交所需文件，如清洁提单、保险单、原产地证书后，由进口国的一家银行承担支付货款。

donate [də(ʊ)'neɪt] *vt.* 捐赠；捐献

Phrase(s): ***donate money to charity***

◇ *The wealthy family decided to donate the inherited land to the country for use as a public park and sports area.* 这个富裕家庭决定把这块继承的土地捐献给国家，作为公共公园和体育运动区。

domestic [də'mestɪk] *adj.* 国内的；*n.* 国货

Phrase(s): ***domestic equity market; domestic exchange***

◇ *Some economists claimed that a British exit from the EU would pose the "biggest domestic risk"to financial stability.* 一些经济学家声称，英国退出欧盟将会对国内金融稳定造成“最大风险”。

◇ *With terrorist attacks occurring more and more frequently around the world, domestic security becomes a big issue in various election campaigns.* 世界各地越来越频繁地发生恐怖袭击，国内安全已经成为各种竞选活动的一大热门话题。

domestic currency [də'mestɪk 'kʌr(ə)nsɪ] *n.* 本国货币

◇ *When the government paper is denominated in the domestic currency and funded by the bank in the same currency, at national discretion a lower specific risk charge may be applied.* 如果政府债券以本币计值，且银行是用本币融资购买的，可根据本国情况适用较低的特定资本要求。

double ['dʌb(ə)l] *adj.* 两倍的；重复的；*v.* 使……加倍；重复

Phrase(s): ***double leasing; double mortgage; double option***

◇*In order to avoid any double counting, there will be no additional capital recognition of the CRM techniques.* 为了避免重复计算，对于信用风险缓释不需要持有额外的资本。

◇ *The new government should double its efforts to increase the minimum wage for blue collar workers rather than please foreign investors by exploiting its people.* 新政府应该加倍努力提高蓝领工人最低工资水平，而不是压榨自己的人民来讨好外国投资者。

Dow Jones average [daʊ dʒəʊnz 'æv(ə)rɪdʒ] *n.* 道·琼斯平均指数

Phrase(s): ***Dow Jones Average Index; Dow Jones Industrial Average***

◇ *The Dow Jones industrial average, which on Tuesday eclipsed its old high from May 2015, gained another 0. 1%, or 24 points, to finish at a new closing high of 18 372. 12.* 道·琼斯工业平均指数，于周二刷新 2015 年 5 月创下的旧高，上涨 0. 1%（24 点），收于 18 372. 12 点，创下新高。

◇ *The Dow Jones industrial average fell Tuesday, with blue chip shares tumbling 108 points, or 0. 6%, the first drop after Brexit.* 道·琼斯工业平均指数星期二下跌，蓝筹股的股价暴跌 108 点（0. 6%），是英国脱欧以后的首次下跌。

downgrade ['daʊngreɪd] *n.* 降级

Phrase(s): ***Sovereign downgrade; credit downgrade***

◇ *After Microsoft's announcement of a latest acquisition deal, Moody's Investor Service immediately warned that it is reviewing the company's credit rating for a potential downgrade from its current AAA score.* 微软宣布了一项新的收购交易后，穆迪投资服务

公司立即警告说，他们正在重新评估该公司的信用评级，可能从目前 AAA 评分做出下调。

◇ *Standard & Poor is warning to give a potential rating downgrade to P&S Holdings due to the substantial drop of its net asset value recently.* 由于近来其净资产价值的大幅下降，标准普尔警告将可能给 S&P 控股公司一个信用评级下调。

downgrade risk ['daʊngreɪd rɪsk] *PHR.* 降级风险

◇ *If the Congress decides to increase the America's debt limit, the country will definitely have a downgrade risk in credit rating by some leading credit agencies in the world.* 如果国会决定增加美国的债务限额，美国一定会有被世界上一些主要信用机构信用降级的风险。

down payment [daʊn 'peɪm(ə)nt] *PHR.* 头期款；预付定金

Phrase(s): ***return of down-payment; cash down payment***

◇ *People buying homes need only make a 20% down payment to obtain a mortgage, except in the five first-tier cities, where they must put down 30%.* 购房者只需要支付 20% 的首期付款获得抵押贷款，除了五个一线城市，在那里他们必须首付 30%。

◇ *Some small lenders even make loans to home buyers to cover their down payments, which adds potential risks to the financial stability in the country.* 一些小银行甚至将贷款发放给购房者，用于支付首付款，这给国家金融稳定增加了潜在风险。

downside ['daʊnsaɪd] *n.* 下降趋势

Phrase(s): ***downside deviation; unlimited downside***

◇ *An official from Federal Reserve said Brexit had pushed global risks even further to the downside and introduced new uncertainties into the global financial market.* 美联储一位官员说英国脱欧推动全球风险进一步下行并为全球金融市场带来新的不确定性。

◇ *Banks, which were majored their business in auto loans, are showing a downside as delinquencies on the securities backed by subprime auto loans have reached the highest level since 2009.* 主营汽车贷款业务的银行，由于次级汽车贷款支持的证券违约率已经达到 2009 年以来的最高水平而呈现下行趋势。

downturn ['daʊntɜːn] *n.* 衰退（经济方面）

Phrase(s): ***economic downturn; cyclical downturn***

◇ *Burberry Group, the well-known British luxury retailer, is getting a new CEO to seek a turnaround amid slumping profit and a downturn in China, hopefully.* 英国著名奢侈品零售商巴宝莉集团，近日上任新的首席执行官，希望为下滑的利润以及在中国市场的衰退寻求转机。

◇ *The purpose of the annual stress tests is to determine whether the nation's biggest banks have enough capital to survive a severe economic downturn in the future.* 年度压力测试的目的是确定国家的大银行是否有足够的资本在未来严重的经济衰退中存活下来。

draft [drɑːft] *n.* 汇票；草稿；*v.* 起草

Phrase(s): ***demand draft; demand bank draft***

◇ *A banker's acceptances an agreement by a bank to pay a sum of money, typically arising when a seller sends a bill or draft to a customer, and the bank will charge the customer a fee for this convenient service.* 银行承兑汇票是银行同意支付的协议，通常在卖家发送账单或汇票给客户的时候发生，而银行将向客户收取服务费。

◇ *One way to obtain a credit commitment from a customer before the goods are delivered is to arrange a commercial draft and require the customer to pay a specific amount by a specified date, otherwise the delivery will not be made.* 卖方在货物交付前获得客户信用承诺的方法之一是开具商业汇票，要求客户在指定日期前支付特定金额，否则将不能交货。

draw [drɔː] *n. & v.* 提款；使用

Phrase(s): ***draw a cheque; draw money***

◇ *Draws on the facility (i. e. assets acquired under a purchase agreement or loans made under a lending agreement) must not be subordinated or subject to deferral or waiver.* 该流动性便利的使用（如按照购买协议购买的资产或按照贷款协议发放的贷款）不能有延期或放弃的规定。

◇ *The originating bank must reflect the likelihood of additional draws in its EAD (Exposure at Default) estimate.* 发起行必须要在其违约风险暴露估计中反映额度被继续使用的可能性。

driving force ['draɪvɪŋ fɔːs] *PHR.* 驱动力；推动力

◇ *As a major driving force for global growth, China has the confidence and capability to promote economic restructuring and maintain medium to high growth at the same time in the new normal.* 作为全球经济增长的主要动力，中国在新常态下具有促进经济结构调整和保持中高增长的信心和能力。

dual ['dju:əl] *n.* 双数；双重；*adj.* 二体的；双重的

Phrase(s): ***dual exchange market; dual trading***

◇ *Many online shopping websites, such as Amazon offer dual factor authentication when you are shopping so that when you log on to your account, the company will send a one-time code to your smartphone for you to input in order to access your account, which greatly increases your security.* 许多在线购物网站如天猫商城，在您购物时提供二元身份认证。当您登录账户时，公司将发送一个一次性的代码到您的智能手机上，您只有输入了这个代码才能访问账户，安全性大大提高。

◇ *On the one hand, it has dual attributes about trading and leasing, and is the representative of innovative finance business, just like other types of financial lease business.* 一方面，它与其他的融资租赁业务类型一样，都具有买卖和租赁的双重属性，都是创新性融资业务的代表。

dual currency bond ['dju:əl 'kʌr(ə)nsɪ bɒnd] *PHR.* 双货币债券

◇ *A dual currency bond is a debt instrument that has coupons denominated in a different currency than its principal amount.* 二重货币债券是一种债务工具，息票以不同于本金的货币币种标识。

due [dju:] *n.* 应付款；应得之物；*adj.* 到期的；由于

Phrase(s): ***due course; due date***

◇ *However,due to insufficient funds, lack of teachers and other factors, the development of new primary schools can't meet the need of the development of basic education.* 但由于经费不足、师资缺乏等因素，新式小学堂的发展无法满足基础教育发展的需要。

◇ *For the purpose of defining the secured portion of the past due loan, eligible collateral and guarantees will be the same as for credit risk mitigation purposes.* 在界定逾期贷款的担保部分时，所采用的合格的抵押物和担保的范围与信用风险缓释技术的范围相同。

due diligence [djuː 'dɪlɪdʒ(ə)ns] *PHR.* 尽职调查

Phrase(s): *cultural due diligence; due diligence investigation; financial due diligence*

◇ *Make sure you use your due diligence when choosing a financial advisor; it is important to see whether he/she has the competence and experience to help meet your investment needs.* 选择财务顾问时确保尽职调查；重要的是看他/她是否有能力和经验来帮助你满足投资需求。

◇ *Institutions should conduct the necessary due diligence to ensure that they are selecting an appropriate solution, be it open source or proprietary.* 机构应该进行必要的尽职调查，以确保他们正在选择一个适当的方案，无论是开源的还是专有的。

dumping ['dʌmpɪŋ] *n.* 倾销

Phrase(s): *persistent dumping; dumping margin; phantom dumping*

◇ *Overcapacity has a damaging effect on International markets, while anti-dumping tariffs will help partially control this problem.* 产能过剩对国际市场具有破坏性影响，而反倾销关税将有助于部分控制这个问题。

◇ *A government research paper says foreign-owned broker-dealers are dumping an average of $170 billion in certain U. S. assets before the end of each quarter in order to appear safer and less levered.* 政府研究报告称外资券商每季度末尾都平均倾销高达 1 700 亿美元的美国资产，以求表面安全和低杠杆。

duration [djʊ'reɪʃ(ə)n] *n.* 久期；持续；期间

Phrase(s): *duration averaging; spread duration; duration gap; key rate duration*

◇ *Throughout the duration of the transaction, including the amortisation period, there is a pro rata sharing of interest, principal, expenses and losses based on the balances of receivables outstanding at the beginning of each month.* 在交易的整个过程中，包括摊还期，应当根据每月月初的应收账款余额，按比例分摊利息、本金、风险以及损失。

◇ *The S&P 500 set a milestone by going 2 607 calendar days without a 20% pullback in April this year, which topped the 2,606-day duration of the bull market that ended in August 1956.* 标准普尔 500 在今年四月树立了一个里程碑，连续 2 607 天没有出现 20% 的拉回，超过了 1956 年 8 月结束的 2 606 天牛市记录。

duty ['dju:tɪ] *n.* 关税

Phrase(s): ***customs duty; customs import duty***

◇ *VAT on self-used articles brought or mailed into China by individuals shall be levied together with Customs Duty*. 个人携带或者邮寄进入中国境内的自用物品的增值税，连同关税一并计征。

E

EAR (effective annual rate) [ɪ'fektɪv 'ænjʊəl reɪt] *abbr.* 实际年利率

Phrase(s): ***estimated EAR***

◇ *The distinction between the stated annual interest rate (SAIR)and the effective annual rate (EAR) frequently confuses students.* 名义年利率和实际年利率的区别经常使学生感到困扰。6（103）

earnings ['ɜːnɪŋz] *n.* 收益；盈利

Phrase(s): ***earnings per share; annual earnings; earnings yield***

◇ *Wells Fargo & Co. said this week its second quarter net income dipped 2. 8% as mortgage banking revenue and equity investment earnings fell.* 美国富国银行本周表示，其第二季度净收入下降了 2. 8%，原因是抵押贷款业务收入和股权投资收益下滑。

◇ *Banks should anticipate the implications of rapid exposure growth and take steps to ensure that their estimation techniques are accurate, and that their current capital level and earnings and funding prospects are adequate to cover their future capital needs.* 银行应该预测贷款迅速增长的影响，并采取步骤来保证自己的估计技术是准确的，当前的资本水平、收益及融资前景都足以满足将来的资本需要。1（83）

◇ *This is the risk of indirect losses to earnings arising from negative public opinion.* 负面的公众舆论会带来盈利间接损失的风险。

easy ['iːzɪ] *adj.* 放松；放宽；分期

Phrase(s): ***easy credit; easy payment; easy money policy***

◇ *"Our entire economy is in danger," he said, carefully explaining how we had gotten to that point: foreign investment in the U. S. , easy credit, a housing boom, irresponsible lending and borrowing.* “我们的整个经济处于危险之中。”他说道，并仔细地解释我们是怎么到达这一步的：在美国的外国投资、宽松的信贷、房地产业的繁荣和不负责任的借贷。14（278）

EAY (effective annual yield) [ɪ'fektɪv 'ænjʊəl ji:ld] *abbr.* 实际年收益率

Phrase(s): ***estimated EAY***

◇ *The annual rate of return is called either the effective annual rate (EAR) or the effective annual yield (EAY).* 年回报率被称作实际年利率或实际年收益率。6（102）

EBIT (earnings before interest and taxes) ['ɜ:nɪŋz bɪ'fɔ: 'ɪnt(ə)rɪst ənd tæksi:z] *abbr.* 息税前利润

Phrase(s): ***EBIT margin***

◇ *Return on capital is typically measured by dividing a company's earnings before interest and taxes, or EBIT, by the sum of the company's common and preferred stock value plus debt.* 资本回报率通常是将一个公司息税前利润除以公司的普通股和优先股的价值加上债务的总和得出来的。

◇ *EBIT is usually called "income from operations" on the income statement and is income before unusual items, discontinued operations or extraordinary items.* 息税前收益在损益表上通常被称为“营运收入”，是指未计不正常项目、停止经营或非常项目前的收入。6（47）

EBITDA (earnings before interest, taxes, depreciation and amortization) ['ɜ:nɪŋz bɪ'fɔ: 'ɪnt(ə)rɪst tæksi:z dɪˌpri:ʃɪ'eɪʃ(ə)n ənd əˌmɔ:taɪ'zeɪʃən] *abbr.* 息税折旧摊销前利润

Phrase(s): ***operational EBITDA***

◇ *EBITDA margin is commonly used as a measure of profitability because it focuses directly on operating cash flows.* 息税折旧摊销前利润率通常被用来衡量盈利能力，因为它直接关注经营性现金流量。

ECN (electronic communications network) [ɪˌlek'trɒnɪk kəmju:nɪ'keɪʃ(ə)n 'netwɜ:k] *abbr.* 电子通讯网络

◇ *Privacy protection issue has long been a big concern of law-makers who are specialized in ECN.* 隐私保护问题长期以来都是电子通讯网络专业立法者们关注的一大问题。

◇ *In a very important development in the late 1990s, the NASDAQ system was opened to so-called electronic communications networks (ECNs). ECNs are basically websites that allow investors to trade directly with one another.* 20 世纪 90 年代末期金融产业有了重大的发展，纳斯达克系统开放了所谓的电子通讯网络。ECN 是允许投资者与其他投资者进行直接交易的基础网站。6（296）

econometrics [ɪˌkɒnə'metrɪks] *n.* 计量经济学

Phrase(s): ***financial econometrics; econometrics toolbox; theoretical econometrics***

◇ *Financial econometrics is the science of modeling and forecasting financial time series.* 金融计量学是一门拟合和预测金融时间序列的科学。5（x）

◇ *Scottish economist Angus Deatonwon 2015 Nobel Prize in Economics for his contribution to finding out the best solutions to measure and analyze welfare and poverty. He was formally an econometrics professor at the University of Bristol.* 苏格兰经济学家安格斯・迪顿荣获 2015 年诺贝尔经济学奖，因为他在发现测量和分析福利和贫困最佳解决方案方面所做出的贡献。他曾经是英国布里斯托大学的计量经济学教授。

EDI (electronic data interchange) [ɪˌlek'trɒnɪk 'deɪtə ɪntə'tʃeɪn(d)ʒ] *abbr.* 电子数据交换

◇ *In financial market, EDIis an electronical exchange platform used to transfer financial information and funds between parties, which terminates the use of paper invoices, paper checks, mailing, and handling.* 在金融市场，EDI 是一个在机构之间转移金融信息和资金的电子交易平台，从而终结了纸质发票、纸质支票、信汇、费用票据。6（841）

EGARCH (exponential generalized autoregressive conditional heteroskedasticity) [ˌəkspə'nenʃ(ə)l 'dʒenərəlaizd ɔ:təʊ'rɪgresɪv kən'dɪʃ(ə)n(ə)l het(ə)rəʊskədæs'tɪsətɪ] *abbr.* 广义自回归条件异方差

Phrase(s): ***EGARCH model***

◇ *Use of the log-conditional variance in EGARCH specification relaxes the constraint of positive model coefficients.* 对数条件方差在 EGARCH 中的使用释放了系数为正的约束。5（302）

◇ *The leverage effect introduced in the EGARCH section is not generated by the FIGARCH model*. EGARCH部分介绍的杠杆效应不能在FIGARCH模型中产生。5(304)

efficiency [ɪ'fɪʃ(ə)nsɪ] *n.* 效率；功效；有效性

Phrase(s): ***Pareto efficiency; work efficiency***

◇ *The data deluge has changed international trade by dealing with orders on internet platforms to improve the efficiency of their operations*. 海量数据改变了国际贸易，通过互联网平台处理订单改善了运营效率。

◇ *Weak efficiency means that the price of the security reflects the past price and trading history of the security*. 弱式有效意味着证券价格反映了证券过去的价格和交易的历史信息。5（171）

◇ *Semistrong efficiency means that the price of the security fully reflects all public information*. 半强式有效意味着证券价格反映了所有公开的信息。5（171）

◇ *Strong efficiency exists in a market where the price of a security reflects all information, whether or not it is publicly available*. 强式有效意味着证券价格反映了所有信息，无论这些信息是否可以公开获取。5（171）

elasticity [elæ'stɪsɪtɪ] *n.* 弹性

Phrase(s): ***price elasticity; elasticity of supply***

◇ *The ratio of the percent change in option price per percent change in stock price is called the option elasticity*. 股票价值每变动1%而带来期权价值变动的百分比就叫作期权弹性。7（578）

element ['elɪm(ə)nt] *n.* 元素；要素；原理；成分；自然环境

Phrase(s): ***inverse element; classical element***

◇ *Common economics often ignores a very important element of inequality between the sexes-unpaid work, such as baby care*. 普通的经济学往往忽视性别间不平等的一个重要部分——无酬工作，比如照顾婴儿。

◇ *Credit derivatives also introduce a new element of risk, which is legal risk*. 信用衍生品也引入风险的新因素，即法律风险。

eligible ['elɪdʒɪb(ə)l] *adj.* 合格的

Phrase(s): ***eligible paper; eligible instruments for open market operations***

◇ *In order to be eligible for the carve-out treatment, an exposure must have an original maturity below three months.* 要符合例外处理的条件，暴露的原始期限必须在3个月以下。1（58）

◇ *Written internal policies must specify all material elements of the receivables purchase programme, including the advancing rates, eligible collateral, necessary documentation, concentration limits, and how cash receipts are to be handled.* 书面的内部政策必须规定在购入应收账款方案中所有重要的因素，包括预付款率、合格的抵押品、必要的文件、集中性限额，以及现金收据如何处理。1（89）

embedded [ɪm'bedɪd] *adj.* 嵌入的；内涵的；内置的

Phrase(s): ***embedded profits; embedded options; embedded value***

◇ *America's success in software innovation gives it a huge advantage in a world in which software is urgently needed to be embedded into hardware, such as smart phones and driverless cars.* 美国在软件创新方面的成功给它带来了世界性的巨大优势，因为当今世界迫切需要软件嵌入硬件的技术，如智能手机、无人驾驶汽车。

emergency [ɪ'mɜːdʒ(ə)nsɪ] *n.* 紧急的

Phrase(s): ***emergency currency; emergency loan; emergency money***

◇ *More than 8 000 surgeries had been cancelled because of this longest doctors' strike in history, only emergency cover was provided; yet they were strongly backed by the public.* 因为这次史上持续时间最长的医生罢工，超过8 000台的手术已经被取消，只有急救治疗得以保留；然而他们却得到了公众的强烈支持。

◇ *The government should be empowered with broader authorities to deal with the failure of a systemically important institution-including the power to inject capital and to make emergency loans.* 应该赋予政府更广泛的权力来解决一个具有系统重要性的机构的破产问题，这包括注入资本和提供紧急贷款的权力。14（446）

emerging market [i'mədʒiŋ 'mɑːkɪt] *PHR.* 新兴市场

Phrase(s): ***emerging capital market; emerging securities market***

◇ *Beside QE (quantitative-easing)programs implemented by the Central Bank, emerging markets are also big buyers of American government bonds as they have built up their foreign-exchange reserves.* 除了央行实行的量化宽松计划，新兴市场也是美国政

府债券的大买家，因为他们已经建立了自己的外汇储备。

◇ *Many emerging markets are facing with challenges of excessive debts, slow growth, plunging currencies and rising inflation.* 许多新兴市场正在面临债务过多、增长缓慢、货币贬值和通货膨胀的挑战。

EMH (efficient market hypothesis) [ɪ'fɪʃ(ə)nt 'mɑːkɪt haɪ'pɒθɪsɪs] *abbr.* 有效市场假说

Phrase(s): *EMH paradox*

◇ *Although EMH is considered as a cornerstone of modern financial theory, it failed to explain some real events in the market; Warren Buffet's investment legend is just one example.* 虽然有效市场假说是现代金融理论的基石，但是它还是无法解释金融市场中的一些真实事件；沃伦·巴菲特的投资传奇就是一个例子。

◇ *All the efficient market hypothesis hold the view that, on average, the manager cannot achieve an abnormal or excess return.* 所有的有效市场假说均认为，通常管理人员不能获得不正常或超额收益。6（443）

empirical [em'pɪrɪk(ə)l] *adj.* 经验主义的；完全根据经验的；实证的

Phrase(s): *empirical method; empirical equation*

◇ *As econometric models are probabilistic models, any model can in principle describe our empirical data.* 因为计量经济学模型都是概率模型，原则上任一模型都能描述我们的经验数据。5（7）

◇ *The criteria used to define facility grades must be grounded in empirical evidence.* 定义贷款级别的标准，必须建立在经验研究基础上。

endogenous [en'dɒdʒɪnəs] *adj.* 内生的；内因性的

Phrase(s): *endogenous variable; endogenous groups*

◇ *Some researchers develop the models of endogenous liquidity risk incorporation, when this type of risk is unique for the agent and presents the effect of liquidated quantity on the prices.* 一些研究者建立内生流动性风险整合的模型，由于这种类型的风险对于机构是独一无二的并呈现清算数量对价格的影响。10（279）

◇ *The recovery rate is endogenous here, as it depends on the value of the firm, time, and debt ratio.* 恢复率在这儿是内生的，因为它取决于公司的价值、时间以及债务比率。

endorse [ɪn'dɔːs] *vt.* 背书；认可；签署；赞同；在背面签名

Phrase(s): ***endorse clause; endorse bill***

◇ *It has been endorsed by financial regulators and bank supervisory committees as a tool designed to quantify and forecast market risk.* 它已被金融监管机构和银行监管委员会用来量化和预测市场风险。5（312）

endowment [ɪn'daʊm(ə)nt] *n.* 捐赠；捐款；财富

Phrase(s): ***capital endowment; endowment fund***

◇ *Like mutual funds, hedge funds also pool and invest the money of many clients. But they are open only to institutional investors such as pension funds, endowment funds, or wealthy individuals.* 像共同基金一样，对冲基金也聚集很多客户的钱去投资。但是他们只开放给机构投资者，如养老基金、捐赠基金或富人。7（48）

◇ *Endowment funds are held by organizations chartered to use their money for specific non-profit purposes.* 捐赠基金是由特许的组织建立，将他们的资金用于特定非营利目的的一种基金。7（755）

enhancement [ɪn'hɑːnsm(ə)nt] *n.* 增强

Phrase(s): ***credit enhancement; edge enhancement; contrast enhancement***

◇ *A credit enhancement is a contractual arrangement in which the bank retains or assumes a securitisation exposure and, in substance, provides some degree of added protection to other parties to the transaction.* 信用提升是一种合同安排，在这样的安排下，银行保留或承担资产证券化的风险，并且在实质上向合同中的其他当事人提供某种程度的额外保护。1（102）

◇ *By credit enhancement it is meant that there is a source of capital that can be used to absorb losses incurred by the asset pool.* 信用增级意味着存在一个资本来源可用于吸收由资产池导致的损失。13（15）

entity ['entɪtɪ] *n.* 实体

Phrase(s): ***legal entity; accounting entity; business entity***

◇ *An SPE(special purpose entity)is a corporation, trust, or other entity organised for a specific purpose；the structure is set to isolate the SPE from the credit risk of an originator or seller of exposures.* 特别目的机构指的是为特定目的而组建的公司、信托机构或其

他类型的实体；其结构在于将特别目的机构同发起人或资产出售人的信用风险分离开来。1（101）

equilibrium [ˌiːkwɪ'lɪbrɪəm] *n.* 均衡；平衡

Phrase(s): ***equilibrium price; market equilibrium; Nash equilibrium***

◇ *In equilibrium, the risk premium on the market portfolio must be just high enough to induce investors to hold the available supply of stocks.* 处于平衡状态时，市场投资组合的风险溢价必须足够高以诱导投资者持有大量股票。7（231）

◇ *The Dow rises as markets look to regain their equilibrium amid new geopolitical risks.* 在新的地缘政治风险中，道指上升期待市场重新获得平衡。

equity ['ekwɪtɪ] *n.* 普通股；抵押资产的净值；公平；公正；平衡法

Phrase(s): ***private equity; equity investment; stockholders equity***

◇ *Portfolio managers who want an estimate of the interest rate sensitivity of a portfolio consisting of both equity and bonds would have to estimate the duration of the equity position in the portfolio.* 投资组合的管理者如果想要估计一个既包括股票又包括债券的组合的利率敏感性，就必须估计其中股票的久期。5（173）

◇ *Compared with private equity, hedge funds have short lockup periods, which means investors can redeem their cash relatively easily whenever they are worried about the performance in the emerging markets or the oil price.* 与私募基金相比，对冲基金有较短的禁售期，这意味着投资者在担心新兴市场表现或者油价时，可以相对容易地赎回现金。

erosion [ɪ'rəʊʒ(ə)n] *n.* 侵蚀；贬值

Phrase(s): ***erosion of the value of money; erosion of value of assets***

◇ *Erosion occurs when a new product reduces the sales and, hence, the cash flows of existing products.* 当一个新产品的出现减少了现有产品的销售量，继而减少现金流时，就发生了侵蚀效应。6（173）

◇ *Nominal interest rates include an inflation premium that compensates the lender for inflation-induced erosion in the real value of principal.* 名义利率包含一个通货膨胀的溢价，用来补偿债权人因为通货膨胀而导致的本金价值的贬值。7（468）

escrow ['eskrəʊ] *n.* 第三方保管契约

Phrase(s): ***escrow account; escrow fees; in escrow***

◇ *The cash proceeds of a short sale are kept in escrow by the broker, and the broker usually requires that the short-seller deposit additional cash or securities to serve as margin (collateral) for the short sale.* 卖空交易的现金收益由经纪人暂为保管，并且经纪人通常要求卖空者存放额外的现金或证券作为卖空的保证金（抵押品）。7（113）

◇ *In the house purchase deal in the USA, it is typical for the purchaser and seller to negotiate for a credit or an escrow allowance for a repair or replacement found during the inspection in relatively small dollar amounts.* 在美国的购房交易中，普遍的做法是买方和卖房就验房时发现的需要修理或者更换的地方协商一笔数额相对较小的由第三方托管的经费。

estate [ɪ'steɪt] *n.* 房地产；财产

Phrase(s): ***real estate; estate agent***

◇ *However, as the real estate market corrected sharply, the put options moved in-the-money, which led to large losses on the super senior debt.* 然而，随着房地产市场大幅修正，看跌期权向价内期权转移，导致超级优先债务的巨额亏损。

◇ *High-volatility commercial real estate (HVCRE) lending is the financing of commercial real estate that exhibits higher loss rate volatility.* 高变动性的商用房地产贷款是一种具有较高损失波动率的商用房地产融资。

estimation [estɪ'meɪʃ(ə)n] *n.* 估计；尊重

Phrase(s): ***precision estimation; estimation procedures***

◇ *Although the time horizon used in PD(probability of default) estimation is one year, banks must use a longer time horizon in assigning ratings.* 尽管估计违约概率的时间段是一年，但是银行评级时必须使用较长的时间段。1（73）

◇ *Different regression models and their estimation methods are presented in this chapter.* 这一章节介绍了各种回归模型和估计方法。5（xi）

◇ *It is clear that evaluating performance is fraught with enormous potential estimation error.* 很明显，评估绩效充满了大量潜在的估计误差。5（24）

estimator ['estɪmeɪtə] *n.* [统计] 估计量；评价者

Phrase(s): ***unbiased estimator; point estimator***

◇ *The Retirement Estimator offered by American Social Security Administration help*

US people figure out exactly how much they will get from the Social Security account when they retire from their jobs. 由美国社会保障管理总署提供的这款退休金计算器能帮助人们算出当他们退休时究竟能从社会保障账户中拿多少钱。

ETF (Exchange Traded Fund) [ɪks'tʃeɪndʒ treɪdɪd fʌnd] *abbr.* 交易型开放式指数基金

Phrase(s): ***ETF securities; cross-border ETF***

◇ *To obtain finer coverage of equity risks, hedgers could use futures contracts on industrial sectors, or exchange-traded funds (ETFs), or even single stock futures*. 为了能够更好地覆盖股票风险，套期保值者可以利用产业部门中的期货合约，或交易所交易型基金（ETF），甚至单一的股票期货。

◇ *Investment giant Carl Icahn recently expressed his concern on high-yield ETFs in an environment of rising interest rates. If the junk bond bubble bursts, small investors who have swarmed to high-yield bond ETFs for juicier returns could suddenly find themselves trapped*. 投资巨头卡尔·伊坎日前表示对利率上升环境中高收益交易型开放基金的担忧。如果垃圾债券泡沫破灭，为了丰厚回报而涌向这些高收益债券开放基金的小投资者会突然发现困在其中。

Eurobond ['juərəuˌbɒnd] *n.* 欧洲债券

Phrase(s): ***Eurobond market; Eurobond denominated in SDR***

◇ *A Eurobondis a bond issued in multiple countries but denominated in a single currency, usually the issuer's home currency*. 欧洲债券是一种在许多国家发行但是以单一货币标价的债券，通常用发行者所在国的本币标价。6（486）

◇ *Eurobond market has nothing to do with euros; it isa large, liquid market for international bonds denominated in dollars and other major currencies*. 欧洲债券市场与欧元没有关系；它是一个大型的以美元或者其他主要货币计价的国际债券流动市场。

eurocurrency ['juərəu'kʌrənsi] *n.* 欧洲货币

Phrase(s): ***eurocurrency banking market; eurocurrency deposits; eurocurrency funds***

◇ *Eurocurrency is money deposited in a financial center outside of the country whose currency is involved*. 欧洲货币是存在一个货币发行国以外的金融中心的货币。6（946）

◇ *For instance, Eurodollars—the most widely used Eurocurrency—are U. S. dollars deposited in banks outside the U. S. Banking System.* 例如，欧洲美元——运用最广泛的欧洲货币——是将美国美元存在美国银行系统以外的银行中。6（946）

EVA (economic value added) [ˌiːkə'nɒmɪk 'væljuː 'ædɪd] *abbr.* 经济增加值；经济附加值

◇ *A company like Intel earns a far higher ROE (return on equity) on its investments in chip making facilities than its cost of capital. The present value of these "economic profits," or economic value added, is a major component of Intel's market value.* 像英特尔这样的公司在芯片生产设施上投资的净资产收益率远远高于其资本成本。这些“经济收益”的现值，或称为经济附加值，是英特尔市场价值的一个重要组成部分。7（433）

evaluate [ɪ'væljʊeɪt] *vt.* 评价；估价；求……的值；*vi.* 评价；估价

Phrase(s): ***evaluate methods; evaluate outcome; evaluate system***

◇ *A qualified professional must evaluate the property when information indicates that the value of the collateral may have declined materially relative to general market prices or when a credit event, such as default, occurs.* 当信息显示抵押品价值相对于一般的市场价格已经大幅度下降或有信贷事件（如违约）发生时，有资格的专业人员必须评估抵押品。1（91）

◇ *To evaluate the validity of the model, we perform diagnostic checks on the residuals with inspection of the structure of the SACF and SPACF of the residuals.* 为了评估模型的有效性，我们考察残差的 SACF 和 SPACF，对残差进行诊断检验。5（270）

event [ɪ'vent] *n.* 事件；大事；项目；结果

Phrase(s): ***event-study methodology; event procedure; external event***

◇ *Operational risk is the risk of loss resulting from failed or inadequate internal processes, systems, and people, or from external events.* 操作风险是由失败的或不充分的内部流程、系统和人员，或外部事件引起的损失风险。

◇ *In the event of the borrower's financial distress or default, the bank should have legal authority to sell or assign the receivables to other parties without consent of the receivables obligors.* 发生借款人财务陷入困境或违约的情况，银行应该拥有不经过应收账款债务人的同意，出售应收账款或将应收账款交给其他方面的法律权利。1（92）

excess [ɪk'ses] *n.* 超过；超额；过度；过量；无节制；*adj.* 额外的；过量的；附加的

Phrase(s): *excess value; excess profit*

◇ *Since most central banks are supported by governments, they could issue fresh bonds to soak up the excess money if the inflation rate went too high.* 由于大多数中央银行在政府支持下，如果通货膨胀率过高，他们可以发行新的债券来吸收多余的钱。

◇ *E-commerce platforms like Alibaba help all kinds of manufacturers in China to sell excess inventory, which also increase job opportunities in production and delivery process.* 像阿里巴巴这样的电子商务平台帮助中国各类厂家销售过剩库存，同时在生产和交付过程中也增加了就业机会。

exchequer [ɪks'tʃekə] *n.* 国库；国家金库

Phrase(s): *exchequer bill; exchequer bonds; Chancellor of the Exchequer*

◇ *British Chancellor of the Exchequer highlightedthe incompatibility between sovereignty and membership in the joint currency; Britain respects other country's democratic right to decide their future as well as the right of the eurozone to set conditions of membership. This contradictory integration is one of the reasons we stay out of the euro.* 英国财政大臣强调主权和共同货币的会员之间的不相容性；英国尊重其他国家的民主决定自己的未来以及欧元区设定会员条件的权利。这种矛盾的整合是我们不加入欧元的原因之一。

◇ *British Chancellor of the Exchequer George Osborne in London reassured British people that with current financial strength, UK was ready to face the market volatility caused temporarily by Brexit.* 英国财政大臣乔治·奥斯本向英国人民保证，以目前的金融实力，英国已准备好面对脱欧带来的暂时性市场波动。

exchange [ɪks'tʃeɪndʒ] *n.* 交换；交流；交易所；兑换；*vt.* 交换；交易；兑换；*vi.* 交换；交易；兑换

Phrase(s): *exchange rate; foreign exchange; stock exchange*

◇ *The merger between the London and Frankfurt stock exchanges have been rejected by shareholders in both countries; now it is the third time to pick up the topic.* 伦敦证券交易所和法兰克福证券交易所之间的合并遭到了两国股东的拒绝；现在这个话题第三

次被拾起。

◇ *Swaps are agreements by two parties to exchange cash flows in the future according to a prearranged formula.* 互换就是交易双方根据预定公式约定未来互换现金流的协议。

ex-date ['eks deɪt] *n.* 除息日

Phrase(s): *on the ex-date*

◇ *In a world without taxes, the stock price would fall by the amount of the dividend on the ex-date.* 在一个没有税收的世界，除息日的股票价格将会减少与股息相同的数额。6（583）

execution [ˌeksɪ'kju:ʃ(ə)n] *n.* 执行

Phrase(s): *execution cost; execution uncertainty; execution stage*

◇ *What has the greatest impact on the execution of the deal is how the senior bonds are structured.* 这次交易执行最大的影响是如何结构化高级债券。13（42）

◇ *An economic analysis of the cost of further enhancement of a structure versus the improved execution of the transaction will be performed by the structurer.* 进一步增强结构和改善交易执行的成本经济分析将由组建者执行。13（105）

exempt [ɪg'zem(p)t] *vt.* 免除；豁免；*adj.* 被免除的；被豁免的；*n.* 免税者；被免除义务者的

Phrase(s): *exempt from tax; exempted institution*

◇ *National supervisors may exempt facilities to certain smaller domestic corporate borrowers from the explicit maturity adjustment if the reported sales (i. e. turnover) as well as total assets for the consolidated group of which the firm is a part of are less than €500 million.* 如果公司是并表集团的一部分，而且它报告的销售（营业额）和总资产不足5亿欧元，各国监管当局可以将银行对这些国内公司借款人的小额贷款期限从直接调整中排除。1（58）

◇ *Corporations can obtain financing from a municipality at the tax-exempt rate because the municipality can borrow at that rate as well.* 企业可以从市政当局以免税的利率融得资金，因为市政当局也能以这样的利率借款。6（560）

exercise price ['eksəsaɪz praɪs] *PHR.* 行权价格；合约价

◇ *If the stock price is greater than the exercise price, then the call is in the money.* 如果股票价格大于行权价格，那么这个买入期权为价内期权。6（682）

◇ *The Merton model views equity as akin to a call option on the assets of the firm, with an exercise price given by the face value of debt.* 默顿模型认为股本就类似于公司资产的一个看涨期权，其行使价格由债务的面值决定。

existing [ɪɡ'zɪstɪŋ] *adj.* 现存的；现有的

Phrase(s): ***existing assets; existing controller; existing state***

◇ *A minimum risk weight of 100% will be applied to private equities where the returns on the investment are based on regular and periodic cash flows not derived from capital gains and there is no expectation of future (above trend) capital gain or of realising any existing gain.* 最低风险权重 100% 适用于非上市公司的股权，持有这类股权的投资收益来自常规和定期的现金流，不是资本收益，也不期望实现将来（向上的趋势）的资本收益或任何现实资本收益。

expected [ɪk'spektɪd] *adj.* 预期要发生的；期望

Phrase(s): ***expected loss (EL); expected return***

◇ *In the IRB framework, banks are permitted to recognise provisions in offsetting the expected loss of risk weighted assets.* 按照内部评级法框架的要求，银行可使用准备冲抵风险加权资产的预期损失。

◇ *For the specific case of facilities already in default, the bank must use its best estimate of expected loss for each facility given current economic circumstances and facility status.* 对已经违约贷款的具体情况，银行必须根据当前经济情况和贷款的法律地位，最妥善地估计每笔贷款的预期损失。1（84）

experiment [ɪk'sperɪm(ə)nt] *vi.* 尝试；进行实验；*n.* 实验；试验；尝试

Phrase(s): ***experiment design; experiment teaching***

◇ *Some leading chipmakers are persistently experimenting with materials beyond silicon, because they believe there must be better conductors than silicon in terms of power usage and speed.* 一些领先的芯片制造商正在不断尝试超越硅材料，因为他们相信，在电力使用和速度方面一定有比硅更好的导体。

expiration [ˌekspɪ'reɪʃ(ə)n] *n.* 呼气；终结；到期

Phrase(s): ***expiration date; automatic expiration***

◇ *A European option differs from an American option in that it can be exercised only on the expiration date.* 欧式期权与美式期权的不同之处在于，它只能在到期日行权。6（681）

◇ *The credit derivative shall not terminate prior to expiration of any grace period required for a default on the underlying obligation to occur as a result of a failure to pay.* 在违约所规定的任何宽限期之前，标的债项不能支付并不导致信用衍生工具终止。1（34）

explicit [ɪk'splɪsɪt] *adj.* 显性的

Phrase(s): ***explicit cost; explicit transaction***

◇ *The African Development Bank handed over $1 billion in the past two years with the explicit aim ofboosting intra-African trade, unfortunately only a few countries in the continent take it seriously.* 非洲发展银行在过去两年中拿出 10 亿美元专门用于振兴非洲国家间贸易，遗憾的是，整个非洲大陆只有少数几个国家认真对待。

exponential [ˌekspə'nenʃ(ə)l] *adj.* 指数的；越来越快的；*n.* 指数

Phrase(s): ***exponential growth; exponential probability distribution; exponential smoothing***

◇ *Moore's Law, put forward by one of the founders of Intel—Gordon Moore, refers to the exponential increase of the number of electronic components which could be crammed into an integrated circuit.* 摩尔定律，是英特尔创始人之一——戈登·摩尔提出来的，是指集成电路上可容纳的电子元件数量呈指数增长。

exposure [ɪk'spəʊʒə] *n.* 风险暴露

Phrase(s): ***exposure at default (EAD); qualifying revolving retail exposures (QRRE); credit exposure***

◇ *The risk weights for sovereign,interbank, and corporate exposures are differentiated based on external credit assessments.* 按照外部信用评级，对主权、银行同业、公司的风险暴露的风险权重各不相同。

◇ *For the first time since the 2008 financial crisis, more institutional investors plan to cut their hedge-fund exposure than to increase it due to the poor performance in hedge fund industry*. 自2008年金融危机以来，由于对冲基金业表现不佳，更多的机构投资者首次计划削减而不是增加他们的对冲基金风险暴露。

external [ɪk'stɜːn(ə)l] *adj.* 外部的；外面的

Phrase(s): ***external rating; external source***

◇ *Many regional trade communities impose a common external tariff on goods of non-members so as to protect the member countries' benefits*. 许多区域贸易共同体对非成员国的商品施加一个共同的外部关税，以保护成员国利益。

◇ *To many countries in the world, military spending is not only for external defence use, but also for internal security concerns*. 对于世界上许多国家来说，军费开支不仅用于对外防御，也用于内部的安全问题。

external financing needed (EFN) [ɪk'stɜːn(ə)l fɪ'nænsɪŋ 'niːdid] *abbr.* 外部融资需求

Phrase(s): ***associated EFN***

◇ *There are many external financing needed calculators online to help companies define exact amount needed; the essential elements are Growth in Assets (GD), Earnings Retained (ER) and Growth in Current Liabilities (GCL)*. 网上有很多外部融资需求计算器帮助企业准确定义资金需求量；所需要素有资产增长、留存收益与流动负债增长。

extraordinary losses [ɪk'strɔːd(ə)n(ə)ri 'lɒsɪz] *PHR.* 非寻常损失

Phrase(s): ***extraordinary gains and losses***

◇ *Stress testing can be described as a process to identify and manage situations that could cause extraordinary losses*. 压力测试可以被描述为一个用来识别和管理可能造成非寻常损失情况的过程。

F

fabricate ['fæbrɪkeɪt] *v.* 制造；伪造

Phrase(s): *fabricate evidence; fabricate an excuse*

◇ *Prosecutors presented evidence on the court to prove that the executives of this company had fabricated the certificate of test which falsely made people believe that their products were not contaminated.* 检察官在法庭上出示的证据证明这家公司的高管们伪造了产品测试证书，错误地使人们相信他们的产品没有被污染。

facility [fə'sɪləti] *n.* 贷款；便利

Phrase(s): *facility letter; loan facility*

◇ *A bank must have a sufficient number of facility grades to avoid grouping facilities with widely varying LGDs into a single grade.* 银行必须具备足够数量的贷款评级，以避免违约损失率变化大的多笔贷款进入同一评级级别。1（72）

factor ['fæktə] *n.* 因子；要素；*n.* 代理商

Phrase(s): *discounting factor*

◇ *To value the payment, we need a discounting factor.* 为了评估支付情况，我们需要一个贴现因子。

◇ *When using factor models to measure risk, banks should ensure that the factors are sufficient to capture the risks inherent in the equity portfolio.* 如果采用因子模型来测量风险，希望银行保证这些因子能够计量出股权组合中的内在风险。

◇ *Risk factors should correspond to the appropriate equity market characteristics (for example, public, private, market capitalisation industry sectors and sub-sectors, operational characteristics) in which the bank holds significant positions.* 风险要素应该与银行持有重要股权头寸的市场特征（例如上市的、非上市的、市场资本化的行业、内部的子行业、操作特征）一致。1（96）

factor loading ['fæktə 'ləʊdɪŋ] *PHR.* 因子负荷

◇ *Factor loadings represent how much a factor explains a variable in factor analysis, loadings usually range from -1 to 1 and they can be positive and negative.* 因子负荷代表因子分析中一个因素对一个变量的解释程度，负荷通常范围从—1 到 1，可以是正也可以是负。

factoring ['fæktərɪŋ] *n.* 保理

◇ *Factoring enables companies to sell their accounts receivable available at a discount to a third-party to raise capital; it is often used by industries which need to wait for a long time to get their receivables.* 保理业务允许公司以一定折扣出售应收账款给第三方以筹集资金；它往往应用于需要等待很长时间来归拢应收账款的行业。

factorization [ˌfæktərai'zeiʃən] *n.* 因子分解；因式分解

Phrase(s): ***factorization method***

◇ *In mathematics, factorization is the decomposition of an object (for example, a number, a polynomial, or a matrix) into a product of other objects, or factors, which when multiplied together give the original.* 在数学中，因式分解就是把一个对象（例如，一个数字、一个多项式或一个矩阵）分解成几个其他的对象或因子，将它们相乘积可以还原。

factory ['fækt(ə)rɪ] *n.* 工厂；制造厂

Phrase(s): ***factory automation***

◇ *The abandoned textile factory close to a higher education park has been turned into a shopping mall with all kinds of facilities to meet the needs of university students and teachers.* 靠近高等教育园的一个废弃纺织厂已经被改造成了一个设备齐全的购物中心，满足学生和教师的需要。

fact sheet [fækt ʃiːt] *PHR.* 事实报告

◇ *A fact sheet is always based on a thorough and objective fact check, otherwise, it will become a cheat sheet*. 事实报告应该总是基于一个全面、客观的事实调查，否则，它将成为一个作弊报告。

fade [feɪd] *vi.* 褪色；凋谢；逐渐消失

Phrase(s): ***fade back***

◇ *This reversal effect,in which losers rebound and winners fade back, suggests that the stock market overreacts to relevant news*. 反转效应，就是指失败者回弹而成功者后退。这个效应意味着股票市场对相关信息的过激反应。7（365）

fair [feə] *n.* 定期集市；博览会

Phrase(s): ***commodity fair; job fair***

◇ *The latest employment fair is a collaborative effort by the Chamber of Commerce and several top-ranking universities; a wide range of businesses will come and seek qualified candidates*. 最新的就业集市是在商会和一些一流大学的共同努力下举办的；很多企业将前来物色人才。

fair value [feə 'vælju:] *PHR.* 公允价值

◇ *The efficient market hypothesis implies that companies hope to receive fair value for securities that they sell; fair here refers to the price they receive from issuing securities is the present value*. 有效市场假说暗示公司希望从出售的证券中获得公允价值；公允在这里指他们发行证券获得的价格是目前的价值。

fait ['feɪt] *n.* 证书；契据

Phrase(s): ***fait of purchase***

◇ *A fait of purchase will be given to the creditors as a certificate for right of claim, creditors are supposed to gain an extra interest as a compensation for the money*. 债权人购买债券后收到一个代表求偿权的购买凭证，他们可以因此获得利息作为补偿。

fake [feɪk] *n.* 假货；赝品

Phrase(s): ***fake bill***

◇ *Many online shoppers trust reviews given by previous shoppers; in reacting to this preference, some shops pay people to write good reviews for them or give gifts to exchange for five stars*. 许多网上购物者信任以前顾客给予的评价；应对这种偏好，一些商店付费请人为他们写好评，或赠送礼物来换取五颗星。

falsify ['fɔ:lsɪfaɪ] *v.* 伪造；撒谎

Phrase(s): ***falsify evidence***

◇ *A financial manager was sentenced to 10 years in prison for a conspiracy to falsify records in a fraud which could be the largest Ponzi Scheme in the US history.* 一个财务经理因为伪造记录、密谋欺诈被判 10 年监禁，该诈骗甚至构成美国历史上最大的庞氏骗局。

Fama-French three-factor model [fama'fren(t)ʃ θri:'fæktə 'mɒdl] *n.* Fama-French 三因子模型

◇ *The Fama–French (1993) three-factor model is an empirically motivated implementation of Ross's arbitrage pricing theory.* Fama-French 三因子模型是罗斯套利定价理论的一个实证研究。6（392）

FASB(Financial Accounting Standards Board) [faɪ'nænʃ(ə)l ə'kaʊntɪŋ s'tændədz bɔ:d] *abbr.* 财务会计准则委员会

◇ *The Enron scandal and other accounting frauds prompted the Financial Accounting Standards Board (FASB) to reexamine the use of off-balance-sheet transactions.* 安然丑闻和其他会计作假事件促使财务会计准则委员会重新审视资产负债表外交易的使用。13（19）

fat tails [fætteilz] *PHR.* 厚尾

◇ *Fat tails is a type of statistical distribution with the opening of the bell stretched out in a bell cruve. Distributions with fatter tails have a greater kurtosis coefficient.* 厚尾是一种统计分布，在钟形曲线图上显示为钟的开口外伸。更厚的尾部分布有更高的峰态系数。

favored [feɪvəd] *adj.* 有利的；受到优待的

◇ *The presidential candidate promises high-speed Internet in every home by 2020, winning a fame of tech's favored candidate.* 总统候选人承诺到 2020 年每个家庭都拥有高速互联网，赢得“高科技宠儿”候选人的声誉。

favourable ['feɪv(ə)rəb(ə)l] *adj.* 有利的；良好的；赞成的；赞许的；讨人喜欢的

◇ *Under the first option all banks incorporated in a given country will be assigned a risk weight one category less favourable than that assigned to claims on the sovereign of that country.* 按照第一个方案，对银行的债权将得到比其所在注册国债权差一个档次的风险权重。1（31）

FDIC(Federal Deposit Insurance Corporation) ['fed(ə)r(ə)l dɪ'pɒzɪt ɪn'ʃʊər(ə)ns kɔːpə'reɪʃ(ə)n] *abbr.* 美国联邦存款保险公司

◇ *FDIC, on behalf of the U. S. government, sold $2. 4b in Citigroup bonds which were issued during 2008 financial crisis, and Citigroup wouldn't make any profit from this sale.* 美国联邦存款保险公司代表美国政府，出售了花旗集团在 2008 年金融危机期间发行的 24 亿美元债券，花旗集团不会从这个交易中赢利。

feasible set ['fiːzɪb(ə)l set] *PHR.* 可行集

◇ *A portfolio in a feasible set offers the highest possible expected return for a given level of risk or the lowest possible risk for a given level of expected return.* 在可行集内的投资组合，对于一个给定的风险会提供尽可能高的预期收益率或者对于一个给定的预期收益水平会提供尽可能低的风险水平。

federal budget deficit ['fed(ə)r(ə)l 'bʌdʒɪt 'defɪsɪt] *PHR.* 联邦预算赤字

◇ *A former U. S. senator was criticized recently for not fulfill his promise to reduce the federal budget deficit.* 一位前美国参议员近日被批评没有履行他的承诺减少联邦预算赤字。

Federal Reserve Board ['fed(ə)r(ə)l rɪ'zɜːv bɔːd] *n.* 联邦储备委员会

◇ *The Federal Reserve Board let savers down when it announced that interest rates would stay at the record low of 0-0. 25 percent which started from 2008 in an effort to boost the economy after the economic crisis.* 联邦储备委员会令储户们大失所望，它宣布将利率保持在 0 —0. 25% 的低点，这个利率是从 2008 年经济危机后为刺激经济而设定的。

fee [fiː] *n.* 费用；酬金；小费

Phrase(s): ***servicing fee; guaranty fee***

◇ *Securitization can be used to allow the originator of loans to convert capital intensive assets to a less capital intensive source of servicing fee income.* 资产证券化能够用来允许贷款的发起人将资本密集的资产转化为对于资本要求相对宽松的服务费收入来源。13（20）

feedback ['fi:dbæk] *n.* 成果；反馈

Phrase(s): ***positive feedback***

◇ *Bank of China has established a 24/7 information hotline to answer questions, receive feedback and solve complaints.* 中国银行已经建立了一个全天候信息热线，用于回答问题，接受反馈并解决投诉。

feed stocks [fi:dstɔks] *PHR.* 原料；能源物质

◇ *Price, volume, growing environment and transportation risk of feedstocks demand attention.* 我们需要关注原材料的单价、数量、生长环境以及运输风险。1（200）

fictitious [fɪk'tɪʃəs] *adj.* 虚构的；假想的；编造的；假装的

Phrase(s): ***fictitious transaction; fictitious capital; fictitious account***

◇ *According to operation, modern economy can be classified into physical economy based on material products operation and fictitious economy based on fictitious capital operation.* 根据运行方式的不同，现代经济可以划分为以物质产品运行为主体的实体经济和以虚拟资本运行为主体的虚拟经济。

Fidelity Magellan Fund [fɪ'delɪtɪ mə'gɛlən fʌnd] *n.* 富达麦哲伦基金

◇ *The Fidelity Magellan Fund is one of the largest mutual funds in the United States; one of its managers — Peter Lynch,once created a legend for generating average annual returns of 29% per year over his 14-year tenure.* 富达麦哲伦基金是美国最大的共同基金之一；富达麦哲伦基金经理彼得·林奇曾创造了一个传奇：在他 14 年的任期内保持了 29% 的年平均回报率。

fiduciary [fɪ'dju:ʃ(ə)rɪ] *n.* 受托人；*adj.* 信托的

Phrase(s): ***fiduciary trust***

◇ *In the financial world, a fiduciary is a financial advisor who agrees legally to put their client's best interests ahead of their own.* 在金融世界中，受托人是在法律协议下同意将其客户的最佳利益置于自身利益之上的财务顾问。

field warehouse financing [fi:ld 'weəhaʊs fɪ'nænsɪŋ] *PHR.* 存仓货物融资

◇ *In field warehouse financing, a public warehouse company supervises the inventory for the lender.* 在仓库场地融资中，由公共仓库公司监督贷款人的库存。6（822）

FIFO method ['faifəu 'meθəd] *abbr.* 先进先出计算法

◇ *In accounting practice, companies may choose either the last-in, first-out (LIFO) or the first-in, first-out (FIFO) method to value inventories.* 在会计实务中，企业可以选择后进先出（LIFO）或先入先出（FIFO）的方法来评估存货价值。

figure ['fɪgə] *n.* 数字；价格

Phrase(s): ***figure out***

◇ *In today's job market, new graduates are generally not well paid, but they will see a salary with more figures in the second or third job with gains both in working experience and networking.* 在今天的就业市场上，刚毕业的人一般薪水都不高，但在第二或第三份工作时伴随着工作经验和人脉的增加，薪水上涨。

filing ['faɪlɪŋ] *n.* 文件归档；文件

◇ *The presidential candidate's filings with regulators and outside estimations suggest that he is a billionaire and he is always seeking to shift away from debt-heavy property.* 总统候选人提交给监管机构的文件和外部的估计表明，他是一个亿万富翁，而且总是寻求摆脱债务沉重的财产。

final settlement date ['faɪn(ə)l 'set(ə)lm(ə)nt deɪt] *PHR.* 最终清算日期

◇ *The future date is called the delivery date or final settlement date.* 未来的日期也叫交割日或到期清算日。

financial [faɪ'nænʃ(ə)l] *adj.* 金融的；财务的；经济的

Phrase(s): ***financial risk management; financial crisis; financial institution***

◇ *London Stock Exchange is famous for its profitable clearing-house business in swaps, bonds and other financial instruments.* 伦敦证券交易所以盈利的互换、债券和其他金融工具结算业务而闻名。

◇ *In order to secure buyers' financial interest, many e-commerce platforms set an intermediate account to temporarily hold customers' money until they have safely received their goods.* 为了保障买家的利益，许多电子商务平台设立中间账户暂时性地持有客户的钱，直到他们安全收到货物。

financial community [faɪ'nænʃ(ə)l kə'mju:nɪtɪ] *PHR.* 财界；金融界

◇ *His achievement in generating long-time high annual returns became a miracle in the financial community.* 他创造长期高年回报率的成绩已经成为金融界的一个奇迹。

financial distress [faɪ'nænʃ(ə)l dɪ'stres] *PHR.* 财务困境

◇ *Some organizations in the U. S. offer you financial education service, helping you tell whether you are in financial distress or a good shape. This service is just like a blood pressure machine to check the health condition of your money.* 在美国，一些组织为你提供金融教育服务，帮助你判断你的财务状况是在困境中还是良好。这项服务就像一个血压仪检查你的金融健康状况。

financial guideline [faɪ'nænʃ(ə)l 'gaɪdlaɪn] *PHR.* 财务指标

◇ *With good financial guideline and strong capability for liquidation, the project has a low risky level. The investment can bring favorable economic and social benefits.* 该项目各项财务指标较好，偿债能力较强，整体风险水平较低，项目投资有良好的经济效益和社会效益。

financial innovation [faɪ'nænʃ(ə)l ˌɪnə'veɪʃn] *PHR.* 金融创新

◇ *Financial innovation is to investors what technological innovation is to customers.* 金融创新之于投资者就如同技术创新之于消费者。

financial integrity [faɪ'nænʃ(ə)l ɪn'tegrɪtɪ] *PHR.* 财政方面的稳健性

◇ *According to a financial integrity investigation report, since 2010 thousands of U. S. homeowners complained that they were cheated by lawyers or marketers who had boasted to renegotiate mortgage loans or help them stave off foreclosure actions.* 一份金融稳健性调查报告显示，自2010年以来，数以千计的美国购房者控诉他们被律师和营销商欺骗，这些人鼓吹可以重新协商抵押贷款并帮助房主避开丧失抵押品赎回权的诉讼。

financial intermediary [faɪ'nænʃ(ə)lˌɪntə'miːdɪərɪ] *PHR.* 金融中介机构

◇ *A U. S. financial advisor was accused of stealing a large amount of money from clients when serving as a third-party financial intermediary in their investment process.* 美国一名财务顾问被指控作为第三方金融中介，在客户投资过程中窃取客户大量金钱。

financial leases [faɪ'nænʃ(ə)l liːsiz] *PHR.* 融资租赁

◇ *In financial leases, the lessee must make all payments or face the risk of bankruptcy.* 在金融租赁中，承租人必须支付所有款项否则将面临破产风险。

financial leverage [faɪ'nænʃ(ə)l 'liːv(ə)rɪdʒ] *PHR.* 财务杠杆

◇ *Financial leverage is the extent to which a firm relies on debt, and a levered firm is a firm with some debt in its capital structure.* 财务杠杆是企业依靠债务的延伸，并且一个有杠杆的企业在它的资本结构中有一些债务。6（410）

financial slack [faɪ'nænʃ(ə)l slæk] *PHR.* 财务宽松

◇ *Financial slack is a favorable condition when companies have sufficient cash,marketable securities, and are ready to obtain debt from the financial markets.* 财务宽松是一种有利状态，公司有足够的现金和有价证券，并准备好从金融市场上获得债务。

financial turmoil [faɪ'nænʃ(ə)l 'tɜːmɒɪl] *PHR.* 金融风暴；金融危机；金融混乱

◇ *IMF recently warned global policy-makers that a potential risk of financial turmoil would happen if no active measures were taken to safeguard the financial system and to reform the monetary policy.* 国际货币基金组织最近警告说，全球决策者如果不主动采取措施保护金融系统、改革货币政策，金融动荡可能发生。

fine [faɪn] *n.* 罚金；罚款；*v.* 罚款；处以罚金

Phrase(s): ***pay a fine; severe fine***

◇ *The pesticide factory was facing a heavy fine due to violations of environmental regulations.* 农药厂因违反环保法规而面临重罚。

finite ['faɪnaɪt] *adj.* 有限的；限定的

Phrase(s): ***finite set***

◇ *We can value a bond with a finite number of coupons over T periods at which time the principal is repaid.* 我们可以利用债券在有限 T 个时期内的利息计算该债券的价值，其中在 T 时期债券的本金会被归还。

FIORI(Financial Institution Operational RiskInsurance) [faɪ'nænʃ(ə)l ɪnstɪ'tjuːʃ(ə)n ɒpə'reɪʃ(ə)n(ə)l rɪskɪn'ʃʊər(ə)ns] *abbr.* 金融机构操作风险保险

◇ *Swiss Re, a global leading wholesale provider of reinsurance, insurance and other insurance-based forms of risk transfer, introduced in 1999 an innovative product called financial institution operational risk insurance.* 瑞士再保险公司，是全球领先的再保险，保险和基于保险的风险转移业务批发供应商，1999 年其引入一个创新的产品叫作金融机构操作风险保险。8（507）

fire ['faɪə] *n.* 磨难；*vt.* 解雇；开除

Phrase(s): ***under fire***

◇ *The president fired his respected finance minister because he failed to lead the monetary policy reform and refused to sign off trade deals which were favored by the president.* 总统解雇了他尊敬的财政部长，因为他未能推进货币政策改革，而且拒绝签署总统青睐的贸易协议。

firm [fɜːm] *n.* 公司；商号；*adj.* 坚定的；牢固的

Phrase(s): ***brokerage firm; firm price; firm market***

◇ *Contra-accounts involve a customer buying from and selling to the same firm. The risk is that debts may be settled through payments in kind rather than cash.* 往来账户涉及从同一家公司买卖的客户。这种风险在于债务可以通过以货代款的方式偿付，而不是通过现金偿付。1（45）

firm quotation [fɜːm kwə(ʊ)'teɪʃ(ə)n] *PHR.* 实际报价

◇ *An improved shopping cart and quotation system were introduced that enable eligible clients to receive a comprehensive and firm quotation in a matter of seconds.* 改进版购物车和报价系统，使合格的客户在几秒钟内就可得到全面的实际报价。

first-of-basket-to-default swap [fɜːst (ə)v'bɑːskɪttudɪ'fɔːlt swɒp] *PHR.* 首次违约互换

◇ *The first-of-basket-to-default swap gives the protection buyer the right to deliver one and only one defaulted security out of a basket of selected securities.* 首次违约互换提供了保护买家的权利，在一篮子可选择的证券中只提供一种可能违约的证券。

first-order effect [fɜːst'ɔːdə ɪ'fekt] *PHR.* 一阶效应

◇ *Duration measures the first-order (linear) effect of changes in yield and the second-order (quadratic) term of convexity.* 久期测量地是收益率的一阶（线性）变化以及凸性的二阶（二次）变化。

fiscal drag ['fɪsk(ə)l dræg] *PHR.* 财政拖累

◇ *Lower interest rates usually boost private sector spending, partially offsetting the fiscal drag from higher taxes and government spending cuts.* 较低的利率水平通常会刺激私营部门的支出，部分抵消增税以及政府减支带来的财政拖累。

Fitch [fɪtʃ] *n.* 惠誉国际

Phrase(s): *Fitch rating agency* 惠誉国际评级机构

◇ *Food giant Heinz had a merger with Kraft Foods Group in 2015;Fitch, one of the American's big three financial ratings firms, rated Heinz' positive on hearing the news of merger.* 食品巨头亨氏公司 2015 年与卡夫食品集团合并；美国三大金融评级机构之一的惠誉在听到合并的消息后给出亨氏积极等级。

fixed [fɪkst] *adj.* 固定的

Phrase(s): *fixed-coupon bonds; fixed interest rate; fixed maturity*

◇ *Banks using the Basic Indicator Approach must hold capital for operational risk equal to a fixed percentage (denoted alpha) of average annual gross income over the previous three years.* 采用基本指标法银行持有的操作风险资本应等于前三年总收入的平均值乘上一个固定比例（用 α 表示）1（121）

◇ *In interest-rate swaps, two parties agree to exchange a fixed-rate payment for a floating rate based on a variable measure; since the counterparties of swaps are usually from the private sector, the fixed-rate element of the swap has tended to pay a higher yield than the equivalent bond, thus greater risk could be involved.* 利率互换指双方同意基于在变化中测量的浮动利率来交换固定利率支付；由于互换交易对手通常来自私营部门，互换的固定利率高于等效的债券收益率，从而可能涉及更大的风险。

fixed-coupon [fɪkst'kuːpɒn] *PHR.* 固定利息

◇ *Fixed-coupon bonds refer to bonds which pay a fixed percentage of the principal every period and finish the remaining as one-time payment at maturity.* 固定利息债券是一种每期偿还固定本金、到期一次清偿的债券。

fixed-income [fɪkst'ɪnkʌm] *PHR.* 固定收入

◇ *Due to the decline in bond trading activities, Morgan Stanley plans to slash 25% fixed-income jobs next week.* 由于债券交易活动的下降，摩根士丹利计划下周削减 25% 的固定收入工作。

fixture ['fɪkstʃə] *n.* 定期存款；定期赛事；*adj.* 固定的

Phrase(s): *fixture rate*

◇ *A fixture is money given to a (banking) institution that earns interest but cannot be withdrawn except after giving notice for a defined period of time (usually 90 days)*. 定期存款就是以获得利息、同时除非在确定时间内（通常90天）通告才能取款的方式存到（银行）机构的钱。

flash [flæʃ] *n.* 闪光；闪现；一瞬间

Phrase(s): ***flash crash; in a flash***

◇ *But when high-frequency traders abandon the market, as in the so-called flash crash of 2010, liquidity can likewise evaporate in a flash*. 但是当高频率交易者退出市场，正如2010年的闪电崩盘事件一样，流动性也立刻蒸发。7（66）

flat [flæt] *adj.* 平的；单调的；不景气的

Phrase(s): ***flat file***

◇ *Shares of the digital tech company stayed flat when it announced a merger plan with a small streaming website, however, the shares plunged when it decided to cut jobs*. 当宣布与一个小的流媒体网站合并计划时，股票平稳，然而当决定裁员时股票跳水。

fleeting ['fliːtɪŋ] *adj.* 飞逝的；转瞬间的

◇*Apple is facing intense competition from global rivals in phone market, tablet market as well as content-selling business; like many other leading companies in history, the age of Apple is also a fleeting one*. 苹果在手机市场、平板电脑市场以及内容销售业务中面临着来自全球的竞争激烈；像许多其他历史上领先的公司，苹果时代也是转瞬即逝。

flexible ['fleksɪb(ə)l] *adj.* 灵活的；有弹性的

Phrase(s): ***flexible pay; flexible mechanisms***

◇ *Many young people in urban China applaud ride-sharing apps like Uber and Didi for their flexible hours, low prices and convenience*. 许多中国城市的年轻人对优步、滴滴等打车软件赞赏有加，因为它们时间上灵活，价格上便宜，而且使用起来方便。

floating rate ['fləʊtɪŋ reɪt] *PHR.* 浮动利率

◇ *Floating-coupon bonds, which pay interest equal to a reference rate plus a margin, reset on a regular basis; these are usually called floating-rate notes*. 浮动利率债券，它的利息等于一个参考利率加上保证金，可以定期重置，这些通常被称为浮动利率票据。

floor [flɔː] *n.* 下限

Phrase(s): ***caps and floors***

◇ *The risk weight on the collateralised portion will be subject to a floor of 20% under two specific conditions*. 除了在两种特定条件下，其余情况下抵押品部分的风险权重底线都是 20%。

floor broker [flɔ: 'brəʊkə] *PHR.* 场内经纪人

◇ *A note on an order tells the floor broker to use his or her own good judgment in filling the order*. 在订单上有一个说明，让场内经纪人用自己的判断来执行订单。

flotation ['fləʊ'teɪʃ(ə)n] *n.* （公司的）成立；创立；开办；（资金的）筹措；（债券的）发行

Phrase(s): ***flotation cost***

◇*Flotation costs arise from the issuance of new securities in publicly traded companies; they can include legal fees, registration fees, underwriting fees, etc*. 发行成本产生于公开上市交易的公司发行新证券时；包括律师费、注册登记费以及承销费等。

flow [fləʊ] *n.* 流动；流量

Phrase(s): ***cash flow***

◇ *If the investor has a direct claim on all of the cash flow and the certificate holder has a proportionate share of the collateral's cash flow, the term pass-through certificate (or beneficial interest certificate) is used*. 如果投资者对所持有的现金流有直接的请求权，而且凭证的持有者对担保品的现金流拥有按比例的份额，则使用过手型的说法。13（30）

flow to equity (FTE) approach [fləʊ tə 'ekwɪtɪ ə'prəʊtʃ] *PHR.* 流动资产的方法

◇ *The flow to equity (FTE) approach is an alternative capital budgeting and valuation approach*. 流动资产的方法是一种可选择的资本预算和价值评估方法。6（561）

fluctuation [flʌktʃʊ'eɪʃ(ə)n] *n.* 波动性

Phrase(s): ***price fluctuation; currency fluctuation***

◇ *Banks are required to adjust both the amount of the exposure to the counterparty and the value of any collateral received in support of that counterparty to take account of future fluctuations in the value of each, occasioned by market movements*. 银行需使用折扣系数，对交易对象的风险暴露和交易对象提供的抵押品的价值进行调整，以考虑市场发生波动时，两者未来价值的波动。1（20）

foam [fəʊm] *n.* 泡沫

Phrase(s): ***capital market foam***

◇ *The Stock Market Foam is the part which is higher than the theoretical stock value and has soared up unreasonably because of stock in speculations.* 股市泡沫是由于股市投机导致股票价格非理性上涨超过股票理论价值的部分。1（199）

forced liquidation [fɔːst lɪkwɪ'deɪʃ(ə)n] *PHR.* 强制清算；平仓

◇ *The furniture company was ordered by the court to make a forced liquidation, so in the coming month, a big sale would be on in its big warehouse.* 家具公司被法院责令强制清算，所以在接下来的一个月里，公司将在其大仓库里进行大甩卖。

forecast ['fɔːkɑːst] *n.* 预测；预报；预想；*vt.* 预报；预测；预示

Phrase(s): ***make forecasts; forecasting model***

◇ *International Monetary Fund, for the second time this year, made negative forecast on the global growth, calling for immediate action to reduce the risk of further recession.* 国际货币基金今年第二次对全球增长做出了负面的预测，呼吁立即采取行动减少进一步衰退的风险。

foreclose [fɔː'kləʊz] *v.* 取消抵押品赎回权

Phrase(s): ***foreclosed assets; foreclose upon***

◇ *If you missed a monthly mortgage payment due to unanticipated expenses, your loan could be called due and payable, and the lender could move to foreclose on your property.* 如果因为意外开支没能还上一个月的按揭贷款，你的贷款变成到期应付，借款人会申请取消你赎回房子的权利。

foreclosure [fɔː'kləʊʒə] *n.* 止赎权

◇ *The foreclosure rate varies from state to state in America; in 2015, around 0. 1% of the housing units had foreclosure filings.* 止赎率在美国各个州都不一样；2015 年全国大约有 0. 1% 的住宅单位申请抵押品赎回权。

forex futures ['fɒrɜks 'fjuːtʃəz] *PHR.* 外汇期权

◇ *Forex futures traders in Citibank and JPmorgan Chase were involved in an attempted manipulation of foreign exchange markets by using electronic chat rooms to plot their moves. They were heavily fined by futures trading commission.* 花旗银行和摩根大通

的外汇期货交易员们利用电子聊天室谋划方案，企图操纵外汇市场。他们被期货交易委员会重罚。

forfeit ['fɔːfɪt] *vt.*（因违反协议、犯规、受罚等）丧失；失去；*n.* 罚金；没收物；丧失的东西；代价；*adj.* 丧失了的；被没收了的

◇ *A former portfolio manager was sentenced to prison for 10 years and was ordered by the court to forfeit millions of illegal profit for inside trading plot.* 一位前组合投资经理因为内幕交易阴谋被判了10年监禁，法庭下令没收其数百万元非法获利。

forgery ['fɔːdʒ(ə)rɪ] *n.* 伪造文书；伪造

Phrase(s): ***forgery currency***

◇ *The mafia-related gang in New York was accused of document forgery,prostitution, cigarette smuggling and illegal gambling.* 与黑手党有关的一个团伙在纽约被指控伪造文件，卖淫，香烟走私与非法赌博。

forgiveness of a debt [fə'gɪvnɪs (ə)v ədet] *PHR.* 免除债务

◇ *The Government has pursued a policy of seeking forgiveness of debts and rescheduling in order to reduce the debt burden.* 为减轻债务负担，政府执行了一项争取减免和重新安排债务的政策。

formula ['fɔːmjʊlə] *n.* 公式

Phrase(s): ***valuation formulas; risk weight formula***

◇ *These haircut numbers will be scaled up using the square root of time formula depending on the frequency of remargining or marking-to-market.* 这些折扣系数将基于盯市频率或保证金调整频率的时间平方根予以再调整。1（21）

◇ *Good managers should always think of increasing working efficiency; adding another pointless regular meeting to everyone's calendar sounds like a formula for time-wasting; furthermore,"One-size-fits-one"assessment is meaningless.* 好经理应该始终考虑如何提高工作效率；给每个人的日历上再加一个毫无要点的例会听起来像是一个浪费时间的公式；而且“一刀切”的评价是没有意义的。

forward ['fɔːwəd] *n.* 远期；*adj.* 远期的

Phrase(s): ***forward contracts***

◇ *Swaps can be viewed as a portfolio of forward contracts.* 互换可以看作是一种远

期合约的组合。

foundation [faʊn'deɪʃ(ə)n] *n.* 基础

Phrase(s): ***solid foundation; foundation approach***

◇ *Under the foundation IRB approach, as a general rule, banks provide their own estimates of PD and rely on supervisory estimates for other risk components.* 按照 IRB 初级法规定，一般而言，银行自己估计违约概率，其他的风险因素取决于监管当局的估计值。1（46）

fraction ['frækʃ(ə)n] *n.* 分数；部分；小部分；稍微

Phrase(s): ***a fraction of***

◇ *Investors prefer investing in a fraction of a pool of mortgage loans to investing in a single residential mortgage loan, just as investors prefer to hold a diversified portfolio of stocks rather than an individual stock.* 比起投资单笔住房抵押贷款，投资者更愿意投在抵押贷款池中的部分组合，就像他们喜欢持有分散性股票组合而不是单个股票一样。13（287）

fragment ['frægm(ə)nt] *n.* 碎片；片断或不完整部分；*vt.* 使成碎片；*vi.* 破碎或裂开

◇ *Europe's financial markets remain highly fragmented. Its stock markets are about half the size of America's, despite the similar size of the two economies; European corporate-bond markets are about a third of the size.* 欧洲金融市场仍然高度分散。股票市场是美国一半的规模，尽管两国的经济规模相似；欧洲企业债券市场的规模约为美国的三分之一。

fragmentation [frægmen'teɪʃ(ə)n] *n.* 破碎；分裂

Phrase(s): ***market fragmentation***

◇ *After Brexit, the whole Europe has witnessed a political fragmentation in various elections, which could threaten the stability and unity in the community.* 英国脱欧以后，整个欧洲在各种选举中见证了政治区隔程度加深，这可能会威胁到这个共同体的安定团结。

framework ['freɪmwɜːk] *n.* 框架

Phrase(s): ***capital adequacy framework***

◇ *There should be a framework that allows the potential lender to have a perfected first priority claim over the collateral.* 应该有一个框架允许潜在的贷款方对抵押品有完全的第一优先权。1（92）

Franc area [fræŋk 'eərɪə] *PHR.* 法郎区

◇ *Because there is free capital mobility between each of the two regions, the CFA franc area can be considered as a single currency area.* 另外，由于这两个区域之间资本自由流动，所以非洲金融共同体法郎区能被认为是一个单一货币区。

franchise ['fræn(t)ʃaɪz] *n.* 专营权；特许权

◇ *Much of the Hollywood movie success in domestic and overseas markets comes from special-event film franchises such as "The Hunger Games" and "Star War".* 好莱坞电影在国内和海外市场上的成功大部分来自于描述特殊事件的系列电影，如“饥饿游戏”和“星球大战”。

fraud [frɔːd] *n.* 欺骗；诈骗

Phrase(s): ***credit fraud; fraud risk***

◇ *Internal fraud refers to losses due to acts of a type intended defraud, misappropriate property or circumvent regulations, the law or company policy, excluding diversity, discrimination events, which involves at least one internal party.* 内部欺诈损失是由于欺诈、挪用财产或规避法律法规、规避公司政策而产生的损失，它不包括多样化投资、价格歧视所带来的损失，其至少包含一个内部团体。1（203）

free [friː] *adj.* 免税的；免费的；自由的

Phrase(s): ***risk free rate; default free securities***

◇ *Although some subsidiaries of Volkswagen in other countries are prosperous and debt-free, it seems to be a very slow technology innovator to meet the environmental needs.* 虽然大众汽车在其他国家的一些子公司经验良好，没有债务，但大众在符合环保要求的技术创新方面却似乎非常缓慢。

frequent ['friːkw(ə)nt] *adj.* 频繁的；时常发生的；惯常的

Phrase(s): ***frequent issuer***

◇ *Among other things, this requires that the issuer be a frequent issuer in the market in order to get its name established in the asset-backed securities market and to create a reasonably liquid aftermarket for trading those securities.* 这要求发行人在市场中是一个

频繁的发行人，已在资产支持证券市场树立自己的名声，并为交易这些证券化产品构建一个有流动性的市场。13（17）

fringe [frɪn(d)ʒ] *adj.* 次要的；附加的；*n.* 边缘；次要

Phrase(s): ***fringe benefit; fringe market***

◇ *Many presidential candidates put forward policies which win mainstream support, however, the establishment of these policies is always in fringe for a few stakeholders.* 许多总统候选人提出的政策赢得了主流的支持，然而，这些政策的建立实施却总是归于边缘，与少数利益相关者。

frontier ['frʌntɪə] *n.* 前沿；边界

Phrase(s): ***efficient frontier; frontier lecture***

◇ *According to MSCI(Morgan Stanley Capital International), there are only 23 stockmarkets qualified as emerging based on their size, liquidity and openness to foreign investors; other stockmarkets in emerging countries are degraded to be "frontier markets".* 根据 MSCI（摩根士丹利资本国际）的标准，基于自身的规模、流动性和外国投资者开放程度，发展中国家只有 23 个股票市场可以称为新兴市场；其他都降级为“前沿市场”。

fulfill [ful'fil] *vt.* 履行；完成；实践；满足

Phrase(s): ***fulfill the criteria; fulfill the obligation***

◇ *The effective maturity of the underlying should be gauged as the longest possible remaining time before the counterparty is scheduled to fulfill its obligation.* 对应风险暴露的有效期限应尽可能按借款人约定履行债务最长的时间段计量。1（37）

full repayment [fʊl rɪ'peɪm(ə)nt] *PHR.* 全额还款

◇ *As long as there are no defaults by obligors that exceed $50 million, then bond class A receives full repayment of its $390 million.* 只要债务人的违约没有超过 5 000 万美元，债务类别 A 就获得 3. 9 亿美元的全额偿付。13（10）

full repricing [fʊl ˌri: 'praisiŋ] *PHR.* 完全重新定价

◇ *The following three methods can estimate the profit and loss (P&L) of a bullet bond: full repricing, duration and duration plus convexity.* 以下三种方法可以估计一次性偿还而且定期支付息票的债券（子弹型债券）的收益和损失：完全重新定价法、久期法

以及久期加凸性法。

function ['fʌŋ(k)ʃ(ə)n] *n.* 函数

Phrase(s): ***discount function; payoff function***

◇ *This section provides three risk weight functions, one for residential mortgage exposures, a second for qualifying revolving retail exposures, and a third for other retail exposures.* 这部分内容规定了三个风险权重函数，第一个是针对住房抵押贷款的，第二个是针对合格的循环零售贷款的，第三个是针对其他零售贷款的。1（59）

fund [fʌnd] *n.* 基金；资金；存款；*vt.* 筹资；融资

Phrase(s): ***pension fund; mutual fund***

◇ *The auditing report exposed that judges had spent hundreds of thousands of dollars from the judiciary expense fund on their own medical bills and insurance.* 审计报告曝光，法官花了司法费用基金里的数十万美元支付自己的医疗费和保险。

◇ *The European Union has to provid more than 90% of the funds for maintaining some museums of ancient civilizations in Greece, since the country itself couldn't no longer afford the protection expenses.* 欧盟已经为维护一些希腊的古代文明博物馆提供了超过 90% 的资金，因为希腊本身已经承担不起保护费用了。

fundamental [fʌndə'ment(ə)l] *adj.* 基本的；根本的；*n.* 基本原理；基本原则

◇ *Predictors include financial ratios such as earning-to-price ratio or book-to-price ratio and other fundamental quantities.* 这些预测变量包括财务比率，比如市盈率、市净率，以及一些其他的基础变量。

funding risk ['fʌndɪŋ rɪsk] *PHR.* 筹资风险

◇ *The defined benefit pension which will provide retirees with a monthly fixed check is facing some funding risk now, which could impact millions of people's lives after retirement.* 固定福利养老金为退休人员提供每月固定收入，目前面临一些筹资风险，这可能会影响数以百万计人的退休后生活。

fund manager [fʌnd 'mænɪdʒə] *PHR.* 基金经理

◇ *A hedge fund manager committed suicide after he was accused of conspiring to get huge profits from insider information.* 一个对冲基金经理自杀，此前他被指控通过内幕信息阴谋获得巨大利润。

future ['fjuːtʃə] *adj.* 未来的；*n.* 期货

Phrase(s): *future value; futures contracts*

◇ *If the exposure and collateral are held in different currencies, an additional downwards adjustment must be made to the volatility adjusted collateral amount to take account of future fluctuations in exchange rates.* 如果风险暴露和抵押品的货币不是一种，则需要考虑未来汇率的变动，应将抵押品的价值向下调整。1（17）

◇ *Futures contracts are standardized, negotiable, and exchange-traded contracts to buy or sell an underlying asset.* 期货合约是标准化的、可协商的，并且在交易所进行买入或卖出潜在资产的交易合同。

G

GDP (gross domestic product) [grəʊs də'mestɪk 'prɒdʌkt] *abbr.* 国内生产总值

◇ *The World Bank calculates that Mexico is one of the most open large economies in the world: exports plus imports are equivalent to 66% of GDP, compared with 26% for Brazil and 42% for China.* 世界银行计算，墨西哥是世界上最开放的大型经济体之一：进出口总量相当于 GDP 的 66%，与之相比巴西的比例是 26%，中国是 42%。

gearing ratio ['gɪərɪŋ 'reɪʃɪəʊ] *PHR.* 杠杆比率

◇ *Gearing ratio represents net debt over equity plus net debt; gearing measures a firm's financial leverage.* 负债率为净债项与股权加净债项之比；负债衡量地是一个公司的财务杠杆。

generalized autoregressive conditional heteroscedasticity model ['dʒenərəlaizd ɔ:təʊ'rɪgresɪv kən'dɪʃ(ə)n(ə)l het(ə)rəʊskədæs'tɪsətɪ 'mɒdl] *PHR.* 广义自回归条件异方差模型

◇ *The ARCH model and its generalization, the generalized autoregressive conditional heteroscedasticity (GARCH) model, provide a convenient framework to study the problem of modeling volatility clustering.* ARCH 模型及其扩展模型——广义自回归条件异方差（GARCH）模型，为我们研究波动集聚的拟合问题提供了一个合适的框架。5（280）

general ledger ['dʒen(ə)r(ə)l 'ledʒə] *PHR.* 总分类账簿

◇ *Procedures for reconciliation of the general ledger accounts and for closing the books were not documented.* 总账账目的对账和结账程序没有制作证明文件。14（146）

global fund ['gləʊb(ə)l fʌnd] *PHR.* 全球基金

◇ *The majority of global fund managers were gloomy about the outlook for government bonds; they also warned that bonds had become ridiculously overvalued.* 多数全球基金经理对政府债券的前景感到悲观；他们还警告说，债券已完全被高估。

globalization [ˌgləʊbəlaɪ'zeɪʃn] *n.* 全球化

Phrase(s): ***globalization of stock markets; globalization and international investing***

◇ *The efficacy of single-country regulation is being tested in the face of increasing globalization and the ease with which funds can move across national borders.* 随着全球化进程的提速，资金跨境转移的日趋便利，单一国家监管的有效性正在被挑战。7（78）

global macro strategy ['gləʊbəl 'mækrəʊ 'strætɪdʒɪ] *PHR.* 全球宏观战略

◇ *A global macro strategy is a fund strategy which closely observes the overall economic and political policies of various countries to adjust holdings, such as long and short positions in equity, fixed income, currency, commodities and futures markets.* 全球宏观策略是一种基金策略，通过密切观察各个国家整体的经济、政治政策来调整持股情况，如长、短仓股票，固定收入，货币，大宗商品和期货市场。

GNP (gross national product) [grəʊs 'næʃ(ə)n(ə)l 'prɒdʌkt] *abbr.* 国民生产总值

◇ *The beautiful GDP figures of Ireland actually include profits of multinational firms who set up subsidiaries here to evade taxes; the country's GNP since 2014 has been flat.* 爱尔兰漂亮的 GDP 数据实际上包括跨国企业的利润，这些公司在爱尔兰设立子公司来逃避税收；该国国民生产总值自 2014 以来一直低迷。

going concern ['gəʊɪŋ kən'sɜːn] *PHR.* 持续经营企业

◇ *In a going concern, shareholders have claim to the part of operating income left after interest and income taxes have been paid.* 在持续经营的企业中，股东对息后税后的营业收入部分有求偿权。7（38）

going private ['gəʊɪŋ 'praɪvət] *PHR.* 私有化

◇ *Going private refers to a process where the employees of a company or other private investors repurchase all of the company's outstanding stock. Going-private transactions and leveraged buyouts have much in common with mergers.* 私有化指的是一个公司的雇员或其他私人投资者回购公司所有已发行股票的过程。私有化交易和杠杆收购与并

购有很多共同之处。6（916）

gold parity [gəʊld 'pærɪtɪ] *PHR.* 金平价

◇ *The value of the dollar naturally varied from its gold parity.* 美元的价值自然不等同于金平价。

golden share ['gəʊldən ʃeə] *PHR.* 黄金股

◇ *The Italian government does not want a foreigner to take control, but it would have difficulty using its golden share to block a European bidder.* 意大利政府不想让外国人来控制，但它却很难用它的黄金股份来阻止一个欧洲的投标人。

goodwill [gʊd'wɪl] *n.* 商誉

◇ *The costs related to safety reserves are opportunity losses such as lost sales and loss of customer goodwill that result from having inadequate inventory.* 这种和安全性储备相关的成本是一种机会性的损失，诸如因为持有不合适的存货数量而导致的销售损失和面向顾客的商誉损失。6（839）

go public [gəʊ 'pʌblɪk] *PHR.* 上市

◇ *Some American companies choose to go public in the London Stock Exchange or other European stock exchanges to reduce expenses.* 美国的一些公司选择在伦敦证券交易所或其他欧洲证券交易所上市以降低费用。

grace period [greɪs 'pɪərɪəd] *PHR.* 宽限期

◇ *The credit derivative shall not terminate prior to expiration of any grace period required for a default on the underlying obligation to occur as a result of a failure to pay.* 在违约所规定的任何宽限期之前，标的债项不能支付并不导致信用衍生工具终止。1(29)

granularity [grænjʊ'lærɪtɪ] *n.* 分散性

◇ *For IRB banks that invest in highly rated securitization exposures, a treatment based on the presence of an external rating, the granularity of the underlying pool, and the thickness of an exposure has been developed.* 对于投资于评级水平高的证券化头寸而且使用内部评级法的银行来说，基于现行的外部评级制度的对策，资产池的分散性和风险暴露的抵御能力都有一定的提升。1（7）

Gresham's law ['græʃəms lɔ:] *PHR.* 格雷欣法则

◇ *You could have a reverse Gresham's Law at work, in which good money drives out bad*. 实践中存在反向的格雷欣法则：良币驱除劣币。

gross profit rate [grəʊs 'prɒfɪt reɪt] *PHR.* 毛利率

◇ *The company predicted gross profit rate to decline, owing to investments in new product launches and the decrease in previous products' sales*. 因投资新产品的发布和之前产品的销量放缓，公司预计毛利率将下降。

gross savings [grəʊs 'seɪvɪŋ] *PHR.* 储蓄总额

◇ *In our analysis of the impact of Japan's demography, we have shown that the current level of private-sector gross savings is indeed higher than we would expect in equilibrium*. 在日本人口影响的分析中，我们发现当前私营部门的储蓄总额的确高于我们预期的均衡状态。

gross-up clause [grəʊsʌp klɔːz] *PHR.* 补偿费条款

◇ *If the country of the bond issuer suddenly imposes new taxes, the issuer may be subject to a so-called gross-up clause that requires it to pay the investor additional money to make up for the new tax*. 如果这个国家的债券发行人突然被要求征收新税，发行人可能受到所谓的补偿费条款的制约，即需要向投资者支付额外的钱来弥补新税造成的损失。

guarantee fund [gær(ə)n'tiː fʌnd] *PHR.* 保证准备金

◇ *This entity, more commonly referred to as the PBGC (Pension Benefit Guaranty Corporation), would collect fees and create a guarantee fund to support insolvent pension plans and their beneficiaries*. 这个实体，通常被称为养老金担保公司，将收取费用并创建一个保证准备金来支持破产养老金计划及其受益者。

H

haircut ['heəkʌt] *n.* 价值折扣；折减；垫头

◇ *Typically, the amount of the collateral will exceed the funds owed by an amount known as the haircut.* 通常，抵押品价值超过资金价值的那部分被称为价值折扣。

◇ *If the collateral is an asset worth $100 but whose value fluctuates, the creditor may apply a 20 percent haircut and credits only $80 worth of collateral to the transaction's net exposure.* 如果抵押品是一个价值 100 美元的资产，因其价值波动，债权人可以应用一个 20% 的价值折扣，只把价值 80 美元的抵押品算作交易的净风险敞口。8（43）

hazard ['hæzəd] *vt.* 赌运气；冒……的危险；使遭受危险；*n.* 危险；冒险；冒险的事

Phrase(s): ***moral hazard; hazard analysis; fire hazard***

◇ *More than 30 000 cabinet drawers of IKEA have been recalled because they can slide out without control and pose a hazard of hitting people.* 宜家召回了超过 30 000 只柜子抽屉，因为它们会不受控制滑出，存在击中人的危险。

◇ *Cheap rooms you found through online booking agencies before traveling may have hidden cameras dodgy electrics and other hazards.* 你在旅行前通过在线预订代理找到的廉价房可能有隐藏的摄像机、有故障的电器和其他危害。

hedge [hedʒ] *v.* 对冲

Phrase(s): ***hedge funds; selling hedge; hedge inventory***

◇ *Argentina government wouldn't be able to borrow on the international credit markets until it paid its four major creditors; among the four, there was one hedge fund.* 阿根廷政府不能在国际信贷市场上借钱，直到其支付四大债权人；其中一个债权人是对冲基金。

◇ *Around the world, governments of many countries, including the U. S. , have issued bonds that are linked to an index of the cost of living in order to provide their citizens with an effective way to hedge inflation risk.* 在世界各地，许多国家的政府包括美国，已发行与生活成本指数挂钩的债券，是为了给公民提供一种对冲通胀风险的有效途径。7（66）

held to maturity [held tə mə'tʃurətɪ] *PHR.* 持有到期

◇ *The zero-volatility spread is a measure of the spread that the investor would realize over the entire Treasury spot rate curve if the security being analyzed is held to maturity.* 如果证券被分析认为是持有至到期型，零波动利差就可以测量出投资者实现整个国债即期利率曲线的价差。13（328）

heterogeneity [ˌhetərəʊdʒi'niːəti] *n.* 异质性

Phrase(s): ***microscopic heterogeneity; heterogeneity model***

◇ *The risk bucketing process will reflect the seller's underwriting practices and the heterogeneity of its customers.* 划分风险栏的过程反映了销售方授信做法及客户的异质性。1（87）

heteroskedasticity [ˌhetərəʊskədæs'tɪsətɪ] *n.* 异方差性

Phrase(s): ***conditional heteroskedasticity***

◇ *Many time series data exhibit heteroskedasticity, where the variances of the error terms are not equal, and in which the error terms may be expected to be larger for some observations or periods of the data than for others.* 许多时间序列数据呈现异方差性，即误差项的方差不相等，且一些观测值或一段时期的数据的误差项预计比其他的大。5（279）

high-quality [ˌhaɪ'kwɒlɪtɪ] *adj.* 优质

Phrase(s): ***high-quality asset; high-quality bond***

◇ *In today's Beer Man column, the star is a Wisconsin stout which has a very clean profile, smoothness and high-quality richness that reminds me of Munich.* 今天的"啤酒人"专栏，明星是来自威斯康星的黑啤酒；它色泽清透，口感醇厚而浓烈，让我想起慕尼黑。

◇ *The securitization debt is generally backed by high-quality assets, cash held in reserve funds, and may be overcollateralized.* 证券化债务一般是由优质资产、储备基金持有的现金和超额抵押做后盾的。13（300）

high-yield ['haɪji:ld] *adj.* 高收益

Phrase(s): ***high-yield debt; high-yield securities***

◇ *The real impetus came around 1996 when the risk-return profile of the high-yield debt market and the pricing of a triple-A rated floater created excellent arbitrage conditions.* 真正的推动力来自 1996 年左右，高收益债券市场的风险收益曲线与 AAA 级浮动利率债券的定价创造了绝佳的套利条件。13（245）

◇ *The balance was shared by high-yield and investment-grade securities.* 该余额由高收益和投资级证券共同分享。13（246）

historical defaults [hɪ'stɒrɪk(ə)l dɪ'fɔ:lts] *PHR.* 历史违约率

◇ *When applying for a house mortgage, my bank told me that I couldn't get a better rate due to some historical defaults.* 申请房屋抵押贷款时，我的银行告诉我，由于历史违约记录我不能得到更好的利率。

historical delinquency rates [hɪ'stɒrɪk(ə)l dɪ'lɪŋkw(ə)nsɪ reɪts] *PHR.* 历史拖欠率

◇ *The sizing of the enhancement for each pool is done based on traditional ABS(Asset-backed Securities) rating principles-historical delinquency rates and loss severity.* 每个池大小的增强是基于传统的资产评估原则，即历史拖欠率和损失的严重程度。13（202）

holding company ['həʊldɪŋ 'kʌmp(ə)nɪ] *PHR.* 控股公司；股权公司

Phrase(s): ***personal holding trust company; family holding listed company***

◇ *Usually, holding companies do not produce goods or services themselves, they form a corporate group by owning shares of other companies.* 通常，控股公司本身不生产商品或服务，它们通过拥有其他公司的股份形成一个集团公司。

home currency [həʊm 'kʌr(ə)nsɪ] *PHR.* 本币

Phrase(s): ***home currency bills receivable; home currency bills payable; home currency bills sold***

◇ *Governments that issue debt in their home currency can in principle always repay that debt, if needed, by printing more money in that currency.* 政府用本国货币发行债券原

则上如果需要的话总是可以靠印刷更多的纸币来偿还债务。7（134）

homoscedasticity ['hɔməuskiˌdæs'tisəti] *n.* 同方差性；［数］方差齐性

Phrase(s): *homoscedasticity of variance*

◇ *In linear regression analysis, a standard assumption is that the variance of all squared error terms is the same. This assumption is called homoscedasticity.* 在线性回归分析中，一个标准的假设是所有平方误差项的方差是相同的。这个假设被称为同方差性。5（279）

HPR (holding period return) ['həʊldɪŋ 'pɪərɪəd rɪ'tɜːn] *abbr.* 持有期收益率

Phrase(s): *holding period abnormal return*

◇ *Holding period return refers to the rate of return over a given period.* 持有期收益率是指在一定持有期内的收益率。6（996）

hybrid ['haɪbrɪd] *n.* 杂交；混合物；*adj.* 混合的；杂交的

Phrase(s): *hybrid cap; hybrid cloud*

◇ *For hybrid pools containing mixtures of exposure types, if the purchasing bank cannot separate the exposures by type, the risk-weight function producing the highest capital requirements for those exposure types will apply.* 对于包含着多种贷款的混合暴露池，如果买入银行不能根据类别分开贷款，这些贷款将采用形成最高资本要求的风险权重函数。

hyperinflation [ˌhaɪpərɪn'fleɪʃ(ə)n] *n.* 恶性通货膨胀

◇ *In order to tame Argentina's hyperinflation, the government tied its currency, the peso, to the U. S. dollar. However,the measure made its exports less competitive in the global market.* 为了控制阿根廷的恶性通货膨胀，政府把其货币比索与美元挂钩。然而，这一措施使阿根廷的出口在全球市场失去竞争力。

hypothecation [haɪˌpɑθɪ'keɪʃ(ə)n] *n.* 抵押；担保契约；质押

Phrase(s): *loan hypothecation; hypothecation institution; legal hypothecation*

◇ *Hypothecation is the pledge of client-owned securities in a margin account to secure a loan.* 抵押权是客户为取得贷款将自有证券放在保证金账户的承诺。

hypothetical [haɪpə'θetɪk(ə)l] *adj.* 假定的

Phrase(s): *hypothetical transaction; hypothetical reasoning*

◇ *The children with city passes are invited to experience jobs in all kinds of public servie centers in a hypothetical situation as adults in real life.* 拥有城市通行证的孩子们被邀请在虚拟环境中体验各种公共服务中心里的工作，就像现实生活中的成年人一样。

I

illustrative ['ɪləstrətɪv] *adj.* 说明的；作例证的；解说的

Phrase(s): ***illustrative chart; illustrative examples***

◇ *This young entrepreneur's story is interesting and illustrative, yet, it is what people in my generation would never try.* 这个年轻企业家的故事既有趣又有说明性，然而却是我们这一代人永远不会尝试去做的。

immaterial [ɪmə'tɪərɪəl] *adj.* 非物质的；无形的；非实质的；不重要的

Phrase(s): ***immaterial asset; immaterial wealth***

◇ *Some exposures in non-significant business units as well as asset classes that are immaterial in terms of size and perceived risk profile may be exempt from the requirements.* 对不甚重要的业务单位和资产类别的一些贷款可以不受这个要求的约束。这些业务单位和资产类别在规模上和可觉察的风险轮廓都不重要。1（48）

immateriality ['ɪmə͵tɪərɪ'ælɪtɪ] *n.* 无形；非物质

Phrase(s): ***immateriality asset***

◇ *Failure to produce an acceptable plan or satisfactorily implement the plan or to demonstrate immateriality will lead supervisors to reconsider the bank's eligibility for the IRB approach.* 如果没有一个可接受的计划或令人满意的实施计划而且证明不力，监管当局将重新考虑银行 IRB 法的资格。1（70）

impact ['ɪmpækt] *n.* 影响；效果

Phrase(s): ***impact on; disparate impact***

◇ *The impact of measuring things differently can be very significant.* 用不同的方法衡量事情带来的影响巨大。

implement ['ɪmplɪm(ə)nt] *vt.* 实施；执行；使生效；实现；落实（政策）；把……填满；*n.* 工具；器械；家具；手段；[法] 履行（契约等）

◇ *Since each country in the world seeks to control what happens within its own borders; governments prefer making their own policies; however, within no globally accepted rules, these policies can not be implemented effectively.* 世界上的每个国家都希望边界以内发生的事情在掌握之中；所以政府喜欢制定本国的政策；然而，没有全球公认的规则，这些政策无法有效实施。

imply [ɪm'plaɪ] *vt.* 意味；暗示；隐含

Phrase(s): ***imply to***

◇ *The premier's speech implied a need for deeper structural changes, such as reducing the dominance of inefficient state-owned firms in vital areas of the economy and giving priority to service industry.* 总理的讲话暗示了更深层次的结构变化的需要，如减少效率低下的国有企业在经济的重要领域的优势，以及重点发展服务业。

impose [ɪm'pəʊz] *v.* 强加；征税；施加影响

Phrase(s): ***impose on; impose a fine***

◇ *Governments in Africa frequently imposed price control on agricultural products, which discouraged peasants' willingness to work on land under extreme weather conditions.* 非洲各国政府经常对农产品实行价格控制，这使农民不愿意在极端天气条件下在田地里劳作。

inadequate [ɪn'ædɪkwət] *adj.* 不充足的；不适当的

◇ *Although he can get all the funding he wants, it may be sill inadequate to prevent him from bankrupting.* 虽然他可以得到所有他想要的资金，但这可能不足以阻止他破产的命运。

incentive [ɪn'sentɪv] *n.* 动机；诱因；刺激；鼓励；*adj.* 刺激性的；鼓励性质的

Phrase(s): ***incentive wage; incentive structure; incentive contract; incentive factor; incentive programs***

◇ *Commercial banks had little incentive to hold large quantities of safe, liquid assets, knowing that the central bank would save them in a panic.* 商业银行没有动力去持有大量安全的流动资产，因为它们知道一旦恐慌出现，中央银行就会出手相救。

◇ *The bank must have techniques for creating incentives to improve the management of operational risk throughout the firm.* 银行必须在全行范围内采取激励手段鼓励改进操作风险管理。1（624）

incidental [ɪnsɪ'dent(ə)l] *adj.* 附带的；偶发的

Phrase(s): *incidental capital loss; incidental charge; incidental condition*

◇ *Facebook users think that reading news on the website is incidental since their main purpose is to browse photos or chat with friends on these popular social networking sites.* 脸谱网用户认为在该网站阅读新闻纯属偶然，因为他们光顾这个流行的社交网站主要是为了浏览照片或与朋友聊天。

income ['ɪnkʌm] *n.* 收入；进款；进来的动作；进入

Phrase(s): *annual income; per capita income*

◇ *Cambodia is still a poor country but develops very quickly. The gross national income per person in 2014 was $1 020; besides, one third of households in big cities have the Internet access.* 柬埔寨仍然是一个贫穷的国家，但发展很快。2014 年人均国民总收入为 1 020 美元；此外，大城市里三分之一的家庭有互联网接入。

◇ *The borrowing entity has little or no other material assets or activities, and therefore little or no independent capacity to repay the obligation, apart from the income that it receives from the asset(s) being financed.* 借款实体基本没有或没有其他实质性资产或业务，因此除了从被融资资产中获得的收入外，基本没有或没有独立的偿还债务能力。1（187）

incontrovertible [ˌɪnkɒntrə'vɜːtɪb(ə)l] *adj.* 无可争议的；无疑的；明白的

Phrase(s): *incontrovertible evidence; incontrovertible proof*

◇ *A guarantee must represent a direct claim on the protection provider and must be explicitly referenced to specific exposures, so that the extent of the cover is clearly defined and incontrovertible.* 担保必须是信用保护提供者的直接负债，而且必须明确对应具体的风险暴露，因此抵补的程度是定义清楚和不可撤销的。1（213）

inconvertible [ɪnkən'vɜːtɪb(ə)l] *adj.* 不可转换的

Phrase(s): *inconvertible paper; inconvertible stock; inconvertible currency*

◇ *Investors can make investment using inconvertible currency, machinery, equipment or other objects, or industrial right, or non-patent technology.* 投资者可以用不可自由兑换货币、机器设备或者其他实物、工业产权、非专利技术等作为投资。

incorporate [ɪn'kɔːpəreɪt] *vt.* 包含；吸收；体现；把……合并；*vi.* 合并；混合；组成公司；*adj.* 合并的；一体化的；组成公司的

Phrase(s): *incorporate with; incorporated business*

◇ *Payment and settlement losses related to a bank's own activities would be incorporated in the loss experience of the affected business line.* 与银行自营业务有关的支付和结算损失将反映到受影响的产品线损失记录当中。1（199）

increase [ɪn'kriːs] *vt.* 增加；增大；增多；*vt.* 增强；增进；*vi.* 增强；增进；增殖；繁殖

Phrase(s): *increase in productivity; pay increase; tax increase*

◇ *The reduction of tariffs in Africa has led to an increase in import costs of products which can not be both manufactured and sources inside the region.* 在非洲内部减少关税反而导致进口成本的增加，因为这些进口产品不能同时在该区域内生产和采购。

independent [ˌɪndɪ'pendənt] *adj.* 独立的；单独的；自主的；不相关连的；无党派的；*n.* 独立自主的人

Phrase(s): *independent of; independent director; financial independent*

◇ *The mapping process to business lines must be subject to independent review.* 产品线对应流程必须接受独立审查。1（201）

◇ *An independent review of the risk measurement system should be carried out regularly in the bank's own internal auditing process.* 在银行内部的审计的程序中，应经常对风险计量系统进行独立评估。1（136）

indicator ['ɪndɪkeɪtə] *n.* 指示器；指标

◇ *Some common economic and financial indicators listed in the Economist magazine are gross domestic product, industrial production, customer prices, unemployment rate, current-account balance, budget balance and interest rates.* 《经济学人》杂志列出的一

些常用经济和金融指标，包括国内生产总值、工业生产总值、消费者价格、失业率、经常账户平衡、预算平衡和利率。

individual [ˌɪndɪ'vɪdjʊ(ə)l] *n.* 个人；个体；*adj.* 个人的；单笔的

Phrase(s): ***individual account; individual exposure; individual proprietorship***

◇ *Thanks to the financial support from asset-based, non-banking financial companies, today, 80 percent of all trucks in India are owned by individuals in small road transport businesses.* 多亏了资产为本的非银行金融公司提供的资金支持，今天，小型私人道路运输公司拥有印度 80% 的卡车。

industry ['ɪndəstrɪ] *n.* 工业；产业（经济词汇）；工业界；勤劳

Phrase(s): ***new industry; industry risk***

◇ *During the 13th five-year development period, Chinese government will put great efforts in cutting excessive industrial capacity in energy industrials such as coal and steel.* 第十三个五年发展期间，中国政府将努力在能源产业如煤炭钢铁和部门进行去产能改革。

ineligibility [ɪnˌelɪdʒə'bɪlətɪ] *n.* 无被选资格；不适任

◇ *This target is not expected to be used as a hard limit that would lead to ineligibility of revolving retail exposures in the case of small or transient deviations.* 这样做的目的不是用这个比率作为硬性限额，硬性限额将导致在发生小的或短暂偏离限额情况下，循环零售贷款无法循环。1（43）

ineligible [ɪn'elɪdʒɪb(ə)l] *adj.* 不合格的

◇ *Boot-camps in the U. S. offer computing courses within a short period of time and prepare students for software-engineering jobs. Their courses and certificates are quite popular in the job market, thus, the Department ofEducationannounced a pilot programme to make federal funds available to boot-camps in 2015, whose students were ineligible for federal aid before that.* 美国的 IT 集训营提供短期计算机课程，培养软件工程方面的专门人才。IT 集训营的课程和证书很受就业市场的青睐，因此，教育部在 2015 年宣布了一项试点计划，将之前不能享受联邦援助的 IT 集训营学生纳入援助计划。

initial [ɪ'nɪʃəl] *n.* 开端；*adj.* 最初的；开头的

Phrase(s): ***initial allowance; initial issue; initial public offerings (IPO);***

initial margin

◇ *One aspect of deregulation is to change the way that initial public offerings (IPOs) are conducted, letting the market decide which companies get to list, when and at what price.* 放松管制的一个方面就是改变首次公开发行（IPO）的进行方式，让市场决定哪些公司、在什么时间、以什么价格上市。

◇ The amount required to open a futures position is called initial margi*n*. 开立期货账户所需的保证金叫作初始保证金。

innovation [ˌɪnə'veɪʃən] *n.* 改革；创新；新观念；新发明；新设施

Phrase(s): ***financial innovation***

◇ *Britain's global reputation in science and innovation is built on the creativity that is inspired when people from different cultures collaborate;thus shutting doors to international students will cost Britain a lot.* 创造力使英国的科技创新享誉全球声誉，来自不同文化背景的人合作才激发了这种创造力；因此，拒绝国际学生到英国学习将使英国蒙受巨大损失。

innovative ['ɪnəvətɪv] *adj.* 革新的；创新的

Phrase(s): ***innovative thinking; innovative ability***

◇ *The percentage of innovative instruments to total Tier 1 would equal 15%.* 创新工具占一级资本的比例为15%。1（169）

input ['ɪnpʊt] *n.* 输入；投入；*vt.* 把……输入

◇ *Most African countries produce a narrow range of goods and there is little trade in inputs and services that might lead to African chains ofproduction.* 大多数非洲国家生产的物品种类少，几乎没有商品和服务贸易能够促成整个非洲范围内的生产链。

insolvent [ɪn'sɒlv(ə)nt] *adj.* 破产的；无力偿付债务的；*n.* 无力偿还债务的人；破产者

Phrase(s): ***insolvent bank***

◇ *Upon any default event, regardless of whether the counterparty is insolvent or bankrupt, the bank has the unfettered, legally enforceable right to immediately seize and liquidate the collateral for its benefit.* 如出现违约事件，不受交易对象无清偿力或破产的影响，银行拥有绝对的、法律上可实施的处置和清算抵押品的权利。1（28）

institution [ɪnstɪ'tju:ʃ(ə)n] *n.* （大学、银行等规模大的）社会事业机构；惯例；制度；规定；建立；< 口 > 名人；名物

Phrase(s): ***financial institution; official institution***

◇ *Institutions must use an internal model that is appropriate for the risk profile and complexity of their equity portfolio.* 银行必须采用适合于自己风险轮廓和股权组合复杂性的内部模型。1（95）

institutional [ɪnstɪ'tju:ʃ(ə)n(ə)l] *adj.* 制度的；制度上的；机构的

◇ *Sustainable mutual funds focus not only on profits but also on the issuers' social and ethical responsibilites. Both institutional and individual investors are optimistic about the mutual benefits between sustainability and profitability.* 可持续基金不仅关注利润也关注债券发行人的社会伦理道德。无论是机构投资者还是散户投资者对可持续性和盈利能力之间的相互利益表示乐观。

instrument ['ɪnstrʊm(ə)nt] *n.* 仪器；工具；手段；法律文件；*vt.* 用仪器装备；向……提交文书

Phrase(s): ***financial instrument; monetary instrument; traditional instrument***

◇ *Heavy-handed rules were urgently needed to make sure that banks in Switzerland did not create "money-like"instruments, however, the government was also worried that the reform in the system would bring costly consequence to this country dependent on finance industry.* 瑞士迫切需要严厉的规则来制止银行推出类似于货币的金融工具，但是政府也担心体制改革将给这个依赖金融产业的国家带来沉重的后果。

◇*Proposals put forward to build a complete banking union in European Union include a tougher central fiscal authority and common debt instruments; unfortunately, these ideas are incompatible with one another since member countries hold different standpoints on interest.* 在欧盟建立一个完整的银行业联盟的提议具体包括建立更严厉的中央财政机构和公共债务工具；不幸的是，这些想法由于各成员国利益不同而互不相容。

integration [ɪntɪ'greɪʃ(ə)n] *n.* 整合；一体化；结合

Phrase(s): ***economic integration***

◇ *There were some great historical projects in the process of European integration, such as the single currency and the passport-free Schengen Agreement.* 欧洲一体化进程中

有一些重大历史项目，如单一货币和免除多次签证的申根协议。

interbank ['ɪntəbæŋk] *adj.* 银行间的；同业的

Phrase(s): ***interbank deposit; interbank borrowing (lending); interbank liquidity***

◇ *The risk weights for sovereign, interbank, and corporate exposures are differentiated based on external credit assessments.* 按照外部信用评级，对主权、银行同业、公司的风险暴露的风险权重各不相同。1（2）

interest ['ɪnt(ə)rɪst] *n.* 利息；利益

Phrase(s): ***interest rate; loan interest***

◇ *Gross income is defined as net interest income plus net non-interest income.* 总收入定义为：净利息收入加上非利息收入。1（216）

◇ *Apple's refusal to unlock the iPhone of a gun shooting suspect in the U. S. did not aim at the immediate interests of the company but the public security policy and its long-term position in global technological market.* 苹果拒绝解开美国一个枪击案嫌疑人的手机锁，并不是瞄准公司的当前利益，而是公共安全政策及其在全球技术市场的长期地位。

interface ['ɪntəfeɪs] *n.* 界面；交界面；<计>接口；*v.*（使通过界面或接口）接合；连接；*vi.* 相互作用（或影响）；交流；交谈

Phrase(s): ***user interface***

◇ *According to a survey, people now have a closer relationship with technological companies than with their governments; a little change on the interfaces or cameras can have a big impact on people's lives.* 据调查，人们现在与科技公司的关系比与政府的关系更密切；界面或相机一个小小的变化都会对人们的生活产生很大的影响。

intermediary [ˌɪntə'miːdɪərɪ] *n.* 中介；中间；中间人；*adj.* 中介的；中间的

Phrase(s): ***intermediary bank; intermediary market; intermediary trade***

◇ *This lady is a licensed intermediary for a big insurance company and has seventeen years' experience in retirement preplanning.* 这位女士是一家大型保险公司的持牌中介，有十七年的退休规划经验。

internal [ɪn'tɜːn(ə)l] *adj.* 内部的；体内的

Phrase(s): ***internal supervisory; internal audit; internal control***

◇ *The EU is currently making it easier for firms in its member countries to borrow, lend and invest across its internal borders, in the hope of reducing funding costs.* 欧盟正在简化其成员国企业在欧盟内部各国间贷款、出借和投资的难度，以降低融资成本。

international [ɪntə'næʃ(ə)n(ə)l] *adj.* 国际的；*n.* 国际组织

Phrase(s): ***international meeting***

◇ *Chinese students are making the largest contingent of all international students in the U. S. ; what's more, in recent years their parents, especially mothers are going with them, buyingproperties or make investments.* 中国学生占据全美国际学生的最大比例；而且，近年来他们的父母（尤其是母亲）和孩子一同前往美国，在当地购买房产或投资。

interpret [ɪn'tɜːprɪt] *vt.* 说明；解释；*vi.* 做解释

Phrase(s): ***exclusively interpret***

◇ *To assist supervisors in interpreting whether a CDR(cumulative default rate) falls within an acceptable range for a risk rating to qualify for a particular risk weight, two benchmarks would be set for each assessment, namely a "monitoring"level benchmark and a "trigger man" level benchmark.* 为帮助监管当局掌握累积违约率是否在可接受范围内，以使相应的风险等级适合于某个特定风险权重，委员会对每个评级结果设定了两个基本标准，一个是监测点标准，另一个是触发点标准。1（172）

inverse floaters ['ɪnvɜːs 'fləʊtəs] *PHR.* 反向浮动利率债券

◇ *Reverse floaters'coupon payments vary inversely with the level ofinterest rates.* 反向浮动利率债券的利息支付随着利率水平反向变动。

investment [ɪn'vestmənt] *n.* 投资；投资额

Phrase(s): ***foreign investment; direct investment; capital investment; investment bank***

◇ *Some South Asian countries encourage women in rural areas to make long-term investment like cash crops growing and tree planting, allowing them to use land as collateral for loans.* 一些南亚国家鼓励农村妇女做长期投资，如种植经济作物和植树造林，允许他们使用土地作为贷款抵押。

◇ *Significant minority and majority investments in commercial entities which exceed certain materiality levels will be deducted from banks' capital.* 对商业企业的大额少数或

多数股权投资，只要超过一定限度，都应从银行的资本中扣除。1（4）

investor [ɪn'vestə] *n.* 投资者；出资者

Phrase(s): ***financial investor***

◇ *The country strived to improve the investment environment, so investors home and abroad would feel that doing business here is a rewarding and enjoyable experience.* 这个国家努力改善投资环境，让国内外的投资者都觉得在这里做生意是一个有回报并令人愉快的经历。

involve [ɪn'vɒlv] *vt.* 包含；使参与；牵涉

Phrase(s): ***involve in***

◇ *The brand-new scheme of the IT giant involves large investment in clouding computing and artificial intelligence.* 这个 IT 巨头的全新发展方案包含在云计算和人工智能方面的大规模投资。

irrespective [ɪrɪ'spektɪv] *adj.* 无关的；不考虑的；不顾的；

◇ *The vacancy is open to all applicants meeting the basic entry requirement irrespective of their disability, sex, marital status, pregnancy, age, family status, sexual orientation and race.* 这个职位空缺面向所有满足基本条件的申请人，不论其是否残疾、性别、婚姻状况、是否怀孕、年龄、家庭状况、性取向和种族。

irrevocable [ɪ'revəkəb(ə)l] *adj.* 不可改变的；不能取消的；不能挽回的

Phrase(s): ***irrevocable letter of credit***

◇ *When it comes to making decisions that may be irrevocable, it's important to seek professional guidance.* 在做出可能是不可撤销的决定时，寻求专业指导非常重要。

isolate ['aɪsəleɪt] *vt.* 使隔离；使孤立

◇ *To stay away from loneliness is to stop isolating yourself and find what you like to do, do it with some friends.* 远离孤独就是别孤立自己，找到你喜欢做的事情并和一些朋友去做。

issue ['ɪʃuː; 'ɪsjuː] *n.* 发行；发行物；问题

Phrase(s): ***bank of issue; issue price; issue bill***

◇ *The most difficult issue to the post-Brexit Britain is how to maintain full access to EU market since half of its exports goes to the rest of EU countries.* 英国脱欧以后最大的

困难是如何维持全面进入欧盟市场，毕竟英国一半的出口流向其他欧盟国家。

◇ *SPEs are commonly used as financing vehicles in which exposures are sold to a trust or similar entity in exchange for cash or other assets funded by debt issued by the trust.* 特别目的机构通常被用作融资工具，通过它将资产出售给信托机构或类似实体，换取现金或其他资产。这些现金或资产是由信托机构发行的债务融资的。1（101）

J

Japanese [ˌdʒæpəˈniːz] *n.* 日本人；日语；*adj.* 日本的；日本人的；日语的

Phrase(s): ***Japanese yen; Japanese interest; Japanese rate; Japanese stocks***

◇ *A dollar-based investor has a portfolio consisting of $1 million in cash plus a position in 1 000 million Japanese yen.* 一个以美元为基础的投资者有一个投资组合，包括 100 万美元的现金加上 10 亿日元的头寸。

◇ What is the current Japanese interest rate? 日元目前的利息是多少？

jeopardize [ˈdʒepədaɪz] *vt.* 危害；使……陷入危地；使……受危困

Phrase(s): ***jeopardize your life***

◇ *Yellen from the Federal Reserve warned that overseas weakness could jeopardize the plans to raise interest rate in 2016.* 美联储主席耶伦警告说，海外市场的衰弱可能会危害 2016 年利率提高的计划。

jitter [ˈdʒɪtə] *vi.* 抖动；［电子］跳动；战战兢兢；神经过敏；*vt.* 紧张地说；使……惶恐不安；*n.* 振动；剧跳；紧张不安

Phrase(s): ***deterministic jitter; beam jitter***

◇ *Being a highly leveraged instrument, CDOs (collateralized debt obligations) are prone to cyclical changes. Once in a while, as the corporate debt scenario worsens, the CDO market gets some jitters.* 作为一种高杠杆的金融工具，担保债务凭证极易发生周期性变化。有些时候，当企业债务情况恶化，担保债务凭证市场会产生剧烈抖动。

13（265）

jobber ['dʒɒbə] *n.* 批发商；股票经纪人；临时工

Phrase(s): ***land jobber; independent jobber; bill jobber***

◇ *A continuous and free market insecurities have been pursued by many countries with varying degrees of success. In Britain, the essential freedom is provided by a special group of Stock Exchange Member Firms, the jobbers, who constitute a unique feature of the Britain market system.* 许多国家都力求建立一个连续、自由的证券市场，并取得不同程度的成功。在英国，证券市场最基本的自由度是证券批发商所提供的。证券批发商是证券交易所成员的一个特殊的群体，他们构成了英国市场体系的一大特色。

joint [dʒɒɪnt] *n.* 关节；接缝；接合处；*adj.* 共同的；联合的；*vt.* 连接；接合；*vi.* 贴合

Phrase(s): ***joint account; joint distribution; joint venture***

◇ *Influenced by the government's free-up policy, the state-owned oil giant was forced to auction off some fields to foreign bidders, and to form joint ventures with foreign firms.* 受到政府开放政策的影响，国有石油巨头被迫通过拍卖转让一些油田给外国投标者，并与国外企业建立合资企业。

jolt [dʒəʊlt] *vt.* 使颠簸；使震惊；使摇动；*vi.* 摇晃；颠簸而行；*n.* 颠簸；摇晃；震惊；严重挫折

Phrase(s): ***jolt table; jolt squeezer***

◇ *The subprime crisis in the summer of 2007 was the first major jolt to the CDO(collateralized debt obligation) business.* 2007 年夏天的次贷危机，是担保债务凭证所遭受的第一次大震荡。13（220）

journal ['dʒɜːn(ə)l] *n.* 分类账

Phrase(s): ***journal entry***

◇ *In accounting, a journal is a chronological listing of the company's transactions, which is also known as the book of original entry.* 在会计学里，分类账是一家公司按时间顺序记录的交易列表，也被称为原始账簿。

judgment ['dʒʌdʒm(ə)nt] *n.* 意见；判断力；［法］审判；评价

Phrase(s): ***the judgment; pass judgment; ethical judgment; direct judgment***

◇ *The choice of each factor needs to be justified as a meaningful driver of risk, based on experience and involving the expert judgment of the affected business areas.* 要将每次因素调整成为有意义的风险要素，应基于实际经验，并征求专家对相关业务领域的意见。1（129）

jump [dʒʌmp] *n.* 跳跃；暴涨；惊跳；*vt.* 跳跃；使跳跃；跳过；突升；*vi.* 跳跃；暴涨；猛增

Phrase(s): ***jump-diffusion***

◇ *Since most importers have to get their dollars on the black market, rather than through the tiny allocations released by the central bank, the price of almost everything in this African country has soared with inflation jumping to almost 16%.* 由于大多数进口商必须从黑市获得美元，而不是通过央行放出的微小拨款，几乎所有东西的价格在这个非洲国家都飞涨，通货膨胀飙升到了 16%。

juncture ['dʒʌŋ(k)tʃə] *n.* 接缝；连接；接合

Phrase(s): ***at this juncture; critical juncture***

◇ *Whether these cyclical and structural developments will bring an overall increase or decline in systemic risk is difficult to assess at this juncture-but there are some indications of increased market and liquidity risk in advanced economies.* 在这个节骨眼上，这些周期性和结构性的发展是否会带来系统性风险总体上的增加或减少难以评估，但确有迹象表明发达经济体中市场和流动性风险的增加。

junior ['dʒuːnɪə] *adj.* 年少的；后进的；下级的；*n.* 年少者；晚辈；地位较低者；大学三年级学生

Phrase(s): ***junior stock; junior secretary***

◇ *Both France and Germany play important roles in deciding major issues in EU such as migration crisis and euro stability; however, when facing each other, Germany's preeminence immediately turned France into a junior member.* 法国和德国在欧盟如移民危机和欧元稳定等重大问题的决策中都起着重要作用；然而当两国相对，德国的强悍实力立即把法国降为初级会员。

junk [dʒʌŋk] *n.* 垃圾；废物；舢板

Phrase(s): ***junk bonds; junk mail***

◇ *Junk bonds are not always garbage; the market is treating different types of junk bonds differently, some still have good yields.* 垃圾债券不是垃圾；市场以不同方法对待不同类型的垃圾债券，其中一些仍然有很好的收益。

jurisdiction [ˌdʒʊərɪs'dɪkʃ(ə)n] *n.* 司法权；审判权；管辖权；权限；权力

Phrase(s): ***territorial jurisdiction; tax jurisdiction; admiralty jurisdiction***

◇ *Subject to national discretion, claims on certain domestic PSEs (public sector entity) may also be treated as claims on the sovereigns in whose jurisdictions the PSEs are established.* 鉴于国别差异，对于非本地公营单位的要求也应与对该单位所在辖区的要求一致。1（8）

just [dʒʌst] adv. 只是；仅仅；刚才；刚刚；正好；恰好；实在；刚要；*adj.* 公正的；合理的；正直的；正义的；正确的；应得的

Phrase(s): ***just over; only just***

◇ *Higher liquidity buffers are strongly recommended for all financial institutions(not just banks) that are reliant on short-term wholesale markets for funding and that engage immaturity transformation.* 对于所有依赖于短期批发市场融资并处于不成熟的转型中的金融机构（不仅仅是银行），强烈建议他们保有更高的流动性缓冲。

justification [dʒʌstɪfɪ'keɪʃ(ə)n] *n.* 理由；辩护；认为有理；认为正当；释罪

Phrase(s): ***economic justification***

◇ *Use of a model obtained from a third-party vendor that claims proprietary technology is not a justification for exemption from documentation or any other of the requirements for internal rating systems.* 采用从拥有专有技术的第三方获得的模型必须形成文件，也不能不符合对内部评级体系的任何其他要求。1（75）

K

key man provision [ki: mæn prə'vɪʒ(ə)n] *PHR.* 关键人条款

◇ *If the team is too thin, the rating agencies often insist on a "key man" provision whereby if a key person leaves the organization, it is treated as an event empowering noteholders to replace the key person.* 如果团队太小，评级机构通常坚持关键人条款，如果一个关键人离开组织，它被视为债券持有人取代关键人物的事件。13（262）

key [ki:] *n.* 关键；钥匙

Phrase(s): ***the key to; key issue***

◇ *The capital structure of the firm is a key piece of a firm's risk profile; and it is supposed to be diversified and based on overall market researches.* 公司的资本结构是描述公司风险轮廓的关键所在，它应该是多元的并基于整体市场研究。

kiting ['kaɪtɪŋ] *n.* 开空头支票；移挪；补空；冒空

Phrase(s): ***kiting cheque***

◇ *Cheque kiting is a form of financial fraud; it cheats by intentionally writing a check for a value greater than the account balance from an account in one bank, then writing a check from another account in another bank, also with non-sufficient funds, with the second check serving to cover the non-existent funds from the first account.* 空头支票是一种金融诈骗；欺诈方式是故意开一张支票，价值高于在一家银行里的账户余额，然后再从另一家银行里的另一个资金不足的账户再开一张支票，用第二张支票覆盖第一个账户里不存在的资金。

knot points [nɒt pɒɪnts] *PHR.* 结点

◇ *The arbitrary points at which the segments are divided are called knot points.* 分割各个片段的任意选定的点称为结点。5（154）

the Kronecker product [ðə k'rəʊnekər 'prɒdʌkt] *n.* 克罗内克积

◇ *The Kronecker product, also called the direct product or the tensor product, is an (mp)×(nq) matrix.* 克罗内克积也称为直积或者张量积，它是一个（mp）×（nq）矩阵。5（340）

kurtosis [kɜː'təusɪs] *n.* [统计] 峰度

◇ *The joint measure of peakedness and tail fatness is called kurtosis.* 峰度是一个联合测量峰值和尾部厚度的指标。5（40）

◇ *The variance is the second central moment, skewness is a rescaled third central moment, and kurtosis is a rescaled fourth central moment.* 方差是二阶中心距，偏度是一个重新定标的三阶中心距，峰度是一个重新定标的四阶中心距。5（40）

L

latency ['leɪtənsɪ] *n.* 潜伏期

Phrase(s): *additive latency*

◇ *Latency refers to the time it takes to accept, process, and deliver a trading order.* 潜伏期是指从接受、处理到提交一个交易订单所需要花费的时间。

large-cap [lɑ:dʒkæp] *n.* 高市值股票；大盘股

Phrase(s): *large-cap fund; large-cap index*

◇ *The long period of large-cap underperformance has caused valuations across the market to become compressed.* 大盘股长期表现不佳导致了市场整体估价紧缩。

law [lɔ:] *n.* 法律；规则

Phrase(s): *law cost; law of bankruptcy*

◇ *Any collateral taken must be legally enforceable under all applicable laws and statutes, and claims on collateral must be properly filed on a timely basis.* 在所有适用的法律、法规下，任何取得的抵押品都必须是可实施的，并且抵押品的债权必须及时登记存档。1（91）

lead manager [li:d 'mænɪdʒə] *PHR.* 首席经理人

◇ *Lead manager can be a commercial or investment bank which holds primary responsibility for organizing a bond or credit issuance; usually the lead manager will form a syndicate with other lenders to finish the task.* 首席经理可以是商业或投资银行，承担债券或信用发行的主要责任；通常它会与其他借款人组成联合共同完成发行任务。

leaseback ['li:sbæk] *n.* 租回已出售财产；售后租回

Phrase(s): ***sale and leaseback***

◇ *The restaurant-chain group plans to increase shareholder value by experimenting with cost-saving sale-leaseback transactions for most of its restaurant locations;proceeds from all of the potential sales will be used to repay debt.* 这个餐饮连锁集团计划通过在其下属大多数餐馆试行店面成本节约型售后回租交易来增加股东利益；未来销售所得收益将用于偿还债务。

leasehold ['li:shəʊld] *n.* 租赁；租赁权

Phrase(s): ***leasehold interest; leasehold property***

◇ *The winner bidder in this lease auction will get the leasehold to drill and extract oil and natural gas from the leased land for three years.* 租赁拍卖中的中标人将获得三年的租赁权，允许其在租赁土地上钻取石油和天然气。

legal ['li:g(ə)l] *adj.* 法律的；合法的

Phrase(s): ***legal charge; legal fee; legal estate***

◇ *The legal mechanism by which collateral is given must be robust and ensure that the lender has clear rights over the proceeds from the collateral.* 抵押品的法律机制必须是健全的，同时保证贷款方对抵押品产生的收益有清晰的权利。1（92）

lend [lend] *n.* 贷方；*vt.* 贷出

◇ *The British firm is lending to many would-be divorcees at a high annual interest for them to cover legal fees; without the loans, these people would settle for much less from their divorces.* 一家英国公司以高年利率借贷给许多即将办理离婚的人，用于支付法律费用；没有这些贷款，这些人从离婚官司中得到的极少。

lending ['lendiŋ] *n.* 出借物；出借

Phrase(s): ***lending bank; securities lending; lending transactions***

◇ *After several years' radical monetary easing, banks' leading margins are under great pressure.* 几年的激进货币宽松政策导致银行的贷款利润率处于巨大的压力之下。

letter ['letə] *n.* 字母；证书

Phrase(s): ***letter of assurance; letter of credit; letter of intent***

◇ *For short-term self-liquidating trade letters of credit arising from the movement of goods (e. g. documentary credits collateralised by the underlying shipment), a 20% CCF will be applied to both issuing and confirming banks.* 对于与货物贸易有关的短期自偿性信用证（如以相应的货运单为抵押的跟单信用证），无论对开证行，还是对保兑行，信用风险换算系数均为 20%。

◇ *The bank has made out an irrevocable letter of credit.* 银行开出了不可撤销的信用证。

leverage ['liːv(ə)rɪdʒ] *n.* 杠杆

Phrase(s): ***leverage ratio; financial leverage;***

◇ *The ratio of assets to equity is a measure of the firm's degree of financial leverage.* 资产权益比率是一种测量公司金融杠杆程度的比率。1（457）

◇ *Losing interest in stockmarket, investors with cash in hand turned to housing market; unregulated online lenders were helping them pile on leverage, even skipping minimum down-payments, which led to bubbles.* 失去对股市的兴趣，手头持有现金的投资者转向房地产市场；不受监管的网上银行帮助他们大举借债，甚至最低首付都不用交，这导致了泡沫。

levy ['levɪ] *n.* 征收；征兵；征税；*v.* 征收；征税

Phrase(s): ***tax levy; capital levy***

◇ *American government would probably levy a fine of 60 billion euros on Volkswagen for cheating its emissions test.* 由于排放测试结果作假，美国政府很可能向大众征收 600 亿欧元的罚款。

liability [laɪə'bɪlɪtɪ] *n.* 负债

Phrase(s): ***liability insurance; liability on tax***

◇ *According to the Company Law, a limited liability company with relatively small number of shareholders and a relatively small scale may have only one executive director.* 按照公司法的规定，规模较小、股东人数较少的有限责任公司可以只设一名执行董事。

LIBOR (London Inter-bank Offered Rate) ['lʌndən ɪn'tɜːbæŋk ɔːfəd reɪt] *abbr.* 伦敦同业拆借利率

◇ *LIBOR is widely used as a reference rate for financial instruments; besides, it is also often used as a benchmark rate that some of the world's leading banks charge for short-*

term loans. 伦敦银行同业拆借利率被广泛用作金融工具的参考利率；此外，它也经常被一些世界顶尖银行作为短期贷款的基准利率。

license ['laɪsns] *n.* 许可证；执照

Phrase(s): *licensed bank; licensing criterion*

◇ *The Trademark Law of the People's Republic of China stipulates that the trademark registrant may, by concluding a trademark licensing contract, authorizes another person to use its registered trademark.* 《中华人民共和国商标法》规定，商标注册人可以通过订立商标许可合同授权他人使用其注册商标。

limit ['lɪmɪt] *n.* 限制

Phrase(s): *limit of value; limited liability*

◇ *The African country has a very limited capacity in agricultural production due to the fact that many agricultural researchers were killed at the horrible genocide.* 这个非洲国家农业生产的能力非常有限，因为在可怕的种族灭绝中失去了很多农业研究人员。

line of credit [laɪn (ə)v 'kredɪt] *PHR.* 信用额度

◇ *Under a line of credit, borrowers are permitted to vary the drawn amount and repayments within an agreed limit.* 在一定的信用额度下，允许借款人在协定的幅度内调整提款金额和还款金额。

liquid ['lɪkwɪd] *adj.* 流动的

Phrase(s): *liquid capital; liquid form of deposit*

◇ *Banks are required to establish reserves for less liquid positions by supervisory authorities.* 监管当局要求银行为流动性较差的头寸建立储备金。

liquidation [lɪkwɪ'deɪʃ(ə)n] *n.* 清算

Phrase(s): *liquidation value; bankruptcy liquidation*

◇ *The liquidation sale of this 40-year old store will continue until the entire inventory and all of its equipment has been sold.* 这家 40 年老店的停业清理拍卖将持续到整个库存及所有设备售出为止。

liquidator ['lɪkwɪdeɪtə] *n.* 清算人；公司资产清理人

Phrase(s): *representative liquidator;liquidator conduct*

◇ *The retail chain filed bankruptcy at the beginning of this year; one its previous rivals acquired five of its stores in Midwest. The liquidator is still selling the rest of the stores.* 这个零售连锁今年初申请破产；之前的一个竞争对手收购了五家在中西部的分店。清算人仍在拍卖其余的分店。

liquidity [lɪ'kwɪdɪtɪ] *n.* 流动性

Phrase(s): ***liquidity preference theory; liquidity premium; liquidity ratio***

◇ *Although CRM(credit risk mitigant) techniques reduces or transfers credit risk, it may also increase other risks to the bank, such as legal, operational, liquidity and market risks.* 尽管风险缓释技术可降低或转移信用风险，但同时也会使银行承担其他的风险，如法律风险、操作风险、流动性风险和市场风险。1（18）

listed ['lɪstɪd] *adj.* 上市的

Phrase(s): ***listed corporation; listed securities***

◇ *Some emerging markets are quite small; their listed companies qualify neither in size nor in liquidity.* 一些新兴市场是相当小的，它们的上市公司既没有规模也没有流动性。

litigation [lɪtɪ'geɪʃ(ə)n] *n.* 诉讼；讼争；打官司

◇ *Europe has many cross-border litigations, which demands lots of time to negotiate which member country should take the lead a particular case.* 欧洲有很多跨国诉讼，因而需要花费很多时间去谈判，以决定每一起特定案件有哪个成员国来主持审理。

loan [ləʊn] *n.* 贷款；借款

Phrase(s): ***loan guarantee; loan bank; collateral loan; loan sharking***

◇ *The Federal Reserve has tightened the lending regulations on bank loans to big firm to avoid impacts on financial stability.* 美联储收紧了银行向大公司提供贷款的规定，以避免对金融稳定的影响。

◇ *Regulators will target on online lenders who help home buyers skirt around government rules and make loans to them to cover down-payments.* 监管者将重点整顿一些网上银行，它们帮助购房者绕过政府规则并向他们发放贷款用于支付首付款。

Lock-Up Agreement [lɒkʌp ə'gri:m(ə)nt] *PHR.* 锁定协议

◇ *A Lock-Up agreement forbids underwriters in a company from selling any stock share within a fixed period of time to ensure the price stability at the start of the trading.* 锁

定协议禁止承销商在固定的时间内出售公司任何股份，以确保交易刚开始时股票价格的稳定。

long [lɒŋ] *n.* 看涨的人；多头

◇ *When traders believe the oil price will not fall further, some will probably build long positions and close their short positions.* 当交易商认为油价不会继续下跌，其中一些人就会买入多头头寸，卖出空头头寸。

longevity [lɒn'dʒevɪtɪ] *n.* 寿命

Phrase(s): ***longevity risk***

◇ *Family businesses which enjoy longevities share something in common; they are hardworking, modest and seeing the gap in the market sharply.* 持久兴盛的家族企业有一些共性；他们勤奋、谦虚，敏锐地发现市场缺口。

long-term [ˌlɔŋ'tɜːm] *adj.* 长期的

Phrase(s): ***long-term debt; long-term rating***

◇ *Among the most common examples of current liabilities are accounts payable, short-term notes payable, the current portion of long-term debt, accrued liabilities, and unearned revenue.* 最常见的流动负债有应付账款、短期应付票据、长期负债的当期部分、应计负债和预收收入。

loss [lɒs] *n.* 损失；亏损

Phrase(s): ***loss ratio; loss aversion; loss given default(LGD)***

◇ *The Japanese bank Nomura plans to cut more than 500 jobs in Europe, where the bank made a loss of $500 m this financial year.* 日本野村银行计划在欧洲裁员 500 人，该银行本财政年度在欧洲市场亏损 5 亿美元。

lottery ['lɒt(ə)rɪ] *n.* 彩票

Phrase(s): ***lottery record; lottery contract; win a lottery***

◇ *When asked what they would do first if they won a lottery prize, most people said they would buy a better house and travel around the world with their families.* 当问人们彩票中奖后要做的第一件事是什么，大部分人的回答是买一处更好的房子并和家人周游世界。

M

maintenance margin ['meɪntɪnəns 'mɑːdʒɪn] *PHR.* 最低保证金；维持保证金

Phrase(s): *maintenance margin requirement*

◇ *If the margin account balance falls below the maintenance margin level, the account balance must be brought back up to the maintenance level.* 如果保证金账户余额低于维持保证金要求，需要追加账户资金以满足保证金要求。

management buyout ['mænɪdʒm(ə)nt 'baɪ'aʊt] *PHR.* 管理层收购

Phrase(s): *state-owned enterprise management buyout*

◇ *A management buyout (MBO) occurs where a company's management team purchases the assets and operations of the business they manage; it usually requires substantial financing.* 管理层收购（MBO）指的是一个公司的管理团队购买他们所管理企业的资产和业务；它通常需要大量的融资。

marginal ['mɑːdʒɪn(ə)l] *adj.* 边际的

Phrase(s): *marginal cost; marginal utility; marginal tax rate*

◇ *Since young employees are receiving the lowest salaries, they are also paying low marginal tax rates.* 因为年轻的员工工资最低，他们支付的边际税率也很低。

◇ *If a young employee starts investing $100 every month in his IRA (individual retirement account)since 21 years old,he could get more than $200 000 by age 67(assuming a 5% annual return and a marginal tax rate of 25%).* 一个年轻职工如果从 21 岁起每月往他的个人退休账户里存入 100 美元，67 岁时就可以获得超过 200 000 美元（假设

年回报率是 5%，边际税率是 25%）。

markdown ['mɑː kdəʊn] *n.* 减价

Phrase(s): ***markdown percentage; markdown sales***

◇ *Many physical bakeries also use their social networking sites for photographic markdown, meaning to post photos of discounted cakes or breads for young customers to order online.* 许多实体的面包店也利用其社交网站进行图片降价，就是把打折的蛋糕或面包的照片传到网页上，方便年轻客户网上订购。

market arbitrage ['mɑːkɪt ˌɑːbɪtrɑːʒ] *PHR.* 市场套利

Phrase(s): ***market arbitrage strategy; market arbitrage mechanism***

◇ *An ill designed treasury future contract will cause increased market arbitrage, increased market risk, market disorder and even market breakdown.* 如果国债期货合约设计不科学、不合理，就会导致国债期货市场过分投机，风险增大，市场秩序混乱，甚至导致国债期货市场的崩溃。

market capitalization ['mɑːkɪtˌkæpɪt(ə)laɪ'zeɪʃ(ə)n] *PHR.* 资本市值；市价总值

Phrase(s): ***tradable market capitalization; market capitalization ratio***

◇ *It is strongly recommended that investors should focus on intermediate-above companies which have a market capitalization of $1 billion or more.* 强烈建议投资者应该关注中等规模以上的公司，即资本市值在 10 亿美元以上。

market-clearing ['mɑːkɪt'klɪərɪŋ] *n.* 市场出清

Phrase(s): ***market-clearing price***

◇ *In economics, there is an important assumption that a market-clearing price can cause quantities supplied and demanded to be equal.* 经济学中有一个重要假设，即通过一个市场出清价格，会使供给量和需求量相等。

market failure ['mɑːkɪt 'feɪljə] *PHR.* 市场失灵

◇ *Market failure means market itselfcannot maintain all the requirements for a competitive situation.* 市场失灵就是市场本身不能够维持竞争所需要的一切条件。

market friction ['mɑːkɪt 'frɪkʃ(ə)n] *PHR.* 市场摩擦

◇ *Market friction includes financial factors like human capital and non-financial factors such as the cost of re-balancing the portfolio.* 市场摩擦包括非财务因素如人力资

本和财务因素如重新平衡投资组合的成本。

market risk ['mɑ:kɪt rɪsk] *PHR.* 市场风险

Phrase(s): *market risk management*

◇ *Risk weighted assets for equity exposures in the trading book are subject to the market risk capital rules.* 交易账户上股权暴露的风险加权资产遵守市场风险资本规则。1（62）

◇ *Any type of VaR model used must be able to capture adequately all of the material risks embodied in equity returns including both the general market risk and specific risk exposure of the institution's equity portfolio.* 无论采用哪种类型的 VaR 模型，都必须能充分计算所有体现在股权收益中的重要风险，包括一般的市场风险和银行股权组合的特殊风险。1（95）

market value ['mɑ:kɪt 'vælju:] *PHR.* 市场价值；市价

Phrase(s): *fair market value*

◇ In fiscal year 2014, the company's market value grew by more than$ 50 billion. 在 2014 财政年度中，这家公司的市值增加了超过 500 亿美元。

◇ *The market value of a convertible bond often fluctuates with the market value of an equivalent number of shares of common stock.* 可转换债券的市价通常会随等值的普通股的市价波动而波动。

mark-to-market ['mɑ:k tə 'mɑ:kɪt] *n.* 逐日盯市

Phrase(s): *mark-to-market risk; mark-to-market accounting rules*

◇ *Independent price verification is distinct from daily mark-to-market. It is the process by which market prices or model inputs are regularly verified for accuracy.* 与逐日按市场价值计价不同，价格独立验证是指将市场价格或模型参数定期进行精确性验证的过程。1（133）

master data ['mɑ:stə 'deɪtə] *PHR.* 主数据

◇ *Master data management (MDM) enables an enterprise to link all of its critical data to one file so as to ensure that it does not use multiple versions of the same master data.* 主数据管理（MDM）使企业把各环节的关键数据归于一个文档，以确保不会使用相同主数据的多个版本。

material risk [mə'tɪərɪəl rɪsk] *PHR.* 重大风险

Phrase(s): ***material tail risk; material misstatement risk***

◇ *Banks are free to choose different types of models as long as the models can capture all the materials risks run by the banks.* 银行可以自由选择不同类型的模型，只要模型能捕获银行所承担的重大风险即可。

maturity [mə'tʃʊərətɪ] *n.* 到期

Phrase(s): ***maturity date; yield to maturity; debt maturity***

◇ *The most common type of fixed-income security is a bond that promises to make a series of interest payments in fixed amounts and to repay the principal amount at maturity.* 最常见的固定收益证券是承诺付出一系列固定数额的利息以及在到期日偿还本金的证券。

measurement criteria ['meʒəm(ə)nt kraɪ'tɪərɪə] *PHR.* 衡量标准

◇ *Banks should have universal measurement criteria for capital.* 银行需要一个统一的资本衡量标准。

mechanism ['mek(ə)nɪz(ə)m] *n.* 机制

Phrase(s): ***market mechanism; incentive mechanism***

◇ *Market mechanism should play a decisive role when allocating resources.* 市场机制在资源配置中要起决定性作用。

medium term ['mi:dɪəm tɜ:m] *PHR.* 中期的；中项

Phrase(s): ***medium term actions; medium term note***

◇ *A well-known global rating agency said that the Brexit referendum outcome would be disruptive for U. S. global banks with significant operations in the U. K. and would weigh on their profitability in the short to medium term.* 全球知名评级机构表示，英国脱欧公投结果将破坏那些在英国业务量大的美国全球银行，将对其中短期盈利能力带来负面影响。

◇ *It is urgent that West African countries should push ahead with more medium term actions to make agriculture a priority since they have a large population to feed.* 西非国家的当务之急是应推进中期措施，优先发展农业，解决大批人口的温饱问题。

medium to long-term funds ['mi:dɪəm tə ˌlɒŋ'tɜ:m fʌndz] *PHR.* 中长期资金

◇ *Banks can raise medium to long-term funds through the issuance of bonds.* 银行可以通过发行债券筹集中长期资金。

merger ['mɜ:dʒə] *n.* 并购

Phrase(s): ***merger and acquisition; business merger***

◇ *Shareholders from both companies have voted to approve the merger, federal regulators' approval will be the next step.* 两家公司的股东都已投票批准合并，下一步将是征得联邦监管机构的批准。

mesokurtic [ˌmɜsəʊ'kɜ:tɪk] *adj.* 常峰的

Phrase(s): ***mesokurtic distribution***

◇ *Normal distribution can be divided into three types: leptokurtic, mesokurtic and platykurtic.* 正态分布可以分为三种类型：尖峰的、常峰的和扁峰的。

mezzanine finance ['mezəni:n 'faɪnæns] *PHR.* 夹层融资

Phrase(s): ***the development of mezzanine financing***

◇ *Mezzanine financing, as one of the private equity investment businesses, has flexible structure.* 夹层融资作为私募股权投资业务品种之一，具有结构灵活的特性。

◇ *Companies need a pretty record in the industry with established reputation, a history of profits and a feasible plan of expansion to realize mezzanine finance.* 公司需要在行业建立良好的声誉，有实现利润的历史记录和可行的扩张计划才可能实现夹层融资。

minimum capital ['mɪnɪməm 'kæpɪt(ə)l] *PHR.* 最低资本

Phrase(s): ***Minimum Capital Requirements***

◇ *Banks may use modelling techniques such as historical scenario analysis to determine minimum capital requirements for banking book equity holdings.* 银行也可以采用建模技术（如历史情形分析）来确定银行账户中对股权持有的最低资本要求。1（95）

minority interest [maɪ'nɒrɪtɪ 'ɪnt(ə)rɪst] *PHR.* 少数权益；少数股东权益

Phrase(s): ***take a minority interest***

◇ *The European publisher has agreed to buy minority interest in an online media company; the financial terms will soon be disclosed.* 一个欧洲出版商已同意购买一家网络媒体公司的少数股东权益，财务条款将很快公布。

◇ *Viacom announced that it would sell the significant minority interest in Paramount Pictures to raise more cash for another business line.* 维亚康姆集团宣布将出售在派拉蒙电影公司的重要少数股东权益，为另一个业务线发展筹集更多资金。

mismatch ['mɪsmætʃ] *v.* 错配

Phrase(s): ***mismatch risk; maturity mismatch***

◇ *Where the residual maturity of the CRM is less than that of the underlying credit exposure a maturity mismatch occurs.* 如果风险缓释的期限比当前的风险暴露的期限短，则产生期限错配。1（21）

mitigate ['mɪtɪgeɪt] *vt.* 使缓和；使减轻；使平息；*vi.* 减轻；缓和下来

Phrase(s): ***mitigate risk; mitigate credit risk***

◇ *A diversified allocation of assets in both domestic and international markets is helpful to mitigate risk and enhance returns.* 在国内和国际市场进行多元化资产配置有助于降低风险和提高收益。

◇ *Many energy consumers in the Mid-west protested that power transmission companies were too lucrative. They are planning to file a lawsuit to help mitigate their utility rates.* 许多中西部能源消费者抗议电力公司太赚钱。他们正计划提起诉讼，以帮助降低电费。

money market ['mʌnɪ 'mɑːkɪt] *PHR.* 货币市场

Phrase(s): ***money market fund***

◇ *Short periods of lending and borrowing are often involved in money market, where high liquidity and short maturities are two important features.* 货币市场往往涉及短期借贷，高流动性和短期限是货币市场的两个重要特点。

money supply ['mʌnɪ sə'plaɪ] *PHR.* 货币供应量

◇ *Money supply represents a country's entire stock of currency and other liquid instruments in a specific time; money supply may impact a country's price level and inflation rate.* 货币供应量是在特定的时间一个国家全部的货币和流动性票据；货币供应量可能会影响一个国家的价格水平和通货膨胀率。

◇ *M2 is a broader gauge of the money supply than M1 because it includes non-cash, highly liquid assets which could be converted to cash quickly if needed.* M2 比 M1 更广泛

地衡量货币供应量，因为它包括非现金的高流动性资产，一旦需要可以快速转换为现金。

monopoly [mə'nɒp(ə)lɪ] *n.* 垄断

Phrase(s): *natural monopoly; monopoly economy*

◇ *Monopoly doesn't provide incentives for healthy competition in the market; even monopolies themselves will not benefit in terms of sustainable development.* 垄断不提供健康的市场竞争激励；甚至垄断企业本身也不会在可持续发展方面受益。

mortgage ['mɔːgɪdʒ] *vt.* 抵押；*n.* 抵押

Phrase(s): *housing mortgage; mortgage loan; subprime mortgage*

◇ *American investors lost billions of dollars when Goldman Sachs mis-sold the mortgage-backed securities between 2005 and 2007.* 高盛银行在 2005 年到 2007 年间不当销售抵押贷款支持证券，造成美国投资者损失了数十亿美元。

multinational corporation [mʌltɪ'næʃ(ə)n(ə)l kɔːpə'reɪʃ(ə)n] *PHR.* 跨国企业

◇ *Large number of Indians came to East African at the beginning of the 19th century; they used their international relations with Asia and Britain to achieve great business success there just like multinational corporations would do today.* 大批印度人在 19 世纪初来到东非；他们用自己与亚洲和英国的关系取得了巨大的商业成功，就像跨国企业今天做的一样。

◇ *Many founders or CEOs of large multinational corporations are continuously ranked in the "Forbes" richest list.* 许多大型跨国企业的创始人或首席执行官一直排在"福布斯"富豪榜上。

multiplier effect ['mʌltɪplaɪə ɪ'fekt] *PHR.* 乘数效应

◇ *It's estimated that every lost job in oil and gas industry leads to three times more job cuts in other industries; this multiplier effect proves the fact that oil and gas people earn a lot and spend a lot.* 据估计，石油和天然气行业每裁员一个人将导致其他行业三倍以上的裁员量，这个乘数效应证明一个事实：石油和天然气行业的人赚得多，花得也多。

municipal bond [mjʊ'nɪsɪp(ə)l bɒnd] *PHR.* 市政券

Phrase(s): *municipal bond market; municipal bond model*

◇ *Municipal bonds are issued by states, cities or other government sections to finance long-term large public projects.* 市政债券由州政府、城市或其他政府部门发行，专为长期的大型公共工程提供融资。

◇ *The Securities and Exchange Commission imposed a heavy fine on a financial firm for overcharging retail customers in the municipal bond sales.* 一家金融公司向零售客户高价销售市政债券，被证券交易委员会处以高额罚款。

mutual fund ['mju:tʃʊəl fʌnd] *PHR.* 互惠基金；共同基金

◇ *Some mutual funds marked down the value of their stake in e-commerce companies due to their frenzy input in logistics and discounts in order to compete for more market share.* 一些共同基金降低了他们在电子商务企业的股份估值，因为这些电子商务企业为争夺更多的市场份额，在物流和折扣上疯狂投入。

N

naked short selling ['neɪkɪd ʃɔːt 'selɪŋ] *PHR.* 无担保沽空

◇ *Naked short selling exists due to loopholes in regulation rules and it causes fluctuations in stock prices.* "裸卖"由于监管规则的漏洞而存在，它会导致股票价格的波动。

narrower profit margin ['nærəʊə 'prɒfɪt 'mɑːdʒɪn] *PHR.* 较小利润幅度

◇ *For commercial banks, to establish a sound mechanism of risk management in SMEs credit extension is not only meaningful to help SMEs to get financing, but also helpful for commercial banks themselves whose narrower profit margin is becoming increasingly narrower.* 商业银行建立合理的中小企业授信风险管理机制不仅对解决中小企业融资难题具有积极意义，对于目前利润空间日益缩小的商业银行也具有很强的现实意义。

nature of business ['neɪtʃə (ə)v 'bɪznɪs] *PHR.* 业务性质

◇ *The nature of business determines the company's high concern on technology innovation and security protection.* 业务性质决定了公司高度重视技术创新和安全保护。

near money [nɪə 'mʌnɪ] *PHR.* 准货币

◇ *Near money is not money but assets with high liquidity such as bank deposits.* 准货币不是货币而是流动性很强的资产，例如银行存款。

negative growth ['negətɪv grəʊθ] *PHR.* 负增长

◇ *Customer survey revealed the factors attributed to the e-commerce company's negative growth and drop in market share: slow delivery and insecured online payment system*. 客户调查显示了这家电子商务公司负增长和市场份额下降的原因是物流速度慢以及不安全的在线支付系统。

negotiable [nɪ'gəʊʃəb(ə)l] *adj.* 可谈判的；可协商的；可商量的；（票据）可兑现的

◇ *Futures contracts are standardized, negotiable, and exchange-traded contracts to buy or sell underlying assets*. 期货合约是标准化的、可转让的、交易性的标的资产买卖合约。

nest egg [nest eg] *PHR.* 养老金

◇ *Be careful: a very tiny increase in investment fees will make a huge difference in your nest egg because this is a long-term investment with accumulated loss*. 小心：即使投资费用只增加一丁点，也会给你的养老金收入带来巨大的差异，因为这是一个长期投资，损失会累积。

net cash flow [net kæʃ fləʊ] *PHR.* 净现金流

◇ *The current value of an outstanding forward contract can be found by entering an offsetting forward position and discounting the net cash flow at expiration*. 一个远期合约的现值，可以通过一个相抵持仓，并在到期时对净现金流进行贴现。

net duration [net djʊ'reɪʃ(ə)n] *PHR.* 净久期

◇ *They release only exposures to major risk factors, such as net duration, net systematic risk, and so on*. 他们只发布了主要风险暴露因子，如净久期、净系统性风险等等。

net income [net 'ɪnkʌm] *PHR.* 净收入

◇ *Net income reflects differences in a firm's capital structure and taxes as well as operating income*. 净收入反映了公司资本结构和税收方面的不同，同时也反映了营业收入方面的不同。6（47）

net leverage [net 'liːv(ə)rɪdʒ] *PHR.* 净财务杠杆；净杠杆比率

◇ *Net Leverage is an important measure for investors to evaluate a company's liquidity*. 净杠杆是投资者评估公司流动性的重要手段。

net position [net pə'zɪʃ(ə)n] *PHR.* 净头寸

◇ *Net position refers to the value of the position subtracting the initial cost of setting up the position.* 净头寸指的是头寸价值减去购买头寸的初始成本。

net premium [net 'pri:mɪəm] *PHR.* 净保费；净贴水

◇ *Ignoring the net premium, the highest potential gain is $2 and the worst loss is $3.* 忽略净贴水的情况下，这个项目最高的潜在收益是 2 美元，最大的损失是 3 美元。

netting agreement ['netɪŋ ə'gri:m(ə)nt] *PHR.* 净额结算协议

◇ *Netting agreement between two or more parties will reduce the number of transactions by calculating the combined value of payments so as to lower the bank fees.* 交易双方或多方通过净额结算协议来计算多次交易收支的合并价值从而减少交易次数，降低银行费用。

non-callable [nɒn'kɔ:ləb(ə)l] *adj.* 不可赎回的

Phrase(s): ***non-callable bond; non-callable securities; non-callable preferred stock***

◇ *The yield to the worst call date is much better than yield to maturity of a non-non-callable bond.* 召回日期最后一天的收益率也要比非提前偿还的债券到期收益率高得多。

◇ *The dividends on both new kinds of shares would be paid in perpetuity, and the securities would be non-callable.* 这两种新型股票是不可赎回的，其股利支付是永久性的。

non-defaulting party [nɒndɪ'fɔltɪŋ 'pɑ:tɪ] *PHR.* 守约方；未违约方

◇ *Netting agreements must provide the non-defaulting party the right to terminate and close-out in a timely manner all transactions upon an event of default, including in the event of insolvency or bankruptcy of the counterparty.* 在交易对象出现包括无力支付、破产等违约事件时，净扣交易必须赋予未违约方及时终止、停止合同的权利。

non-firm offer [nɒnfɜ:m 'ɒfə] *PHR.* 虚盘或非确定报价

◇ *They have made us a non-firm offer for their new products with an intention to raise the price as long as we place an order.* 他们就新产品向我们报了虚盘，一旦我们下订单就会考虑提高价格。

normal distribution ['nɔ:m(ə)l dɪstrɪ'bju: ʃ(ə)n] *PHR.* 正态分布

◇ *Typical choices for the distribution of ε are normal distribution, t-distribution, and stable non-Gaussian distribution.* 典型的 ε 分布选择的是正态分布、t 分布和稳定性好的非高斯分布。5（5）

NPV (net present value) [net 'prez(ə)nt 'vælju:] *abbr.* 净现值

◇ *Fixed-income securities can be valued by, first, laying out their cash flows and, second, computing their net present value (NPV) using the appropriate discount rate.* 固定收益证券通过以下两点进行估值：第一，测定其现金流；第二，用适当的折现率计算净现值（NPV）。

null hypothesis [nʌl haɪ'pɒθɪsɪs] *PHR.* 零假设

◇ *The hypothesis to be tested is called the null hypothesis or simply the null.* 即将被检验的假设被称作零假设。5（85）

◇ *Null hypothesis usually assumes that there is no relationship between two measured phenomena or groups. Rejecting the null hypothesisis a central task in science.* 零假设通常假定两个被测量的现象或群体之间没有关系。否定零假设是科学界的中心任务。

O

obligor ['ɒblɪgɔː] *n.* 债务人

Phrase(s): obligor rating; specific obligor; secondary obligor

◇ *In the event of the borrower's financial distress or default, the bank should have legal authority to sell or assign the receivables to other parties without consent of the receivables obligors.* 发生借款人财务陷入困境或违约的情况，银行应该拥有不经过应收账款债务人的同意，出售应收账款或将应收账款交给其他方面的法律权利。1（92）

odd-lot [ɒdlɒt] *n.* 零星交易

Phrase(s): ***odd-lot trading; odd-lot dealer***

◇ *With the help of online trading platforms, disposing of odd lots is much easier and less expensive than it used to be.* 有了在线交易平台，处理零星交易要比过去更容易也更便宜。

OECD(Organization for Economic Cooperation and Development) [ˌəuiːsiː'diː] *abbr.* 经济合作与发展组织

Phrase(s): ***OECD governance framework***

◇ *As a leading international economic body, OECD's forecast for global growth has drawn world attentions.* 作为一个领先的国际经济体，经合组织对全球经济增长的预测引起了世界的关注。

offer ['ɒfə] *n.* 报价；出价

Phrase(s): ***offer rate***

◇ *Global investors have to accept the government's offer, though they are not satisfied with the payment terms; otherwise, they would get nothing.* 全球投资者不得不接受这个政府的提议，虽然他们并不满意还款的条约；否则，他们什么也得不到。

◇ *Under extreme weather conditions, African countries should investment more in irrigation equipment and offer some insurance for crops to reduce farmers' loss in bad seasons.* 极端天气条件下，非洲国家应该在灌溉设备上做更多的投资，并为农作物提供保险，以减少农民在灾害季节的损失。

offset ['ɔːfset] *v.* 补偿；抵消

◇ *The bank reported a big fall in net income due to lower interest earnings; fortunately, the revenues gained from consumer banking offset the loss in investment banking.* 银行报告，由于较低的利息收益，净收入大幅下降；幸运的是，消费者业务的利润抵消了投资业务的亏损。

offshore ['ɒfʃɔː] *adj.* 离岸的；［海洋］近海的；吹向海面的；*adv.* 向海面；向海

Phrase(s): ***offshore finance; offshore trade***

◇ *Many multinational corporations use offshore tax heavens to evade huge taxes in their registered countries.* 许多跨国企业利用离岸避税天堂逃避在注册国家的巨额税收。

oligopoly [ˌɒlɪ'gɒp(ə)lɪ] *n.* 寡头垄断

Phrase(s): ***oligopoly market; oligopoly price***

◇ *Mineral Lithium , used to be an oligopoly, now becomes a "gold zone" for all kind of miners due to its increasing use in electric vehicle battery production.* 矿物质锂过去被寡头垄断，现在由于广泛应用于电动汽车的电池生产，成为各种采矿人争夺的“黄金地带”。

◇ *Despite many advantages, free market system could also lead to a high degree of market concentration with game winners becoming oligopolies.* 尽管有许多优点，自由市场体系也会导致高度的市场集中，使游戏赢家成为垄断寡头。

omission [ə(ʊ)'mɪʃ(ə)n] *n.* 疏忽；遗漏；省略；冗长

Phrase(s): ***material omission***

◇ *Oscar awarding ceremonies in recent years have triggered controversial discussions for its omissions in colored actors.* 由于对有色演员的忽略，奥斯卡颁奖仪式近年来引发具有争议性的讨论。

open ['əʊp(ə)n] *n.* 未平仓的

Phrase(s): ***open interest***

◇ *The open interest is the number of long positions or, equivalently, the number of short positions.* 未平仓合约是指期货市场上的所有的多头头寸数量，这个数量也等于所有空头头寸的数量。

option ['ɒpʃ(ə)n] *n.* 期权；选择权

Phrase(s): ***European option; call option; option premiums***

◇ *A clean-up call is an option that permits an originating bank or a servicing bank to call the securitisation exposures (e. g. asset-backed securities) before all of the underlying exposures have been repaid.* 清收式赎回是一种选择权，它允许发起行或服务行在资产池中的资产未被全部偿还的情况下召回资产证券化风险暴露（如资产支持型证券）。1（100）

◇ *Due to wet weather, grain production is bound to decline this year; luckily, the futures and options market help farmers to lock in profitable prices as the stockpile of grains in the country is getting small.* 因潮湿天气，今年粮食生产势必减少；幸运的是，由于国家储备粮食正在减少，期货和期权市场帮助农民锁定了盈利的价格。

order ['ɔːdə] *n.* 订货；订单； *v.* 命令

Phrase(s): ***order form; shipping order***

◇ *The maker of planes and trains announced billions of net losses due to its shrinking in order book and write-downs.* 这个飞机和火车制造商宣布，由于订单减少造成数十亿的净亏损和资产减值。

◇ *The fuel efficiency technology may bring the car manufacture more orders from Chinese market.* 燃油节省技术可能会给这家汽车制造商带来更多中国市场的订单。

out [aʊt] *adj.* 虚值的

Phrase(s): ***out-of-the-money option***

◇ *With an "out-of-the-money" call stock option, the current share price is less than the strike price so there is no reason to exercise the option.* 对于虚值看涨期权来说，当前价

格是比执行价格低的，因此没有理由去行权。

outflow ['aʊtfləʊ] *n.* 流出；流出量

Phrase(s): ***outflow of capital***

◇ *The outflow of capital spending and high paying jobs, as manufacturers shift more production overseas, will be a problem.* 在制造商将更多的生产转移至海外之际，资本支出和高薪工作岗位外流将是个问题。

◇ *While China is promoting a wave of infrastructure construction with abundant national capital resources, the outflow of domestic capital searching for foreign resources becomes inevitable.* 在中国掀起基础设施建设大潮，国家资本充足的背景下，国内资本走出国门，在世界范围内搜罗资源成为必然。

outgoing ['aʊtgəʊɪŋ] *n.* 外出；流出；开支；*adj.* 外向的；即将卸任的

Phrase(s): ***outgoing partner***

◇ *The outgoing CEO will retire in September this year, but he will remain as board chairman for another session.* 即将离任的首席执行官将于今年九月退休，但他仍将留任下一期的董事会主席。

output ['aʊtpʊt] *n.* 输出；产量；*v.* 输出

Phrase(s): ***industrial output; hourly output; average output***

◇ *Africa's share only accounts for less than 3% in global manufacturing output; it lacks many things that a successful manufacturing sector needs.* 在全球制造业产出中，非洲的份额只占不到 3%，它缺乏很多一个成功的制造业需要的东西。

outside [aʊt'saɪd] *adj.* 外部的；*n.* 外部；*prep.* 在……范围之外

Phrase(s): ***outside dealing; outside information***

◇ *After China began Opening-up and Reform in lte 1970s, great changes have taken place in various aspects of social life.* 上个世纪 70 年代末，中国开始了改革开放，社会生活的各个方面发生了巨大的变化。

◇ *Twenty years ago, a large proportion of African's wealth was held outside the continent; thanks to increasing political stability, now much of the wealth are returning to Africa in real estate and other businesses.* 二十年前，大部分非洲的财富在非洲大陆以外；由于政治稳定性的提高，现在大部分的财富正在返回非洲，投资于房地产和其他企业。

outsold [ˌaʊt'səʊld] *v.* 超卖；卖得比……多

◇ *According to the sales report of this car manufacturer, its hybrid cars outsold gasoline-fueled cars in the first quarter of 2015.* 根据该汽车制造商的销售报告，其混合动力汽车销量在 2015 年第一季度超过汽油为燃料的汽车。

◇ *The launch of iPhone 6 and 6 plus gave Apple a jump in smartphone market share; though iPhone outsold iPhone 6 plus greatly.* 苹果 iPhone 6 和 6+ 推出以后，苹果公司在智能手机市场的份额突飞猛进；虽然 iPhone 6 销量大大超过 iPhone6+。

outstanding [aʊt'stændɪŋ] *adj.* 杰出的；显著的；未解决的；未偿付的；*n.* 未偿贷款

Phrase(s): *outstanding cheque*

◇ *If qualifying residential mortgage loans are past due but specific provisions are no less than 50% of their outstanding amount, the risk weight applicable to the remainder of the loan can be reduced to 50% at national discretion.* 对于逾期的合格住房抵押贷款，如果专项准备达到贷款余额的 50% 或 50% 以上，监管当局可自行决定，将扣减处理后贷款的风险权重降低到 50%。1（13）

overallotment [ˌəʊvə'lɒtm(ə)nt] *n.* 超额配售权

Phrase(s): *overallotment agreement; overallotment right*

◇ *If the demand for a company's share is high and the trading price is higher than the offering price, then the issuing company may authorize underwriters to exercise the overallotment option.* 如果一个公司的股票需求量大，交易价格高于发行价格，那么发行公司可授权承销人行使超额配售权。

◇ *A good chunk of that money will come from the $20 billion in proceeds the firm could raise in the IPO on Friday, provided that the whole overallotment is sold.* 一大部分所需资金将源自周五 IPO 所募得的 200 亿美元，但条件是公司出售所有超额配售权。

overbuy [əʊvə'baɪ] *v.* 超买；买空

◇ *Christmas sales are always attractive, but don't overbuy.* 圣诞节促销总是很有吸引力，但不要买得太多哦！

overcollateralization [əʊvəkə'læt(ə)r(ə)laɪzeɪʃ(ə)n] *n.* 超额抵押

◇ *The aim of overcollateralization is increasing its credit rating from internal credit enhancement.* 超额抵押的目的是从内部增信的角度提高信用评级。

overdraft ['əʊvədrɑːft] *n.* 透支

Phrase(s): ***overdraft of an account; overdraft on banks;***

◇ *Overdrafts will be considered as being past due once the customer has breached an advised limit or been advised of a limit smaller than current outstandings.* 若客户违反了规定的透支限额或者新核定的限额小于目前的余额，各项透支将被视为逾期。1（80）

◇ *Authorized overdrafts must be subject to a credit limit set by the bank and brought to the knowledge of the client.* 授权透支必须在银行信贷限额以内，同时必须告之客户。1（81）

overdue [əʊvə'djuː] *adj.* 过期的；未兑的

Phrase(s): ***overdue interest; overdue payment***

◇ *People in America think that passing a gun control bill is much more important than analysis of former gun shootings, because we don't know where the next massacre will be.* 在美国，人们认为通过控枪法案远比分析之前的枪击事件更为重要，因为我们不知道下一个大屠杀将在哪里发生。

◇ *In a wise family budget plan, paying overdue income taxes should go before next overseas holiday traveling; otherwise, your passport could be revoked due to tax scofflaws.* 明智的家庭预算应该先计划补缴所得税，再计划下一次海外度假旅游；否则，你的护照可能因为税收违法而被吊销。

overhang [əʊvə'hæŋ] *n.* 积压

Phrases(s): dollar overhang; debt overhang

◇ *A large overhang of photovoltaic products were stranded at the port due to the unsettled dispute on dumping between the two countries.* 由于这两个国家之间悬而未决的倾销纠纷，大量积压的光伏产品被滞留在港口。

◇ *The housing price is still going up while there is a large overhang of apartments for sale.* 虽然有大量积压公寓等待出售，住房价格仍然上涨。

overhead [əʊvə'hed] *n.* 间接费用

Phrase(s): ***overhead cost***

◇*High overhead cost in IPO had a substantial reduction in total profit of the company.*

高昂的 IPO 间接费用严重缩减了公司的总利润额。

overnight [əʊvə'naɪt] *adj.* 隔夜的

Phrase(s): ***overnight liquidity assistance; overnight margin; overnight position; overnight rate***

◇ *My landlord boosted the rent from 2 000 rmb to 4 000 rmb overnight, which pushed me to save harder for the down-payment of a house mortgage loan.* 房东一夜之间把租金从 2 000 元涨到 4 000 元，逼得我拼命存钱付住房抵押贷款的首付。

◇ *Traders pay at different margin rates for "day"and "overnight" positions in currency futures trades.* 在货币期货交易中，交易者为日间交易和隔夜交易支付不同的保证金。

overrun [əʊvə'rʌn] *n.* 泛滥成灾；超出限度；*vt.* 泛滥；超过；*vi.* 泛滥；蔓延

Phrase(s): ***overrun cost***

◇ *Don't let one single hot stock overrun your portfolio; diversify your investments if you predict a bear market is on the way.* 不要让一个热门股票在你的投资组合中份额过大；如果你预测熊市即将到来，必须分散你的投资。

overseas [əʊvə'siːz] *adj.* 外国的；在海外的；adv. 国外；向国外

Phrase(s): ***overseas currency balance; overseas interest; overseas financial institution***

◇ *Many Chinese emigrants are returning to invest the money they earned in overseas market; they often chose coastal cities as their business locations.* 许多中国移民回国投资他们在海外市场赚来的钱；他们经常选择沿海城市作为自己的经营地点。

◇ *Many Hollywood films chose European countries as the destinations of their overseas premieres because of shared culture and language foundation.* 因为相似的文化和语言基础，许多好莱坞电影选择了欧洲国家作为他们海外首映的目的地。

oversight ['əʊvəsaɪt] *n.* 监督；照管；疏忽

Phrase(s): ***legislative oversight***

◇ *A credit risk control unit must assume oversight and supervision responsibilities for any models used in the rating process, and ultimate responsibility for the ongoing review and alterations to rating models.* 信用风险控制部门必须对评级过程中使用的模型承担监控和监督责任，并且对将来的检查和评级模型的改变承担最终责任。1（78）

overtax [əʊvə'tæks] *vt.* 负担过度

Phrase(s): ***overtax oneself***

◇ *Some businesses neglected the change in federal tax rate and still overtaxed their customers after the notification from the state tax agency for several times.* 一些企业忽视联邦税率的变化，在州税务局多次通知以后，仍然向顾客多收税。

over-the-counter ['əʊvəðə'kaʊntə] *adj.* 场外的；柜台的

Phrase(s): ***over-the-counter market; over-the-counter trading***

◇ *Banks will be required to calculate the counterparty credit risk charge for OTC(over-the-counter) derivatives, repo-style and other transactions booked in the trading book, separate from the capital charge for general market risk and specific risk.* 监管当局要求银行除了计算一般市场风险和特定风险的资本要求外，还要对交易账户上反映的场外衍生工具、回购协议类产品和其他交易工具等计算信用风险资本要求。1（134）

ownership ['əʊnəʃɪp] *n.* 所有权；物主身份

Phrase(s): ***land ownership; ownership interest; mixed ownership***

◇ *Companies registered in this country are forced to verify their clients' beneficial-ownership information; some politicians warned that businesses would flow to other countries under such strict regulations.* 在这个国家注册的公司被迫核实他们客户的受益所有权信息；一些政治家警告说，在这样严格的规定下这些企业将流向其他国家。

◇ *The former president was accused of concealing his ownership of two overseas properties.* 前总统被指控隐瞒他在海外的两处物业所有权。

P

package ['pækɪdʒ] *v.* 打包（资产）；*n.* 包裹

◇ *Banks often packaged customers' mortgage loans into securities and sold to investors.* 银行通常把顾客的抵押贷款打包成证券并出售给投资者。

◇ *The world well-known magazine is looking for a chief editor and the successful candidate will be offered a competitive six figure package.* 这家世界知名杂志社正在招聘主编，应聘成功者将会获得六位数的年总收入。

package deal ['pækɪdʒ di:l] *PHR.* 总价交易；套餐交易

◇ *The travel agency offered us a package deal to Japanese, including air tickets,hotels and local tour guide service.* 旅行社为我们提供了一个日本旅游套餐，包括机票，饭店和当地导游服务。

padding ['pædɪŋ] *n.* 虚报开支项目

◇ *In times of high unemployment rate and inflation rate, consumers learnt to save more, padding their balances to prepare for another economic difficulty.* 在高失业率和通货膨胀率的艰难时代，消费者学会了节省、补充余额，为下一个经济困难时期做准备。

paid-in ['peid'in] *adj.* 已缴；认缴；实缴

Phrase(s): ***paid-in capital; paid-in surplus***

◇ *Shareholder structure of multilateral development banks is comprised of a significant proportion of sovereigns with long term issuer credit assessments of AA- or better, or the majority of the fund-raising are in the form of paid-in equity/capital and there is little or no leverage.* 从多边开发银行的股东结构看，大多数是主权国家，并且这些主权国家的长期信用评级为 AA- 或以上；或者主要的资金来源是实收资本，并且没有或只有很小的杠杆效应。1（8）

paid-in capital ['peid'in 'kæpɪt(ə)l] *PHR.* 投入股本

◇ *In order to be eligible for a 0% risk weight, multilateral development banks should demonstrate a strong shareholder support by the amount of paid-in-capital.* 多边发展银行需要证明强有力的股东支持，即股东提供了足够的实收资本，才能适用 0% 的风险权重。

panel data ['pæn(ə)l 'deɪtə] *PHR.* 面板数据

◇ *Panel data usually consists of observations of numerous phenomena that are collected over time for a group of units, such as household and governments.* 面板数据是指随着时间的推移收集一组单位（如家庭和政府）的多个截面进行样本观测。

panic ['pænɪk] *n.* 恐慌

Phrase(s): ***panic stations; financial panic***

◇ *The failure of one financial institution can lead to a contagion to other financial institutions because of the financial panic as happened with the collapse of Lehman Brothers.* 金融恐慌会导致一家金融机构的失败蔓延到其他机构，比如雷曼兄弟的破产就是这样。10（24）

paper loss ['peɪpə lɒs] *PHR.* 账面损失

◇ *Due to poor performance in the stock market this year, investors suffered a huge paper loss, which would probably become a real loss if the market stays flat.* 由于今年股票市场表现不佳，投资者遭受了巨大的账面损失，如果市场持续不景气，账面损失将可能变成真正的损失。

paper market ['peɪpə 'mɑːkɪt] *PHR.* 期货和期权合同市场

◇ *The paper market is an essential supplement to money market in China.* 在中国，票据市场是货币市场的必要补充。

paper money ['peɪpə 'mʌnɪ] *PHR.* 纸币；票据

◇ *China began to issue true paper money in Song Dynasty, but only in a small amount and in a limited area.* 中国真正开始发行纸币是在宋朝的时候，当时只是在一定地区少量发行。

paper profit ['peɪpə 'prɒfɪt] *PHR.* 账面利润

◇ *Paper profit means unrealized capital gains in an investment; gains can only be realized after the securities being sold.* 账面利润意味着在投资中未实现的资本收益；证券被出售后收益才能实现。

paradigm ['pærədaɪm] *n.* 范例；样式；模范

Phrase(s): ***a new paradigm of production***

◇ *This crisis led to a new investment paradigm, hence modifying our market risk perception and management.* 这次的危机产生了一种新的投资模式，从而修正的我们对市场风险的认知和管理。10（21）

parallel ['pærəlel] *adj.* 平行的

Phrase(s): ***parallel calculation; parallel structure***

◇ *Banks adopting the foundation or advanced approaches will be required to calculate their capital requirement using parallel calculation.* 采用 IRB 初级法和 IRB 高级法的银行应当进行平行计算。

pari passu ['pɛərai 'pæsju:] *PHR.* 以相同速度；按相同比例

◇ *The "pari passu" clause in the original bond contracts requires the government should make the bonds that they issued to pay their defaulted debt be available to all the investors.* 原债券合同里的“同等权利”条款要求政府面向所有的投资者发行债券，以偿还他们拖欠的债务。

partial collateralization ['pɑ:ʃ(ə)l kə'læt(ə)r(ə)laɪzeɪʃ(ə)n] *PHR.* 部分抵押

◇ *Banks may operate under either, but not both, approaches in the banking book, but only under the comprehensive approach in the trading book. Partial collateralisation is recognised in both approaches. Mismatches in the maturity of the underlying exposure and the collateral will only be allowed under the comprehensive approach.* 对银行账户，银行可选择两种方法的一种，不可同时选用两种方法。但对于交易账户，只能选择综合法。两种方法都认可部分抵押。只有综合法才可处理风险暴露和抵押品之间期限错配。

partial equilibrium ['pɑ:ʃ(ə)l ˌi:kwɪ'lɪbrɪəm] *PHR.* 部分均衡

◇ *Our analysis of individual market is a partial equilibrium analysis because we are taking the factors that may influence demand as fixed except for the price.* 我们对单个市场

的分析是局部均衡分析，因为我们假定除价格之外其他影响需求的因素是固定不变的。16（16）

participant [pɑ:'tɪsɪp(ə)nt] *n.* 参与者

Phrase(s): ***market participant***

◇ *Some market participants will take recent price increases as an indication of higher future assets prices.* 一些市场参与者认为近期的价格增长预测着未来会有更高的资产价格。

party ['pɑ:tɪ] *n.* 当事人；党派；交易方

◇ *Rating assignments and periodic rating reviews must be completed or approved by a party that does not directly stand to benefit from the extension of credit.* 评级和定期评级复议，必须由不能直接从贷款中受益的一方来完成和批准。1（75）

par value [pɑ: 'vælju:] *PHR.* 票面价值

◇ *Par value means face value of stocks or bonds. During initial offering period, the selling price can not be lower than par value so investors would have confidence in the issuer.* 票面价值指的是股票或债券的面值。在最初的发售期间，销售价格不能低于票面价值，确保投资者对发行人有信心。

pass book ['pɑ:s bʊk] *PHR.* 银行存折

◇ *Pass book is a record of deposits and withdrawals and interest held by a depositor at a bank. Nowadays, many young people prefer using bank cards to do transactions on ATMs.* 存折是银行的存款人存款、取款和利息收入的记录。如今，许多年轻人喜欢使用银行卡在自动取款机上进行交易。

past-due ['pæst'du:] *n.* 逾期

Phrase(s): ***past-due loans; past-due bills***

◇ *An important innovation of the standardised approach is the requirement that loans considered past-due be risk weighted at 150%, unless a threshold amount of specific provisions has already been set aside by the bank against that loan.* 标准法的一项重大创新是将逾期贷款的风险权重规定为150%，除非针对该类贷款银行已经计量了达到一定比例的专项准备。1（3）

patent ['pæt(ə)nt] *n.* 专利

◇ *Telecommunication companies pay very high patent royalties to keep their products and services updated.* 电信公司支付很高的专利使用费，及时更新它们的产品和服务。

pawnbroker ['pɔːnbrəʊkə] *n.* 典当商

◇ *A pawnbroker can be either a person or a business. It lends money to people in exchange for the borrower's property as collateral. If the money can't be paid back in due time, the property will be sold to offset the lender's loss.* 典当商可以是一个人或一个企业。它借钱给人们以交换借用人的财产作为抵押物。如果钱不能及时归还，财产将被出售，以抵消贷款人的损失。

pay [peɪ] *v.* 支付；*n.* 工资；报酬

Phrase(s): ***pay back; pay check; pay day***

◇ *Credit events include bankruptcy, insolvency or inability of the obligor to pay its debts.* 信用事件包括破产、丧失偿债能力或债务人无力偿还债务。

payback ['peibæk] *n.* 投资的回收；偿付

Phrase(s): ***pay back period; payback period of investment***

◇ *With the students union's efforts, the university is going to make a $4 million payback to students because it improperly charged them in facilities fee.* 在学生会的努力下，这所大学将向学生偿还征收不当的 400 万元设施费。

payback period ['peibæk 'pɪərɪəd] *PHR.* 回收期

◇ *Investors usually don't like projects with long payback period; housing construction industry is a typical example of long payback period.* 投资者通常不喜欢有较长的投资回收期的项目；住房建筑业就是一个投资回收期长的典型例子。

payee [peɪ'iː] *n.* 收款人

Phrase(s): ***fictions payee; payee name; contingent payee***

◇ *A child who is eligible for Social Security financial support needs to have an adult representative payee to help him/her manage the payments.* 一个领取社会保障财政补助的孩子需要有一个成人作为收款人代表来帮助他 / 她管理收款。

payment ['peɪm(ə)nt] *n.* 支付

Phrase(s): ***payment term***

◇ *The primary source of the cash flows in income-producing real estate (IPRE) would generally be lease or rental payments or the sale of the asset.* 产生收入的房地产中现金流的主要来源是出租、租赁收入，或是资产销售。

peak [piːk] *n.* 商业周期的波峰

◇ *Oil price has fallen by over 50% from its peak two years ago, leading to a GDP growth slowdown in this oil exporting country.* 油价从 2 年前的峰值已经下跌了超过 50%，导致这个石油出口国的 GDP 增长放缓。

peculation [ˌpekju'leiʃən] *n.* 贪污；挪用

◇ *The financial manager was accused of peculation and would be sentenced to prison for 10 years.* 财务经理被指控侵吞公款，将被判入狱 10 年。

pension funds ['penʃ(ə)n fʌndz] *PHR.* 养老基金

◇ *Due to overall economic slowdown and a contraction in coal and mining industry, many miners' health and pension funds are at a risk of insolvency.* 由于整体经济放缓和煤炭开采业的萎缩，许多矿工的健康和养老基金存在破产风险。

◇ *In order to avoid insolvency, the state Pension Fund proposed to slash payments to retirees by up to 50%; if the proposal was approved, senior people's lives would be under great pressure.* 为了避免破产，该州养老基金提出退休金最高削减 50% 的提案；一旦提案通过，老年人的生活将承受很大的压力。

percentage [pə'sentɪdʒ] *n.* 百分比

Phrase(s): ***percentage basis***

◇ *The total capital reserves required by the financial entity are determined as a percentage of the total risk-weighted asset values.* 金融实体所需的总资本储备是总风险加权资产的一个百分比。13（55）

percentile [pə'sentaɪl] *n.* 百分位

◇ *In calculating the haircuts, a 99th percentile one-tailed confidence interval is to be used.* 在计算折扣系数时，使用单尾的 99% 的置信度。1（25）

perfect hedge ['pɜːfikt hedʒ] *PHR.* 完美对冲

Phrase(s): ***perfect hedge method; operation perfect hedge***

◇ *A perfect hedge is an investment strategy aiming to protect an asset portfolio against all potential losses. There are many ways to realize a perfect hedge, such as defensive stocks purchase and options.* 完美对冲是一种投资策略，其目标是避免资产组合遭受潜在损失。实现完美对冲方法很多，如购买防御性股票和期权。

performance [pə'fɔːm(ə)ns] *n.* 表现

Phrase(s): ***historical performance; poor performance***

◇ *In financial market, past performance is not always a reliable indicator of future results.* 在金融市场中，过去的表现不一定总是未来业绩的可靠指标。

perks [pɜːks] *n.* 特权；额外津贴（perk 的复数）；特别待遇

Phrase(s): ***special perks***

◇ *"Perks", also called "other compensations"are paid to corporation CEOs along with fat paychecks, options grants. Perks can either be large amounts of money or the right to use company properties.* "津贴"，也叫"其他补偿"，是公司随着工资、期权等一并支付给首席执行官的特别待遇。额外津贴可以是大量的金钱或使用公司财产的权利。

permissible [pə'mɪsɪb(ə)l] *adj.* 获得准许的

◇ *If the credit derivative covers obligations that do not include the underlying obligation, section below governs whether the asset mismatch is permissible.* 如信用衍生工具覆盖的债项未包括标的债项，则下面条款决定资产错配是否能接受。1（33）

permission [pə'mɪʃ(ə)n] *n.* 准许，认可

◇ *In some countries, having a second child in a family needs permission from the governments; otherwise, it will be difficult for the child to have access to public resources like education and medical care.* 在一些国家，一个家庭生第二个孩子需要政府的许可；否则，这个孩子将面临教育和医疗等公共资源使用困难。

perpetual bond [pə'petʃʊəl bɒnd] *PHR.* 永久债券

◇ *Perpetual bond has no maturity date. They are not redeemable, instead, they pay a steady stream of interest forever.* 永久债券没有到期日也不可赎回，但可提供永久的利息收入。

persistent earnings [pə'sɪst(ə)nt 'ɜːnɪŋz] *PHR.* 持续盈利

◇ *Companies are pursuing persistent earnings so they can have a sustainable development.* 公司追求的是持久的盈利，这样他们才可以可持续发展。

personal trust ['pɜːs(ə)n(ə)l trʌst] *PHR.* 私人信托

Phrase(s): *Boston Personal Property Trust; personal holding trust company*

◇ *There are specific entities to exercise personal trust, which help beneficiaries meet their financial objectives.* 私人信托由专门机构来运作，它有助于受益人实现其财务目标。

PF (project finance) [prə'dʒekt faɪ'næns] *abbr.* 项目融资

◇ *Project finance (PF) is a method of funding in which the lender looks primarily to the revenues generated by a single project, both as the source of repayment and as security for the exposure.* 项目融资是一种融资方法，贷款人主要将单个项目产生的收益作为还款来源和贷款安全性的保障。1（40）

phase [feɪz] *n.* 阶段

◇ *The construction of the solar-energy collection plant has three phases; the first phases went very well and the second one hasn't started due to lack of money.* 太阳能采集工厂的建设分三个阶段，第一阶段进展很好，第二个阶段由于缺乏资金还没有开始。

physical assets ['fɪzɪk(ə)l 'æsets] *PHR.* 实物资产

◇ *Object finance refers to a method of funding the acquisition of physical assets (e. g. ships, aircraft, satellites, railcars, and fleets) where the repayment of the exposure is dependent on the cash flows generated by the specific assets that have been financed and pledged or assigned to the lender.* 物品融资指的是收购实物资产（如轮船、飞机、卫星、有轨车辆、船舶）的一种融资方式，这种融资方式下贷款的偿还依靠已经用来融资、抵押或交给贷款人的特殊资产创造的现金流。1（40）

plant asset [plɑːnt 'æset] *PHR.* 固定资产

◇ *Plant assets, sometimes called fixed assets, can be land, buildings, equipment or furniture;however, they must be within useful lives for effective accounting records.* 固定资产可以是土地、建筑物、设备或家具，然而他们必须在有效的使用期内才能在记录中体现。

◇ *After a period of time, the depreciation of plant assets should be taken into consideration. Some owners will dispose of them by sale, retirement or trade-in.* 固定资产使用一段时间后要考虑其折旧。一些固定资产所有者将它们出售，报废或者折价处理。

plunge [plʌn(d)ʒ] *v.* 突然减少；骤降

◇ *The de-capacity in large state-owned coal and steel corporations should be carried out as soon as possible in this countries before these debt-ridden industries plunge into irrevocable crisis.* 在这些债务缠身的行业陷入无可挽回的危机之前，这个国家的大型国有煤炭企业和钢铁企业应尽快化解过剩产能。

policy-making ['pɒləsɪ'meɪkɪŋ] *adj.* 制定政策的

◇ *As a policy-making institution, the Education Ministry should establish a fair system to distribute education resources despite the imbalanced development in different regions.* 作为一个决策机构，教育部应建立公平的教育资源分配制度，尽管不同地区的发展不平衡。

pool [puːl] *n.* 资产池

Phrase(s): ***the underlying pool; pool of assets***

◇ *The purchasing bank has a claim on all proceeds from the pool of receivables or a pro-rata interest in the proceeds.* 购入银行对所有应收账款的收益或按比例分摊的收益拥有债权。1（45）

◇ *The world well-known company has long seen people as their biggest asset, establishing talent pool with professionals from all over the world.* 这家世界知名公司一直认为人是他们最大的资产，建立了来自世界各地的专业人才库。

pooled basis/pool of exposures [puːld 'beɪsɪs; puːl (ə)v ɪk'spəʊʒə] *PHR.* 贷款库

◇ *The retail exposure must be one of a large pool of exposures, which are managed by the bank on a pooled basis.* 零售贷款必须是大的贷款库其中的一部分，而整个贷款库由银行管理。1（42）

pool of issuer [puːl (ə)v 'ɪʃjuːə] *PHR.* 发行人

◇ *Supervisors should assess the size and scope of the pool of issuers that each ECAI (external credit assessment institution) covers, the range and meaning of the assessments that it assigns, and the definition of default used by the ECAI.* 监管当局应当评估每一个外部评级机构覆盖的发行人的规模和范围，所发布的评级的级别和含义，以及外部评级机构所使用的违约的定义。

portfolio [pɔːt'fəʊlɪəʊ] *n.* 资产组合；券投资组合

Phrase(s): ***portfolio theory; portfolio strategy; portfolio management; portfolio investment***

◇ *Be careful with the companies whose valuations are exceeding their potential; their stocks could be poisonous to your portfolio.* 要小心那些估值超过其潜力的公司，他们的股票可能成为你投资组合的毒药。

◇ *Crude oil investors have been influenced by continuous oil price drop with significant net income loss on their portfolio.* 原油投资者受到持续油价下跌的影响，导致投资组合的净收益损失显著。

◇ *CAPM (Capital Asset Pricing Model) and APT (Arbitrage Pricing Theory) models are two fundamental models of modern portfolio theory.* 资本资产定价模型和套利定价模型是现代资产组合理论的两个基本模型。

portion ['pɔːʃ(ə)n] *n.* 部分；*vt.* 把……分成份额

◇ *Ten years ago, few people were willing to pay for online music or film resources; now the paying portion is growing rapidly although the amount is still quite small.* 十年前，很少有人愿意为在线音乐或电影资源花钱；现在付费人群比例正在迅速增长，虽然金额仍然很少。

position [pə'zɪʃ(ə)n] *n.* 头寸

Phrase(s): ***a first loss position; subordinated securitisation positions***

◇ *For banks using the standardised approach, unrated securitisation positions must be deducted from capital.* 对于采用标准法的银行，未评级部分的证券化头寸必须从资本中扣除。1（7）

◇ *The financial analyst valued the e-commerce company's stake at $30 a share and the cash position at about $8 a share.* 这位金融分析师看好电子商务公司的股份，估价每股30美元，现金头寸约为每股8美元。

position data [pə'zɪʃ(ə)n 'deɪtə] *PHR.* 头寸数据

◇ *A review of the overall risk management process should take place once a year and should specifically address, at a minimum: the accuracy and completeness of position data.* 综合的风险管理程序评估应每年开展一次，并且要针对具体的问题，至少要达到：

头寸数据的精确性和完整程度。1（26）

positive ['pɒzɪtɪv] *adj.* 积极的；正的；*n.* 正面；正量

Phrase(s): ***positive increase; positive position***

◇ *One positive effect of releasing all tax returns to the public is that government can prove its hard work in seeking balance in social wealth.* 向公众公布所有纳税收入的一个积极影响是：政府可以证明自己在追求社会财富平衡方面所做的工作。

possession [pə'zeʃ(ə)n] *n.* 财产；所有权

Phrase(s): ***take possession of; legal possession***

◇ *The legal mechanism by which collateral is pledged or transferred must ensure that the bank has the right to liquidate or take legal possession of it, in a timely manner, in the event of the default, insolvency or bankruptcy (or otherwise-defined credit event set out in the transaction documentation) of the counterparty (and, where applicable, of the custodian holding the collateral).* 抵押品抵押或转移的法律机制必须确保在借款人违约、无力偿还或破产时（或借款合同中明确定义的信用事件），银行能有权及时地对交易对象（如可行，持有抵押品的托管人）的抵押品进行清算或收为己有。1（19）

possible consumption bundles ['pɔsɪb(ə)l kən'sʌm(p)ʃ(ə)n 'bʌnd(ə)ls] *PHR.* 可能的消费组合

◇ *When analyzing possible consumption bundles of consumers, we must consider the time, location and other contextual circumstances of their consuming activities.* 在分析消费者可能的消费组合时，我们必须考虑消费活动发生的时间、地点和其他背景情况。

post [pəʊst] *v.* 宣布（作为抵押物）

◇ *The credit exposure or potential credit exposure is hedged in whole or in part by collateral posted by the counterparty or by a third party on behalf of the counterparty.* 信用风险暴露或潜在的信用风险暴露，全部或部分地以交易对象或代表该交易对象的第三方的抵押品所抵补。1（19）

post-audit [pəʊst'ɔːdɪt] *n.* 事后审计；*adj.* 审计后的

◇ *In China, for a long time, completed final account (estimate) audit of construction project has been featured with a significant post-audit.* 长期以来，我国工程项目竣工结（决）算审计带有明显的事后审计特征。13（56）

◇ *Post-audit review is set to check whether the management has addressed the concerns and recommendations in the Audit report within agreed time. If the first review fails to pass, then the second one will be scheduled for further check.* 审计后审查是检查管理层在商定的时间内是否已处理审核报告中提出的注意点和建议。如果第一次审查未能通过，则安排第二次审查来进一步检查。

post office savings bank [pəʊst'ɒfɪs 'seiviŋz bæŋk] *PHR.* 邮政储蓄银行

◇ *Post office savings bank is a state-owned bank in China, which is much smaller in business scope than the four major state-owned banks.* 我国邮政储蓄银行属于国有，但业务范围要比四大国行小得多。

potential [pə'tenʃl] *n.* 可能；可能性；*adj.* 潜在的；可能的

Phrase(s): ***potential price volatility***

◇ *There may be the potential for ECAIs to use unsolicited ratings to put pressure on entities to obtain solicited ratings.* 外部评级机构也可能会利用被动评级来对评级对象施加压力，使其接受付费的主动评级。1（17）

◇ *As a further alternative to standard supervisory haircuts and own-estimate haircuts banks may use VAR models for calculating potential price volatility for repo-style transactions.* 除标准化的监管折扣系数和自己估计折扣系数外，银行还可使用 VAR 模型计算规定的回购交易的潜在价格波动。1（21）

potential GDP [pə'tenʃl ˌdʒiːdiː'piː] *PHR.* 潜在 GDP

◇ *Generally speaking, potential GDP is higher than real GDP, because it hypothesizes that all the resources are 100% utilized in the operation process.* 一般来说，潜在 GDP 高于实际 GDP，因为它假设所有的资源都在操作过程中得到 100% 的利用。

◇ *Potential GDP can't be fully realized due to unemployment, inflation, major natural disasters and so on; all these factors could impact production efficiency.* 由于失业、通货膨胀、重大自然灾害等因素潜在GDP不能完全实现；所有这些因素都会影响生产效率。

pound [paʊnd] *n.* 英镑

◇ *Strong pound may prevent people from other countries from traveling to or studying in UK despite its reputation in higher education and pub culture.* 强势英镑可能会阻止其他国家的人到英国旅行或学习，尽管它的高等教育和酒吧文化蜚声全球。

practitioner [præk'tɪʃ(ə)nə] *n.* 从业者

Phrase(s): ***bank practitioner; private equity practitioner***

◇ *Currently, this country has too many financial practitioners to play money games, but too few nurse practitioners to take care of the sick and the disabled.* 目前，这个国家有太多的金融从业人员玩金钱游戏，但太少的医生护士照顾病人和残疾人。

predictability [priˌdiktə'biliti] *n.* 可预测性

◇ *The Midwestern city, which is very close to bankruptcy, is forced to buy interest-rate swaps from several global banks to increase predictability for the city budget; it used to provide variable-rate mortgage loans to its citizens.* 这个濒临破产的中西部城市，被迫从几家全球银行购买利率互换来增加城市预算的可预见性；它过去曾向市民提供可变利率抵押贷款。

preference ['pref(ə)r(ə)ns] *n.* 偏好；偏爱；优先权

Phrase(s): ***consumer preference; investment preference***

◇ *A financial strategist on stock market analysed his preference towards stocks with yield at a reasonable price; overvalued stocks usually have difficulty in maintaining long-term high yields.* 股票市场金融战略家分析他为什么优先选择收益合理的股票；过高估值的股票通常很难维持长期的高收益。

preferred bundle of goods [prɪ'fɜːd 'bʌndl (ə)v gʊdz] *PHR.* 偏好的商品组合

◇ *However the preferred bundle of goods are modeled and analysed, the prerequisite should always be the consumer's purchasing power in a certain context.* 无论怎么建模来分析偏好的商品组合，前提始终应该是消费者在一定背景下的购买力。

preferred stock [prɪ'fɜːd stɒk] *PHR.* 优先股

◇ *Banks or other financial institutions, in a moral sense, shouldnot release fake information on their preferred stocks to mislead investors; furthermore, they will involve themselevs into legal cases.* 在道德意义上，银行或其他金融机构不应该发布优先股的虚假信息，误导投资者；而且这样做也会使他们自己卷入法律案件中。

premise ['premɪs] *n.* 房屋；厂房；厂址

Phrase(s): ***commercial premises***

◇ *Mortgages on office and/or multi-purpose commercial premises and/or multi-*

tenanted commercial premises may have the potential to receive a preferential risk weight of 50% under certain conditions. 以写字楼、多用途商业建筑物或多方承租的商业建筑物抵押的贷款，在某些特定条件下有可能获得 50% 的优惠风险权重。1（12）

premium ['priːmɪəm] *n.* 保险费；附加费；*adj.* 优质的；高昂的

Phrase(s): ***insurance premium***

◇ *Customers are only willing to premiums for products which are effectively integrated; they don't want to repeat their computer problems again and again on a long-distance call to Philippines where the after-sales service is outsourced.* 客户只愿意为有效整合的产品付保费；他们不想在通往菲律宾的长途电话上一遍又一遍地重复他们的计算机问题；有些厂家会把售后服务外包给菲律宾。

prepayment [ˌpri'peimənt] *n.* 预付款

Phrase(s): ***prepayment penalty; prepayment mode; prepayment behavior; rational prepayment***

◇ *The new ACT benefits small businesses with long-term loans as well as low interest rates; however, if these small businesses renew their previous loans before the due date, they will face a prepayment penalty.* 新法案将有利于小企业做低利率的长期贷款；但是，如果这些小企业在到期日之前重新贷款，它们将面临提前还款罚款。

◇ *It makes no difference whether you will make a prepayment of your credit card debt or pay it at the due date, for the bank won't charge you any interest within the agreed period.* 你提前偿还信用卡债务还是到期再还没有区别，因为在约定的期限内银行不会向您收取任何利息。

prescribe [prɪ'skraɪb] *v.* 指定；规定

◇ *The calculation of the counterparty credit risk charge for collateralised OTC derivative transactions is the same as the rules prescribed for such transactions booked in the banking book.* 有抵押场外衍生产品交易对手方的信用风险资本要求的计算，与银行账户上此类交易的规定一致。1（134）

pretax [priː'tæks] *adj.* 税前的

◇ *The world famous bank just announced a $600 million pretax loss in the second quarter of this year; the domestic business is shrinking dramatically and they also sold* *many overseas branches.* 这家世界知名银行刚刚宣布今年第二季度 6 亿美元的税前亏损；其国内业务大幅缩水，还出售了许多海外分支机构。

◇ *The two world-leading oil and gas companies had an all-stock merger recently; they are aiming to achieve a $500million goal in pretax cost synergies within five years.* 两个世界领先的石油和天然气公司最近达成全股合并；它们的目标是在 5 年内实现税前 5 亿美元的成本协同效应（即通过互补节省运营成本）。

prevail [prɪ'veɪl] *v.* 流行；盛行

◇ *The information on the salary is for reference only. The entry pay, terms of appointment and conditions of service to be offered are subject to the provisions prevailing at the time the offer of appointment is made.* 薪资信息仅供参考。起薪、任期和服务条件都以录用时的规定为准。

price bubble [praɪs 'bʌb(ə)l] *PHR.* 价格泡沫

◇ *People are worried about the consequences of the current price bubble in the real estate market; developers cope with this situation by targeting different income-level buyers with different types of houses.* 人们担心目前房地产市场价格泡沫的后果；为了应对这种局面，开发商向不同收入水平的买家推荐不同类型的房屋。

price ceiling [praɪs 'siːlɪŋ] *PHR.* 价格上限

◇ *Price ceilings are generally set by governments in the form of laws or regulations; they are intended to protect people from being overcharged for essential expenses, such as rent, electricity& water bill and tuitions of non-compulsory education.* 价格上限一般是由政府以法律或法规的形式规定；其目的是保护人们免受乱收费、乱开价之苦，价格上限多见于必要开支领域，如租金、水电费和非义务教育学费。

price discovery [praɪs dɪ'skʌv(ə)rɪ] *PHR.* 价格发现

Phrase(s): ***delay price discovery effect***

◇ *Price discovery is a method to determine the price for a specific commodity or security; it is greatly affected by supply and demand relations in the market.* 价格发现是一种确定特定商品或证券价格的方法，它受市场供求关系的影响很大。

price floor [praɪs flɔː] *PHR.* 价格下限

◇ *The minimum wage standard is a typical example of price floor, which is set by government to protect people's basic interests.* 最低工资标准是最低价格的一个典型例子，由政府设定来保护人民的基本利益。

price searcher [praɪs 'sɜːtʃə(r)] *PHR.* 价格寻求者

◇ *Generally speaking, price searchers don't have many competitors in the market and they have power to set and adjust the prices of their own products so as to maximize profit.* 一般来说，价格寻求者在市场上的竞争对手不多，而且他们有权来设置和调整自身产品的价格，以实现利润最大化。

price war [praɪs wɔː] *PHR.* 价格战

Phrase(s): ***price-war game theory***

◇ *A price war hurts an industry's overall profits in the short run and consumers' interests in the long run; price war leads to disordered competition and imbalanced market share distribution.* 价格战从短期讲伤害了一个行业的整体利润，从长期看伤害了消费者利益；价格战导致了无序竞争和市场份额的失衡分配。

pricing ['praisiŋ] *n.* 定价

Phrase(s): ***pricing of petro***

◇ *Arbitrage Pricing Theory is the most fundamental principle of the capital markets, which predicts an asset's return by observing the relationship between the asset and common risk factors.* 套利定价理论是资本市场最基本的理论，它通过观察资产和各种常见风险因子之间的关系来预测资产的收益。

prime [praɪm] *adj.* 最好的；非次级的

Phrase(s): ***prime mortgage; prime loan***

◇ *The CEO of an online lending company resigned yesterday for violating the company's business practices; he approved $20 million prime loans to an institutional investor which faked its credit rating.* 一个网络借贷公司的首席执行官因为违反公司的商业惯例昨天辞职；他批准了2 000万美元贷款给一家伪造了信用评级的机构投资者。

principle ['prɪnsɪp(ə)l] *n.* 准则

Phrase(s): ***accounting principle***

◇ *GAAP stands for generally accepted accounting principles; In the U. S. , it includes the basic accounting principles and guidelines, the detailed standards and other rules issued by the Financial Accounting Standards Board as well as generally accepted industry practices.* GAAP 全称是通用会计准则；在美国，它包括基本会计原则和准则，由财务会计准则委员会发布的其他规则以及公认的行业惯例等。

pristine ['prɪsti:n] *adj.* 原始的；初始的

Phrase(s): ***pristine big banks***

◇ *Homeowners who want to move to a new home would use their pristine credit and adequate equity in their current home to apply for a short-term bridge loan for a smooth transfer.* 想搬新家的房主可以使用他们的初始信用和他们目前房屋足够的股权来申请短期过桥贷款，以确保顺利过渡。

private firms ['praɪvət fɜ:ms] *PHR.* 私人企业

◇ *In some European countries, private companies can run airlines, trains or power plants on a state-owned network, thanks to the governments'privatization policy.* 在一些欧洲国家，由于政府的私有化政策，民营公司可以在国有网络上运营航空公司、火车线路或发电厂。

private value auction ['praɪvət 'vælju: 'ɔ:kʃ(ə)n] *PHR.* 私人价值拍卖

◇ *Private value auction and common value auction are different in the way of setting the reserve price.* 私人价值拍卖和共同价值拍卖中的底价设置方式不同。

probability [prɒbə'bɪlɪtɪ] *n.* 概率

Phrase(s): ***probability of default (PD)***

◇ *Probability of default (PD) measures the likelihood that the borrower will default over a given time horizon.* 违约概率测量特定时间段内借款人违约的可能性。1（4）

problem mortgages ['prɒbləm 'mɔ:gɪdʒs] *PHR.* 问题抵押贷款

◇ *Fannie Mae and Freddie Mac，two American major financial institutions in housing mortgage loans, were deeply trapped into problem mortgages since 2008 financial crisis.* 自 2008 金融危机以来，房利美和房地美这两家专门提供住房抵押贷款的金融机构被困于问题抵押贷款中。

prod [prɒd] *v.* 刺激；促使

◇ *Federal Reserve sent out the signal that one piece of report on job gains would not prod it to increase interest rate; policymakers want to see a gradual growth in job markets, in wage and in productivity.* 美联储发出信号，仅凭一份就业增加的报告不会促使他们提高利率；政策制定者们希望看到就业市场、工资和生产率的逐步增长。

producer surplus [prə'dju:sə 'sɜ:pləs] *PHR.* 生产者剩余

◇ *Producer surplus is actually the benefit that the producer receives for selling the good in the market; it is the difference between the price the producer is willing and able to sell a good for and the price he actually receives.* 生产者剩余实际上是生产商在市场出售商品的收益；它是生产者能够卖得价格与其实际卖得价格之间的差异。

product ['prɒdʌkt] *n.* 工具；产品

Phrase(s): ***financial product; credit product***

◇ *Recommend a quality product made in your hometown on this forum with a description of its appearance and functions.* 在这个论坛上推荐一个在你的家乡制造的优质产品，并描述它的外观和功能。

product flaws ['prɒdʌkt flɔ:s] *PHR.* 产品缺陷

◇ *A high degree of homogenization is one of the product flaws of this range.* 产品同质化程度高也是此类产品的缺陷之一。

production function [prə'dʌkʃ(ə)n 'fʌŋ(k)ʃ(ə)n] *PHR.* 生产函数

◇ *Production function shows the relationship between inputs and outputs for a business; it usually considers physical factors like capital and labor.* 生产函数显示一个企业的投入与产出之间的关系；它通常考虑资本和劳动力等物质因素。

productive input [prə'dʌktɪv 'inpʊt] *PHR.* 生产要素

◇ *Productive input such as raw materials and equipment for manufacturing is included in the duty-free importation item list.* 生产原料和设备等生产要素被列入免税进口物品清单。

profit ['prɒfit] *n.* 利润

Phrase(s): ***net profit; gross profit***

◇ *The government imposed a series of entry barriers for international airlines to do business inside the country, so most of the profits are concentrated within domestic airlines.* 政府实施了一系列的进入壁垒，以限制国际航空公司在其国家做生意，因此大部分的利润都集中到国内的航空公司。

profit maximization ['prɒfɪt ˌmæksimai'zeiʃən] *PHR.* 利润最大化

◇ *Profit maximization cannot always be realized by reaching the highest sales level; it basically depends on the difference between the marginal revenue and the marginal cost.* 最高的销售水平不一定能实现利润最大化；它基本上取决于边际收益和边际成本之间的差异。

profit taking ['prɒfɪt 'teɪkɪŋ] *PHR.* 获利抛售

◇ *Chinese shares have encountered aggressive profit taking, losing more than 20 percent in two weeks to fall to a two-month low.* 中国股市近期遭遇强劲获利抛盘局面，大盘两周内狂泻 20%，至两个月来最低点。13（158）

progressive tax [prə'gresɪv tæks] *PHR.* 累进税

◇ *A progressive tax aims to impose higher taxes on high-income earners and keep tax rates low for low-incomers.* 累进税的目的是对高收入者征收更多的税，对低收入者保持低税率。

promissory note ['prɒmɪs(ə)rɪ nəʊt] *PHR.* 本票

◇ *A promissory note is a written promise by one party to pay a definite sum of money to another party either on demand or at a fixed date in the future.* 本票是一方支付给另一方确定金额的书面承诺，可以见票即付也可以承诺在未来某一个固定时间支付。

prompt date [prɒm(p)t deɪt] *PHR.* 交割日

◇ *Different trading markets have different rules on prompt date, so make sure you know where you are trading and what the system is.* 不同交易市场对交割日的规定不同，所以要搞清楚你在哪个市场交易，它的交易体系是什么。

property ['prɒpətɪ] *n.* 财产；地产

Phrase(s): *commercial property; private property; public property*

◇ *It has long been proved that commercial property lending was the cause of troubled assets in the banking industry over the past few decades, the Basel Committee holds to the view that mortgages on commercial real estate do not, in principle, justify other than a 100% weighting of the loans secured.* 过去几十年的经历已经证明，商业房地产贷款一直是造成银行业不良资产问题的原因，因此，巴塞尔委员会认为，在原则上商业房地产抵押贷款只适合给予 100% 的风险权重。1（47）

◇ *Protecting intellectual property should be conducted on an international network.* 应在国际交流网络框架下进行知识产权保护。

property right ['prɒpətɪ raɪt] *PHR.* 产权

◇ *Property right is believed to be the basic right of American citizen, however, some people intentionally abuse their property rights by skirting around regulations and turning residence property into commercial use.* 产权被认为是美国公民的基本权利，然而，有些人故意滥用自己的财产权利，绕开法规把住宅物业转为商业用途。

proprietary trading [prə'praɪət(ə)rɪ 'treɪdɪŋ] *PHR.* 自由资金交易；自营

◇ *Some investment banks have proprietary trading for making more profit on their own account beside commissions and fees from clients.* 除了从客户交易中提取佣金和费用，一些投资银行还用自己账户上的钱投资来获取更多利润。

proprietorship [prə'praiətəʃip] *n.* 独资企业

◇ *In general, a corporate exposure is defined as a debt obligation of a corporation, partnership, or proprietorship. Banks will be permitted to distinguish separately exposures to small-and medium-sized enterprises (SME).* 通常，公司贷款被定义为公司、合伙制企业、独资企业的债务义务，允许银行单独区分中小企业的贷款。1（39）

prospectus [prə'spektəs] *n.* （招股）说明书

◇ *The giant broadcasting company is planning to split off its radio business into a separate public company; the latest prospectus detailed the IPO procedures, assets structure and potential risks of this independent business.* 广播公司巨头计划把它的广播业务分拆成一个独立的上市公司；最新的招股说明书详细介绍了该独立业务的上市程序、资产结构和潜在风险。

protection purchaser/protection provider [prə'tekʃ(ə)n 'pɜːtʃɪsə(r); prə'tekʃ(ə)n prə'vaɪdə] *PHR.* 信用保护的购买者 / 提供者

◇ *If the protection purchaser's right/ability to transfer the underlying obligation to the protection provider is required for settlement, the terms of the underlying obligation must provide that any required consent to such transfer may not be unreasonably withheld.* 如果信用保护的购买者要求执行将标的债项转移给信用保护提供者的权利，标的债项的条款一定不能对这样的转移无理由地拒绝。1（34）

protocal ['prəʊtəkɒl] *n.* 拟定草案；礼仪

◇ *Leading tech companies have such advanced technology in secure FTP (File Transfer Protocol) transfers that even governments can do nothing in data mining.* 领先的技术公司在安全（文件传输协议）传输方面拥有如此先进的技术，即使政府想挖掘数据也无能为力。

proven ['pru:vən] *adj.* 经过验证或证实的

◇ *There are not so many proven links between the bank and this type of financial product;some illegal online lending firm may steal its name.* 银行和这类金融产品之间没有太多可证实的联系；一些非法的网络借贷公司可能假冒其名。

provision [prə'vɪʒ(ə)n] *n.* 准备（金）

Phrase(s): ***specific provisions; call provisions***

◇ *Both on and off-balance sheet retail exposures are measured as the amount legally owed to the bank, gross of specific provisions or partial write-offs.* 表内、表外的零售贷款以法律上欠银行的贷款数量为准，含专项准备或部分冲销的贷款。1（61）

◇ *Many securitisations of revolving retail exposures contain provisions that call for the securitisation to be wound down if the quality of securitised assets begins to deteriorate.* 许多循环零售风险暴露的证券化都包括一些条款，其规定如果证券化资产的质量下降，证券化必须收回。1（7）

proxy ['prɒksɪ] *n.* 委托书

Phrase(s): ***proxy war; proxy fight; proxy access***

◇ *A proxy war(battle) refers to a conflict between two nations or two companies while neither of them is directly involved into the fight.* 代理战争是指两个国家或两个公司之间的冲突，而双方没有发生正面交锋，不直接对抗。

prudential [prʊ'denʃ(ə)l] *adj.* 谨慎的

Phrase(s): ***prudential reasons; prudential attitude***

◇ *The evolution of the prudential regulations on the control of financial risks is a direct consequence of the various financial crises and their impact on their solvency.* 在控制金融风险中做到审慎监管是各种金融危机及其偿付能力影响的直接结果。10（24）

◇ *Many financial institutions prefer adding"Prudential"into their names to emphasize their cautiousness towards business.* 许多金融机构喜欢在自己的名字里加入“审慎”二字来强调他们对业务的谨慎。

PSE (public sector entities) ['pʌblɪk 'sektə 'entɪtɪs] *abbr.* 公共部门实体

Phrase(s): ***claims on non-central government public sector entities (PSEs); PSE loans***

◇ *Subject to national discretion, claims on certain domestic PSEs may also be treated as claims on the sovereigns in whose jurisdictions the PSEs are established.* 各国还可自行决定，对某些国内公共部门实体的债权也视为对主权的债权，但前提是这些公共部门实体是按照该国政府的授权设立的。1（8）

◇ *Claims on domestic PSEs will be risk-weighted at national discretion.* 对国内公共部门实体债权的风险权重由各国自行决定。1（8）

public accounting ['pʌblɪk ə'kaʊntɪŋ] *PHR.* 公共会计

◇ *Public accounting usually refers to external accounting firms who offer accounting services to clients. These services include auditing, consultancy, tax planning, etc.* 公共会计通常是指外部会计师事务所向客户提供会计服务。这些服务包括审计、咨询和缴税计划等。

public goods ['pʌblɪk gʊdz] *PHR.* 公共物品

◇ *Public goods are goods and services that are consumed by people regardless of whether or not they paid for them.* 公共产品是不管人们是否支付相关费用都能消费的产品和服务。16（25）

publicity [pʌb'lɪsɪtɪ] *n.* 公众信息；宣传效用

Phrase(s): ***advance publicity; government publicity campaigns***

◇ *Large corporations usually have Public Relations section to establish and maintain sound relations with all stakeholders; in addition, PR also deals with media for publicity and crisis management.* 大公司通常有公共关系部门，其建立并保持与利益相关方的良好关系；此外，公关部门还要和媒体打交道开展公关宣传和危机管理。

publicly ['pʌblɪklɪ] adv. 公开地

Phrase(s): ***publicly quoted daily***

◇ *A publicly traded holding is defined as any equity security traded on a recognised security exchange.* 上市交易的股票是指在认定的证券交易所交易的所有股票。1（62）

publicly traded firms ['pʌblɪklɪ treɪd fɜːms] *PHR.* 上市交易的公司

◇ *For publicly traded firms, implicit costs are typically only the opportunity cost of equity owners'investment in the firm.* 对上市交易的公司，隐性成本仅仅包含了股权所有者对公司投资的机会成本。6（53）

public offering price ['pʌblɪk 'ɒf(ə)rɪŋ praɪs] *PHR.* 公开发行价值

◇ *Underwriters will have a 30-day option to purchase from our company up to an additional 2 million shares of common stock, at the initial public offering price.* 承销商会有一个 30 天的选择权，以首次公开发行价购买我们公司的普通股，最多可购买额外的两百万股。13（162）

purchase ['pɜːtʃəs] *v.* 购买

Phrase(s): ***purchase order***

◇ *Chinese state-owned ChemChina recently purchased a Swiss seeds and pesticides company so as to counter food safety problems.* 中国国有化工集团公司最近购买了一个瑞士的种子和农药公司以应对食品安全问题。

purchasing bank ['pɜːtʃəsɪŋ bæŋk] *PHR.* 购入银行；买入行

◇ *Purchased retail receivables, provided the purchasing bank complies with the IRB rules for retail exposures, are eligible for the"top-down"approach as permitted within the existing standards for retail exposures.* 如果购入银行符合 IRB 法有关零售贷款的规定，那么在现行的零售贷款标准中允许购入的零售应收账款可使用“自上而下”的方法。1（45）

purchasing power ['pɜːtʃəsɪŋ 'paʊə] *PHR.* 购买力

Phrase(s): ***purchasing power parity***

◇ *Family traveling during summer holiday time is very trendy in Chinese cities nowadays; target consumers who are in their 30s have strong purchase power and desire to relax from stressed work.* 如今暑假期间进行家庭旅行在中国城市里很时髦；目标消费者是三十多岁的人群，他们有很强的购买力且希望在紧张工作之余放松自己。

pursue [pə'sjuː] *v.* 追偿

◇ *On the qualifying default/non-payment of the counterparty, the bank may in a timely manner pursue the guarantor for monies outstanding under the documentation governing the transaction, rather than having to continue to pursue the counterparty.* 在确认债务人违约或不支付的条件下，银行可迅速向担保人追偿合同规定的款项而不必向交易对象追偿。1（33）

◇ *By making a payment under the guarantee the guarantor must acquire the right to pursue the obligor for monies outstanding under the documentation governing the transaction.* 担保人支付款项后，必须有权向债务人追偿合同规定的款项。1（33）

put-call parity [pʊtkɔːl 'pærɪtɪ] *PHR.* 买卖权平价；买卖差价

◇ *Put-call parity applies to European options only, and the put options and the call options compared must have the same expiration date.* 买卖差价只适用于欧式期货，相比较的买权和卖权必须具有相同的到期日。

PWG [piː'dʌbljuːdʒiː] *abbr.* 总统的金融市场工作小组

Phrase(s): *the President's Working Group on Financial Markets*

◇ *The PWG included the chairs of the Federal Reserve Board, the Securities and Exchange Commission (SEC), and the Commodity FuturesTrading Commission.* 总统的金融工作小组包括美联储主席、证券交易委员会主席和商品期货交易委员会主席。14（60）

Q

Q [kjuː] *abbr.* 女王；王后（Queen）；问题；季度；*n.* 英文字母 q 的大写形式

Phrase(s): ***q factor; Regulation Q***

◇ *The implementation of Regulation Q was partly for encouraging people to put money into money market; termination of it was for banks to increase reserves for potential financial risks.* 实施 Q 条例部分是为了鼓励人们把钱投入到货币市场；终止它是为了让银行增加储备以应对潜在的金融风险。

◇ *Q: In 2nd Q. this year, Warren Buffet bought Apple's stocks but Carl Icahn sold them, both in large quantities; who should we follow?* 问：今年第二季度，沃伦·巴菲特买了苹果的股票，卡尔·伊坎卖掉了苹果的股票，都是大数量交易；我们应该跟从谁呢？

QDII(Qualified Domestic Institutional Investor) ['kwɒlɪfaɪd də'mestɪk 'ɪnstɪ'tjuːʃ(ə)n(ə)l ɪn'vestə] *abbr.* 合格境内机构投资者

Phrase(s): ***Qualified Domestic Institutional Investor Scheme***

◇ *In China, QDII is a qualification awarded by government regulators which will permit domestic institutional investors to make investments in some foreign security markets.* 在中国，合格境内机构投资者资格由政府监管机构授予，允许国内机构投资者在国外证券市场进行投资。

QFII(Qualified Foreign Institutional Investors) ['kwɒlɪfaɪd 'fɒrɪn ɪnstɪ'tjuːʃ(ə)n(ə)l ɪn'vestəs] *abbr.* 合格境外机构投资者

Phrase(s): ***QFII Shareholding; QFII investor***

◇ *It is the first time for Saudi Arabia to open its stock market directly to foreign investments. The Middle East country is looking for qualified foreign institutional investors or individual investors to diversify the economy and create more jobs.* 沙特阿拉伯首次直接向外国投资开放其股票市场。这个中东国家正在寻找合格的外国机构投资者或个人投资者，以使经济多元化并创造更多的就业机会。

quadruple [ˌkwɒ'druːpəl] *adj.* 四倍的；四重的；*n.* 四倍；*v.* 使……成为四倍

Phrase(s): ***quadruple the amount; a quadruple medal***

◇ *The health insurance costs in this area quadrupled in the past decade due to high inflation rates; and the current government is determined to lower its citizens'financial burden.* 由于高的通货膨胀率，这个地区在过去的十年中健康保险费用增长了三倍；本届政府决心要降低其公民的经济负担。

quadratic [kwɒ'drætɪk] *adj.* [数] 二次的；平方的；*n.* 二次方程式；二次项

Phrase(s): ***quadratic sum; quadratic equation***

◇ *The quadratic term could be neglected if the increment is too small.* 如果增加太小，二次项可以忽略不计。

qualification [ˌkwɒlɪfɪ'keɪʃ(ə)n] *n.* 资格；条件；限制；赋予资格

Phrase(s): ***professional qualification; enterprise qualification***

◇ *Only those bonds which can meet specific qualifications can be exempt from the federal tax when redeemed. You'd better refer to your financial advisor for details.* 只有满足特定条件的债券才可以在赎回时免除联邦所得税。你最好就细节咨询一下你的财务顾问。

◇ *Facing an everchanging market and complicated regulatory documents, many investors found their investment qualifications are limited.* 面对不断变化的市场和复杂的法规性文件，很多投资者发现他们的投资资历非常有限。

qualified ['kwɒlɪfaɪd] *adj.* 合格的；有资格的；*v.* 限制（qualify 的过去分词）；描述；授权

Phrase(s): ***qualified certificate; qualified accounts***

◇ *A qualified professional must evaluate the property when information indicates that the value of the collateral may have declined materially relative to general market prices or when a credit event, such as default, occurs.* 当信息显示抵押品价值相对于一般的市场价格已经大幅度下降或有信贷事件（如违约）发生时，有资格的专业人员必须评估抵押品。1（91）

◇ *The full list of athletes who are qualified for 2016 Rio Olympics is released to public by the National Sports Bureau today.* 国家体育局今天对外公布了具有 2016 年里约奥运会参赛资格的运动员名单。

qualify ['kwɒlɪfaɪ] *vt.* 限制；使具有资格；证明……合格；*vi.* 取得资格；有资格

Phrase(s): ***Monday qualify; qualify round***

◇ *To qualify for the "top-down" treatment of default risk, the receivable pool and overall lending relationship should be closely monitored and controlled.* 为了有资格对违约风险进行“自上而下”的处理，应该紧密监督和控制应收账款池和整个的贷款关系。1（87）

◇ *Under the new law, female workers in chemical plants will qualify for early retirement due to their poor physical reactions towards the working environment.* 根据新的法律，在化工厂工作的女职工由于她们的身体对工作环境的不良反应将获得提前退休。

qualitative ['kwɒlɪtətɪv] *adj.* 定性的；质的；性质上的

Phrase(s): ***qualitative analysis; qualitative research; qualitative change***

◇ *Regardless of whether a KPI is qualitative or quantitative in nature, all KPIs need to say something useful about the running of the business.* 不管 KPI 本质上是定性的还是定量的，所有的 KPI 都需要能够展现出一些有关业务运转的有用信息。

◇ *Financial institutions should conduct regularly comprehensive exercises aimed at estimating risk appetite, using stress tests and a combination of qualitative and quantitative factors.* 金融机构应该通过压力测试并结合各种定性定量因素对风险偏好定期进行综合性评估。

quality ['kwɒlɪtɪ] *n.* 质量；［统计］品质；特性；才能；*adj.* 高品质的；<英俚>棒极了

Phrase(s): ***high quality; quality policy***

◇ *This country should focus on improving the quality of universities so their graduates can be recognized in the world job market*. 这个国家应该着力提高高校的质量，让毕业生在全球就业市场得到认可。

◇ *The quality of many artworks couldn't be fairly measured by their market values at the time of creation*. 许多艺术品的质量在创造的时候无法被市场价值公平地衡量。

quant ['kwɒnt] *n.* 数据专家

◇ *TheStreet is a leading American digital financial media company;its Quant Ratings service provides professional and unbiased quantitative stock ratings for subscribers all over the country*. The Street 是一家领先的美国数字金融媒体公司；其量化评级服务为全国各地的用户提供专业和公正的定量股票评级。

quantify ['kwɒntɪfaɪ] *vt.* 量化；为……定量；确定数量；*vi.* 量化；定量

Phrase(s): ***quantify precision; metage quantify***

◇ *The survey is an effective way for the company to quantify investors' confidence towards its future growth*. 这个调查有效地帮助公司量化了投资者对其未来增长的信心。

quantile ['kwɒntaɪl] *n.* [计] 分位数；分位点

Phrase(s): ***quantile regression; quantile function***

◇ *Quantile statistics provide the information whether the values of a column are clustered or not*. 分位数统计信息提供关于一个列中的值是否聚合的信息。

quantitative ['kwɒntɪˌtətɪv] *adj.* 定量的；量的；数量的；能用数量表示的；能测量的

Phrase(s): ***quantitative assessment; quantitative linguistics***

◇ *Supervisors will allow banks to use own-estimate haircuts only when they fulfill certain qualitative and quantitative criteria*. 监管当局在银行达到特定的定性和定量要求后，允许银行使用估计的折扣系数。1（21）

quantity ['kwɒntɪtɪ] *n.* 量；数量；大量；总量

Phrase(s): ***quantity delivered; quantity discount***

◇ *In the USA, companies who generate hazardous waste can be classified into different levels, such as Very Small, Small and Large, based on the quantities of the waste they produced every year*. 在美国，产生有害垃圾的公司可以分为不同的级别（如非常小、小和大），定级主要基于它们每年有害垃圾的排放量。

quart [kwɔːt] *n.* 夸脱（容量单位）；一夸脱的容器

◇ *The old man loves making pickles very much, so you can see all kinds of quart and pint jars at his home.* 老人非常喜欢制作泡菜，所以你可以在他家看到各种各样的以夸脱品脱为计量单位的罐子。

quarter ['kwɔːtə] *n.* 季度；四分之一；一刻钟；地区；（美式足球的）一节；*vt.* 把……四等分；供……住宿；使（士兵）驻扎

Phrase(s): ***three quarters; residential quarter***

◇ *We pay electricity & water bills by quarter.* 我们按季度缴纳水电费。

◇ *It is predicted that African population will increase to 2.5 billion by 2050, accounting for a quarter of the total population in the world; with such a big number, this long forgotten land should prosper.* 据预测，非洲人口到 2050 年将增加到 25 亿，占世界总人口的四分之一；如此多的人聚集在这里应该会让这片早已被遗忘的土地繁荣起来。

quartile ['kwɔːtaɪl] *n.* 四分位数；四分点

Phrase(s): ***upper quartile; quartile range***

◇ *The performance of equity funds are not stable, and just a few of them can stay in the top quartile within two years' period.* 股票型基金的表现不稳定，只有少数基金能够在两年期内保持顶尖状态。

◇ *It is obvious that people who are in the highest income quartile and those who are in the lowest income quartile will have a huge difference in the standard of living after retirement.* 很明显，收入在前四分之一水平的人和那些收入在后四分之一水平的人在退休后生活标准将有天壤之别。

quasilinear ['kwɑːzi'liːnɪə] *adj.* 准线性的；拟线性的

Phrase(s): ***quasilinear function; quasilinear characteristics***

◇ *For small movements around the initial yield of 6%, however, the relationship is quasilinear.* 然而，最初的收益率有 6% 左右的小幅波动，是拟线性的关系。

quasi-random ['kwɑːzi'rændəm] *n.* 拟随机；*adj.* 拟随机的

Phrase(s): ***quasi-random sequence; quasi-random access; quasi-random point***

◇ *Quasi-random integration rules that integrate exactly some class of functions are constructed.* 构造了一系列对某一函数集会精确成立的“拟随机”积分公式。

queen ['kwiːn] *n.* 女王；王后；（纸牌中的）皇后；（蜜蜂等的）蜂王；*vt.* 使……成为女王或王后；*vi.* 做女王

Phrase(s): ***The Queen; Queen bee***

◇ *Ice cream maker Dairy Queen recently promoted a miracle treat day on which most of the profits will be donated to children's charity for difficult diseases treatment.* 冰淇淋乳品生产商“冰雪皇后”近期推出了一个治疗奇迹日，这一天大部分的销售利润将捐赠给儿童慈善组织，用于治疗儿童重病患者。

query ['kwɪərɪ] *n.* 疑问；质问；疑问号；［计］查询；*vt.* 询问；对……表示疑问；*vi.* 询问；表示怀疑

Phrase(s): ***spatial query; flashback query***

◇ *The Federal Reserve today queried the financial consultants of the healthcare products company, investigating the company's potential manipulations on the stock price.* 美联储今天对这家医疗保健产品公司的财务顾问进行了质疑，调查该公司对股票价格是否存在操纵。

question ['kwestʃ(ə)n] *n.* 问题；疑问；询问；疑问句；*vt.* 询问；怀疑；审问；*vi.* 询问；怀疑；

Phrase(s): ***complex question; Roman Question; question mark***

◇ *Sometimes, legislators couldn't predict problems after certain laws were passed; so they had no ready solutions to them but to hand the tough questions over to the court.* 有时，立法者无法预测一些法律颁布后产生的问题；所以他们没有现成的解决方案，只得把棘手的问题交给法院。

◇ *The CEO was questioned by the Federal Reserve on the company's violation of financial regulations in information disclosure.* 该首席执行官遭到美国联邦储备委员会的质疑；怀疑其公司在信息披露方面违反金融法规。

quick [kwɪk] *n.* 核心；伤口的嫩肉；*adj.* 快的；迅速的；敏捷的；灵敏的；*adv.* 迅速地

Phrase(s): ***quick ratio; quick dry***

◇ *Among some quick business update ideas, opening an online shop while downsizing the physical shop is a popular one with small fashion shops.* 快速进行业务更新的办法中，开网店并缩小实体店规模的建议受到小型服装店的青睐。

◇ *Due to tight schedules on weekdays, many white collar managers prefer a quick and easy lunch near their workplaces.* 由于工作日紧张的日程安排，许多白领经理更喜欢在工作地点附近选择方便快捷的午餐。

quiesce [kwai'es] *vi.* 静默

Phrase(s): ***terminal quiesce; quiesce database***

◇ *Quiesce, generally meaning pause, is an important command in many software applications.* Quiesce 是很多软件程序中一个重要的命令，基本意思是暂停。

quiescence [kwai'esns] *n.* 静止；沉默

Phrase(s): ***Quiescence Search; still quiescence***

◇ *International investors who were worried about the performance in European stock markets have gone into quiescence thanks to good returns and effective regulations in Europe.* 之前担心欧洲股市表现的国际投资者们已经归于平静，这得益于欧洲市场良好的回报和有效的监管。

quintal ['kwɪnt(ə)l] *n.* 公担（等于 100 千克）

◇ *Quintal is a weight unit; one quintal equals to one hundred kilograms.* 公担是重量单位；一公担等于一百千克。

quintuple [kwɪn'tup(ə)l] *adj.* 五倍的；五重的；五部分组成的；*n.* 五倍；*v.* 使……成为五倍

Phrase(s): ***quintuple the amount; a quintuple medal***

◇ *The number of monthly active users of the social networking site has quintupled since it was established in 2004; even many senior citizens downloaded its app to their smart phones.* 这个社交网站自 2004 年建立以来，月度活跃用户人数已经增长了四倍；甚至许多老年人都在智能手机上下载了它的应用程序。

quit [kwɪt] *vt.* 离开；放弃；停止；使……解除；*vi.* 离开；辞职；停止；*n.* 离开；[计] 退出；*adj.* 摆脱了……的；已经了结的；*n.* (Quit) 人名；（英）奎特

Phrase(s): ***quit rent; quit one's job***

◇ *This company treats people as their most precious assets by proving them withcomfortableworking and traveling environment; so few employees miss work or quit in the past five years.* 这个公司把人作为最宝贵的资产，给他们提供舒适的工作和出差环境；因此在过去的五年中很少有员工耽误工作或者辞职。

◇ *Facing the accounting scandal, the CFO said he would rather quit than acknowledge that the wrongdoing was under his direction.* 面对会计丑闻，首席财务官说他宁愿放弃也不愿意承认错误是在他的指示下酿成的。

quite [kwaɪt] adv. 很；相当；完全

Phrase(s): ***q; quite sensibly; quite reasonably***

◇ *The distribution of credit loss is quite complex.* 信贷损失的分布非常复杂。

◇ *No one is quite sure where the artificial intelligence will lead us before it really happens.* 在真正发生之前，没有人能确信人工智能将把我们带向何方？

quitter ['kwɪtə] *n.* 轻易放弃的人；懒人

◇ *Despite ups and downs, we believe you will calm down and keep practicing the piano every day, because you are no quitter.* 不论个中曲直，我们相信你会冷静下来，继续每天练习钢琴，因为你不是一个轻易放弃的人。

quorate ['kwɔːrət] *adj.* （英）够法定人数的

◇ *The election result was invalid because the shareholder's meeting was not quorate.* 因股东大会不够法定人数，故该选举结果无效。

quota ['kwəʊtə] *n.* 配额；定额；限额

Phrase(s): ***import quota; quota management***

◇ *Quota system has many different meanings in different countries and different periods; it could be a system of limiting immigrants from particular countries or setting limits of goods imported from other countries.* 配额制度在不同国家和不同时期有许多不同的意义；它可能是一个限制来自特定国家移民数量的制度；也可能是限制从其他国家货物进口数量的制度。

◇ *Thanks to gender quota system, women in Scandinavian countries have more higher education opportunities, smaller salary gaps with male colleagues and more seats in governments than women in other countries.* 得益于性别配额制度，北欧国家的妇女，比起其他国家的妇女，有更多的高等教育机会，与男同事的工资差距更小，同时在

政府任职的席位也更多。

quotation [kwə(ʊ)'teɪʃ(ə)n] *n.* 引用；引证引语；语录；［商业］行情（报告）；牌；报价单；估价单

Phrase(s): ***quotation spread; indirect quotation; direct quotation***

◇ *We also assume no transaction costs, that is, zero bid–ask spread on spot and forward quotations as well as the ability to lend and borrow at the same risk-free rate.* 我们还假设没有交易成本，也就是说，现货市场和期货市场上的报价差额为零，以及以相同的无风险利率借贷的能力。

quote [kwəʊt] *vt.* 报价；引述；举证；*vi.* 报价；引用；引证；*n.* 引用

Phrase(s): ***introductory quote; quote sheet***

◇ *Most CDS (negotiable certificates of deposit) contracts are quoted in terms of an annual spread, with the payment made on a quarterly basis.* 大部分的大额可转让定期存单以每年差价报价，并以季度为基础来支付。

◇ *Market practice and government regulations sometimes contradict with each other; best quotes submitted to the regulators are not always obtainable in practice.* 市场实践和政府法规有时互相矛盾；提交给监管机构的最好的报价不一定总能在实践中获得的。

quotient ['kwəʊʃ(ə)nt] *n.* [数] 商；系数；份额

Phrase(s): ***quotient space; quotient rule***

◇ *To our surprise, the grocery chain surpassed Amazon in corporate reputation, according to a leading website in reputation quotient study.* 令我们惊讶的是，据一家领先的公司声誉调查网站统计，一家食品杂货连锁店居然超过亚马逊排名第一。

◇ *Many parents are only concerned about the employment rate of the universities which their children attend; actually, a school's happiness quotient is also worth studying.* 许多家长只关心孩子所上的大学就业率怎么样；实际上，一所学校的幸福指数也值得研究。

R

rally ['rælɪ] *n.* 价格回升；集合；*vi. & vt.* 召集；聚集；重整

◇ *But true to form, last year's rally brightened investors' spirits and by January they were expecting 10% returns.* 但是一如往常，上一年度的价格回升使投资者重燃热情，一月的预期收益率为 10%。7（241）

◇ *Due to serious air pollution, coal has been gradually replaced by natural gas and other alternatives in the main commodities rally in developed countries.* 由于严重的空气污染，煤炭在发达国家已逐渐被天然气和其他新能源所替代，不再属于主要商品范畴。

random ['rændəm] *adj.* [数] 随机的；任意的；胡乱的；*n.* 随意

Phrase(s): ***random vectors; random variable; random process***

◇ *This hypothesis, also known as the random walk theory, implies that the conditional distribution of returns depends only on current prices, and not on the previous history of prices.* 这种假说，也就是随机游走理论，认为收益的条件分布仅取决于当前价格，和历史价格无关。

range [reɪn(d)ʒ] *n.* 范围；幅度；*vi.* 平行；延伸；*vt.* 漫游；归类于

Phrase(s): ***range from; price range***

◇ *Each policy had a specified deductible (or, in insurance terms, a"retention") in an amount that ranged between zero and $6 million.* 每个保单都有特别的扣除项（保险术语是保留率），其范围从 0 到 6 百万美元。4（3）

RAROC(Risk Adjusted Return On Capital) [rɪsk ə'dʒʌstɪd rɪ'tɜːn ɒn 'kæpɪt(ə)l] *abbr.* 风险调整资本回报率

Phrase(s): ***RAROC performance valuation***

◇ *Some activities may require large amounts of risk capital, which in turn requires higher returns. This is the essence of risk-adjusted return on capital (RAROC) measures.* 很多经济活动会需要大量的风险资本，相应地要求更高的回报，这是风险调整资本回报率指标的实质。

◇ *RARCO is the ratio of risk-adjusted return to economic capital; by using this measure, the risks involved in an investment can be accurately calculated.* 风险调整资本回报率是风险调整收益对经济资本的比率，使用这个指标可以精确计算投资所涉及的风险。

rate [reɪt] *n.* 比率

Phrase(s): ***interest rate; unemployment rate***

◇ *It is plausible for interest rates or unemployment rates to rise severely in an economic crisis.* 在经济危机时利率或者失业率会大幅上涨看似是合理的。13（4）

rate of change [reɪt (ə)v tʃeɪn(d)ʒ] *PHR.* 变动率；［计划］变化速度

◇ *Rate of change (ROC) measures the percentage increase or decrease in price over a given period of time.* 变动率衡量的是在给定的期间内，价格上升或下降的百分比。10（39）

◇ *The minimum value of ROC is −100% because securities can only decline by 100% to have zero value.* 变动率的最小价值为 −100%，因为证券价格至多能下降 100%，价值为 0。10（40）

rating ['reɪtɪŋ] *n.* 等级；等级评定

Phrase(s): ***credit rating; rating agency***

◇ *We explain that the amount of credit enhancement required to obtain a targeted credit rating is set by the rating agencies.* 信用增强需要获得目的性的信用评级，而这样的信用评级一般由评级机构做出。13（16）

ratio ['reɪʃɪəʊ] *n.* 比率；比例

Phrase(s): ***exchange-stock ratio; hazard ratio***

◇ *It is a quest that models should describe financial time series such as prices, returns, interest rates, financial ratios, defaults, and so on.* 模型必须能够描述价格、收益、利率、财务比率、违约等金融时间序列。5（16）

rationale [ˌræʃə'nɑːl] *n.* 基本原理；原理的阐述

Phrase(s): ***investment rationale; economic rationale***

◇ *What kind of marketing rationale drove so many celebrities into business, though some of them have lost most of the money earned in their original zone.* 什么样的营销理念让这么多名人投身经商大潮，尽管他们中的一些人已经失去了在原来圈子里赚到的大部分钱。

◇ *This acquisition deal allowed investors to know more about the company's investment rationale.* 这一收购交易使投资者更多地了解到公司投资的理论基础。

realizable ['riːəlaɪzəbl] *adj.* 可变现的

Phrase(s): ***realizable property; realizable value***

◇ *Some significant attributes of the operating entity in a whole securitization are (1) entry barriers, (2) demonstration of successful presence, (3) maintainability of future profits, (4) realizable asset value, (5) brand name, and (6) stable management and efficient internal controls.* 整体资产证券化中，经营实体显著的属性有：（1）进入壁垒；（2）成功的示范；（3）未来收益的可维持性；（4）可变现资产的价值；（5）品牌名称；（6）稳定的管理和有效的内部控制。13（208）

realization [ˌriːəlaɪ'zeɪʃən] *n.* 变现；实现；变卖

Phrase(s): ***realization of gains; realization of property; assets realisation; net realisation***

◇ *For example, an investor may swap from one bond that has decreased in price to another similar bond if realization of capital losses is advantageous for tax purposes.* 例如，如果资产损失的实现对税收是有利的，投资者可以用一个已经降价的债券来交换一个类似的债券。7（37）

◇ *Equities that are recorded as a loan but arise from a debt/equity swap made as part of the orderly realization or restructuring of the debt are included in the definition of equity holdings.* 作为债务正常实现或债务重组的一部分，按照贷款来记录，同时由于债务/

股权掉期产生的股权，也包括在股权的定义中。1（44）

real-time [ˌrɪəl'taɪm] *adj.* 即时的；实时的

Phrase(s): ***real-time delivery versus payment; Real-Time Gross Settlement System***

◇ *CFOs will need real-time financial information to make crucial decisions fast.* 首席财务官需要实时财务信息来快速地做关键性决定。6（88）

◇ *The international organization for migration uses real-time intelligence from NATO navy alliance to cooperate with Greece, Turkey and other European countries for refugee solutions.* 国际移民组织使用北约海军联盟实时情报与希腊、土耳其以及其他欧洲国家合作，解决难民危机。

realty [rɪ'ælɪtɪ] *n.* 房地产；不动产

Phrase(s): ***realty business; realty management***

◇ *Brokerage firms or agencies which are in residential real estate business can also be called realtors, which provide full service to home buyers.* 住宅房地产业务的中介机构也可以被称为房地产经纪人，它们为购房者提供全面的服务。

real-valued [ˌrɪəl'vælju:d] *n.* 实值

◇ *A real-valued set function defined over* Ω *is said to be measurable with respect to a σ-algebra* I*, if the inverse image of any Borel set belongs to* I. 对于一个 σ 代数 I，如果任何 Borel 集的原象属于 I，则定义在 Ω 上的一个实值函数被称为可测的。5（55）

◇ *Random variables are real-valued measurable functions.* 随机变量是实值可测函数。5（55）

reassessment [ˌri:ə'sesmənt] *n.* 重新评定

Phrase(s): ***strategy reassessment; risk reassessment***

◇ *But the estimate is highly sensitive to the input values, and even a small reassessment of their prospects would result in a big revision of price.* 但是估计结果和输入值高度相关，对预期值一个小的重新评估都可能导致价格出现很大的变动。7（274）

rebate ['ri:beɪt] *vt.* 减少；打折扣；*n.* 折扣

Phrase(s): ***tax rebate; commission rebate; cash rebate***

◇ *Sometimes the option offers a rebate if it is knocked out.* 如果期权的价值被敲空，它有时会提供一个折扣。

◇ *Good news! IKEA's annual kitchen sales just begin. If you just moved in to a new home, a 15% rebate is waiting for you.* 好消息！宜家的年度厨房用品大促销刚刚开始。如果你刚搬新家，15% 的折扣等着你呐。

rebound [rɪ'baʊnd] *v.* 回升；反弹；*n.* 振作；回升

Phrase(s): ***rebound strongly; rebound in prices***

◇ *The coastal city forecast a job rebound later this year when several world top 500 enterprises set up assembly lines here.* 这个沿海城市预计今年稍后会出现就业反弹，主要是因为几个世界 500 强的企业在这里建了装配线。

◇ *Forced by 30% shrink in sales, the fast food company expected a business rebound by making several animated short films to attract young guys and children.* 迫于销售量缩水 30%，这家快餐公司希望通过制作几部动画短片来吸引年轻人和孩子们，让生意回升。

recall [rɪ'kɔːl] *vt.* 召回；回想；*n.* 召回；回想

Phrase(s): ***recall ratio; recall level***

◇ *Small kids were seriously affected by the contaminated four due to E. coli bacteria; the mill has had four recalls since the first complaint.* 被污染面粉里的大肠杆菌对小孩子们影响最严重；自从第一起投诉到现在，面粉厂已经四次召回其产品了。

recapitalization [riˌkæpɪt(ə)laɪ'zeɪʃən] *n.* 资本重组；资本额的调整

◇ *Target management will often issue debt to pay out a dividend-a transaction called a leveraged recapitalization.* 目标管理将会发行债券来支付股利，称为杠杆资本重组。6（907）

◇ *The price will rise only if the firm's debt level before the recapitalization was below the optimum, so a levered recapitalization is not recommended for every target.* 只有重组前公司的债务水平低于最佳，价格才会上升，所以杠杆重组并不适合于任一目标。6（907）

receipt [rɪ'siːt] *n.* 收到；收据；收入

Phrase(s): ***American depositary receipt (ADR); receipt voucher; shopping receipt***

◇ *Qwnership over the receivables and cash receipts should be protected against bankruptcy "stays"or legal challenges that could materially delay the lender's ability to liquidate/assign the receivables or retain control over cash receipts.* 应收账款的所有权和

现金收据应该被保护，防止破产发生或出现法律上的挑战，这些挑战将实质性延误贷款方在清算应收账款（给应收账款评级）或保留对现金收据控制方面的能力。1（88）

◇ *Facing a slowdown in economy, the government promised to reduce corporate tax by 10% so as to increase foreign or domestic investment and eventually get more tax receipts.* 面对经济的放缓，政府承诺减少 10% 的公司税，以增加外国或国内投资，并最终获得更多的税收收入。

receivables [rɪ'siːvəblz] *n.* 应收账款；应收票据

Phrase(s): ***receivable account***

◇ *Rapid sales growth requires increased assets in the form of accounts receivable, inventory, and fixed plant, which, in turn, require money to pay for assets.* 快速的销售增长要求应收账款账户、存货和固定厂房设备的增长，反过来又要求有资金用来购买这些资产。6（75）

◇ *The bank must be able to monitor both the quality of the receivables and the financial condition of the seller and servicer.* 银行必须能监控应收账款的质量及销售方、服务方的财务状况。1（88）

receive [rɪ'siːv] *vt.* 收到

Phrase(s): ***receive dividends; receive from***

◇ *The bank must receive timely and sufficiently detailed reports of receivables agings and dilutions.* 银行必须接受及时的和足够详细的关于应收账款账龄及稀释状况的报告。1（88）

◇ *Car owners who were affected by VW emission test scandal would receive thousands of dollars in compensation.* 受大众汽车排放测试丑闻影响的车主将获得数千美元的赔偿。

recent ['riːs(ə)nt] *adj.* 最近的；近代的

Phrase(s): ***recent progress; recent epoch***

◇ *Operational risk in securitization transactions has been the highlight of attention in recent years.* 在最近几年，资产证券化的操作风险受到了高度重视。13（143）

recession [rɪ'seʃ(ə)n] *n.* 衰退；不景气

Phrase(s): ***growth recession; inflationary recession***

◇ *During an economic recession, there is less disposable income to spend and many more loan defaults are likely to occur at the same time.* 在经济不景气时期，人们可用于自由支配的收入减少，同时贷款违约事件也会增加。15（5）

reciprocal [rɪ'sɪprək(ə)l] *n.* 倒数；*adj.* 倒数的；相互作用的

Phrase(s): ***reciprocal rule; reciprocal trade***

◇ *In calculating the capital ratio, the denominator or total risk weighted assets will be determined by multiplying the capital requirements for market risk and operational risk by 12. 5 (i. e. the reciprocal of the minimum capital ratio of 8%) and adding the resulting figures to the sum of risk-weighted assets compiled for credit risk.* 在计算资本比率时，市场风险和操作风险的资本要求乘以 12. 5（即最低资本比率 8% 的倒数），再加上针对信用风险的风险加权资产，就得到分母，即总的风险加权资产。1（6）

recognized ['rekəgnaɪzd] *adj.* 合格的

Phrase(s): ***recognised guarantors***

◇ *Similarly, the standardized approach expands the range of recognised guarantors to include all firms that meet a threshold external credit rating.* 此外，标准法还扩大了合格担保人的范围，使其包括符合一定外部评级条件的各类公司。1（3）

reconciliation [ˌrek(ə)nsɪlɪ'eɪʃ(ə)n] *n.* 和解；调和；对账

Phrase(s): ***reconciliation statement; budget reconciliation***

◇ *The back office deals with trade processing and reconciliation as well as cash management.* 后台处理交易过程、对账和现金管理。

recourse [rɪ'kɔːs] *n.* 追索权；追索补偿

Phrase(s): ***recourse loan; recourse liability***

◇ *The estimates for PD and LGD (or EL) must be calculated for the receivables on a stand-alone basis; that is, without regard to any assumption of recourse or guarantees from the seller or other parties.* 必须逐笔计算应收账款的违约概率、违约损失率（或预期损失），但不考虑追索权、卖方或其他方保证。1（65）

recovery [rɪ'kʌv(ə)rɪ] *n.* 回收率；恢复

Phrase(s): ***recovery value; quick recovery***

◇ *The portion that is expected to be recovered is called the recovery value and the portion that is expected to be lost is the loss given default (LGD).* 将被收回的部分被称作

回收价值，将要损失的部分被称作违约损失。15（7）

◇ *The recent recovery in oil price at least gave investors some confidence, yet, they wouldn't expect this recovery to be staying long.* 最近石油价格的复苏至少给了投资者一些信心，但他们也不会指望这种复苏会保持长久。

recurrent [rɪ'kʌr(ə)nt] *adj.* 经常性的；循环的

Phrase(s): ***recurrent account; recurrent revenue; recurrent cost***

◇ *Technical analysis is essentially the search for recurrent and predictable patterns in stock.* 技术分析在本质上是研究股票经常性和可预计的部分。

recursive [rɪ'kɜːsɪv] *adj.* 递归的；循环的

Phrase(s): ***infinite recursive; recursive model***

◇ *We can look at econometric models from a perspective other than that of the recursive generation of stochastic paths.* 除了递推生成的随机路径，我们可以从其他的角度来看待这些计量模型。5（29）

redeemable [rɪ'diːməbl] *adj.* 可赎回

Phrase(s): ***redeemable bond; redeemable charge; redeemable securities***

◇ *Preferred stock can be callable by the issuing firm, in which case it is said to be redeemable.* 当优先股可以被发行方赎回时，称作可赎回优先股。7（40）

◇ *If you are going to send shopping cards to your friends on holiday time, make sure these cards are redeemable for online shopping, not just physical shops.* 如果你要在节日期间送购物卡给你的朋友，最好确保这些卡在网上购物时也可以使用，而不只是在实体商店使用。

redemption [rɪ'dem(p)ʃ(ə)n] *n.* 赎回；拯救；偿还；

Phrase(s): ***redemption fund; redemption value***

◇ *There is a particularly simple relationship for consols, or perpetual bonds, which are bonds making regular coupon payments but with no redemption date.* 统一公债或永久债券的关系是特别简单的，债券进行常规的利息支付但没有赎回期。

◇ *The girl is seeking help in a rehabilitation center for redemption and farewell to drugs and prostitution.* 这个女孩正在寻求戒毒所的帮助，希望得到拯救，彻底告别毒品和卖淫。

redirected [ˌri:dəˈrektɪd] *v.* 重新传入；重新寄送（redirect 的过去分词形式）

Phrase(s): ***redirected restore; redirected server***

◇ *The principal is redirected to pay off the other bond classes.* 本金被重新定向以用来支付其他级别的债券。13（90）

redistribute [ˌri:dɪˈstrɪbju:t; ri:ˈdɪstrɪbju:t] *vt.* 重新分配；再区分

Phrase(s): ***redistribute risks; redistribute wealth***

◇ *The risks redistributed in the case of agency CMOs(Collateralized Mortgage Obligations)is prepayment risk and interest rate risk.* 抵押担保债券的风险重新分配主要是指预付风险和利率风险的风险重新分配。13（16）

◇ *An efficient economy should try its best to narrow the wealth gap and an efficient government should try all means to redistribute social wealth in a fairer way.* 一个有效率的经济体应该尽最大努力缩小贫富差距，一个高效的政府应尽一切办法以更公平的方式重新分配社会财富。

redistribution [riˌdɪstrɪˈbju:ʃ(ə)n] *n.* [经] 重新分配

Phrase(s): ***the redistribution; redistribution of prepayment; redistribution of cash flows***

◇ *The securitization of conforming loans result in the creation of agency mortgage-backed securities and the redistribution of cash flows to create collateralized mortgage obligations (CMOs).* 合格贷款的资产证券化创造了机构抵押贷款支持的证券，同时，现金流的重新分配则又创造了抵押担保债券。13（16）

reduce [rɪˈdju:s] *vt.* 减少；降低；使处于；把……分解；*vi.* 减少；缩小；归纳为

Phrase(s): ***reduce by; reduce expenditure***

◇ *An amortizing swap is employed to reduce the risk of overhedging.* 分期偿还的互换是可以用来减少过度对冲风险。13（141）

◇ *How to reduce housing costs such as rents and mortgages is a big issue for young people who pour into large cities for better job opportunities.* 如何降低住房成本（如租金和抵押贷款）是那些涌入大城市寻找更好的就业机会的年轻人所面临的一大问题。

reference [ˈref(ə)r(ə)ns] *n.* 参考

Phrase(s): ***external reference; reference rate***

◇ *Bond class FL is the floater and has the typical coupon reset formula of a reference rate plus a quoted margin.* 债券 FL 是一种浮动债券，它有着典型的利息重置公式，这个公式就是参考利率加上一个报价边际利率。13（78）

refinance [riː'faɪnæns] *vt.* 再供……资金；再为……筹钱

Phrase(s): ***refinance credits; refinance loan***

◇ *A fixed rate mortgage can be prepaid when mortgage rates decline below the loan rate as the borrower can refinance the mortgage at the prevailing lower rate.* 当现行的抵押贷款利率低于债务人借款时的抵押利率时，可以提前偿还固定抵押贷款，这样债务人就可以以现行的低利率再融资了。13（52）

◇ *If your mortgage interest rate is too high and you need cash to pay other debts, then it is the right time for you to refinance your mortgage because of historically low rate and preferential rules.* 如果你的抵押贷款利率太高，又需要现金偿还其他债务，那么现在就是你转抵押贷款的好时候，因为历史上较低的利率和优惠规定。

refinement [rɪ'faɪnm(ə)nt] *n.* 修改内容

◇ *Other refinements focus on banks'review of concentration risks, and on the treatment of residual risks that arise from the use of collateral, guarantees and credit derivatives.* 其他一些修改内容突出反映在银行对风险集中的审查和对使用抵押、担保和信用衍生品而带来的剩余风险的处理上。1（9）

refundable [rɪ'fʌndəbl] *adj.* 可退还的；可偿还的

Phrase(s): ***refundable credits; refundable bonds***

◇ *Visitors who rent cottages or lodges along the lakeside in our town need to pay $100 non-refundable deposit from today for maintenance reserves.* 从今天起，游客租我们镇上湖边的村舍或小屋需要支付 100 美元不可退还的押金作为维修储备金。

◇ *A refundable purchase discount would therefore imply an LGD of zero and, hence, the exposure that is covered by such collateral would carry a zero capital charge.* 可退还的买方折扣违约损失率是零，以这种抵押覆盖的贷款其资本要求是零。1（65）

regime [reɪ'ʒiːm] *n.* 政权；政体；社会制度；管理体制

Phrase(s): ***regime change; currency regime***

◇ *Many countries have cut the diplomatic relations with the country because the current president's regime has been threatening to use nuclear power for military purpose.*

许多国家已经切断了与该国的外交关系，因为现任总统的政权威胁要在军事目的中使用核能源。

regional ['riːdʒənl] *adj.* 地区的；局部的

Phrase(s): ***regional economic; regional fund***

◇ *Banks/finance include both money center banks and regional banks, savings and loans, brokerage firms, insurance companies, and finance companies.* 银行 / 金融机构包括货币中心银行和地区性银行、储蓄和贷款经纪公司、保险公司和金融公司。5（41）

registration [ˌredʒɪ'streɪʃ(ə)n] *n.* 注册；登记

Phrase(s): ***registration fee***

◇ *Registration is often required byinvestors as a precondition for investing.* 投资者进行投资时往往要求以登记为前提。

regress [rɪ'gres] *vi.* 逆行；倒退；复归；*n.* 回归；退回

Phrase(s): ***logistic regress; nonlinear regress***

◇ *Stock market is a powerful equalizer; if you purchase all the companies'stocks, then your return would regress to the mean of them all.* 股市是一个强大的均衡器；如果你购买所有公司的股票，那么你的回报将回归到它们的平均值。

regression [rɪ'greʃ(ə)n] *n.* 回归；退化；逆行；复原

Phrase(s): ***regression analysis; linear regression model***

◇ *Regressions are about dependence between variables.* 回归是关于变量之间的依赖性。5（79）

◇ *Regression models show that consumer spending didn't grow rapidly although oil price had a dramatic fall; this result implies that there are other factors influencing their spending plans.* 回归模型表明，虽然石油价格已经大幅下降，但消费者开支并没有迅速增长；这意味着，还有其他因素影响他们的支出计划。

regulated ['regjʊleɪtɪd] *v.* 规定（regulate 的过去分词）；管理；管制

Phrase(s): ***regulated rent; regulated prices***

◇ *For regulated financial entities, securitization is a tool for managing risk-based capital requirements.* 对于被监管的金融实体，资产证券化是一个它们用来管理风险基础资本要求的工具。13（45）

regulatory ['regjulətəri] *adj.* 管理的；控制的；调整的

Phrase(s): *regulatory risk; regulatory arbitrage*

◇*In the development of an investment policy, the following factors must be considered: client constraints, regulatory constraints, and tax and accounting issues.* 制定投资发展政策时，必须考虑以下因素：客户约束、监管约束以及税收和会计问题。5（43）

Regulatory risk ['regjulətəri rɪsk] *PHR.* 监管风险

Phrase(s): *regulatory risk differentiation*

◇ *Regulatory risk are the result of changes in regulations or interpretation of existing regulations that can negatively affect a firm.* 监管风险是由于监管的变动或者是对现存监管条文解释的改变，对公司造成的不利影响。9（520）

reimbursement [ˌriːɪm'bɜːsmənt] *n.* 退还；偿还；赔偿

Phrase(s): *claim reimbursement; reimbursement standards*

◇ *The company would receive reimbursement for losses in excess of the $30 million annual aggregate retention under the contract.* 合同中规定，如果每年的累积存留损失超过 3 千万美元，公司将得到赔偿。4（6）

reinvestment [ˌriːɪn'vestmənt] *n.* 再投资

Phrase(s): *automatic reinvestment; reinvestment services*

◇ *Generally speaking, average investors can expect a 7% annual return rate in stock market including dividend reinvestment; this rate is much higher than term deposit rate.* 一般来说，普通投资者在股票市场可以预期 7% 的年回报率包括股息再投资；这个利率比定期存款利率高很多。

related [rɪ'leɪtɪd] *adj.* 有关系的；有关联的；讲述的；叙述的；*v.* 叙述（relate 过去式）

Phrase(s): *related investment; related factor*

◇ *There are numerous types of third-party credit enhancements available and they include monoline insurance companies, letters of credit, and related-party guarantees such as that of the originator/seller.* 通过第三方加强信用的方法有很多种，包括通过保险公司的单一险种保险，信用证和相关第三方的担保，比如发行人或者卖方。13（91）

relative frequency ['relətɪv 'fri:kw(ə)nsɪ] *PHR.* 相对频率

◇ *Probability as relative frequency is the standard interpretation of probability in the physical science.* 相对频率是物理学界中对概率的标准解释。5（49）

◇ *The two interpretations of probability—as intensity of belief and as relative frequency—are therefore complementary.* 这两种概率的解释——置信的强度和相对频率——是互补的。5（49）

Relative PPP(theory of purchasing power parity) ['θɪərɪ (ə)v 'pɜ: tʃəsɪŋ 'paʊə 'pærɪtɪ] *PHR.* 相对购买力平价理论

◇ *Relative PPP tells us that the exchange rate will rise if the U. S. inflation rate is lower than the foreign country's.* 相对购买力平价说明如果美国通胀率低于他国，外汇汇率将会上升。6（955）

◇ *Relative purchasing power parity does not tell us what determines the absolute level of the exchange rate. Instead, it tells us what determines the change in the exchange rate over time.* 相对购买力平价没有说明什么决定了外汇的绝对水平，而是说明在一段时期内什么决定了汇率的变动。6（953）

release [rɪ'li:s] *vt.* 释放；发射；让与；允许发表；*n.* 释放；发布；让与

Phrase(s): ***release lever; delivery release***

◇ *The presidential candidate recently released an unaudited sheet on his wealth, which couldn't convince the public, for most of his other incomes were not included.* 总统候选人最近公布了其未经审计的财富报表，却不能说服公众，因为他的大部分其他收入不在其列。

relevant ['reləvənt] *adj.* 有关的；中肯的；有重大作用的

Phrase(s): ***relevant range; relevant works***

◇ *The relevant parameters for a normal distribution are the mean standard deviation.* 正态分布的相关参数是均值和标准差。4（5）

◇ *The housing tax reform is only relevant to low and middle-level incomers; and the tiny increase can't impact wealthy people at all.* 房地产税改革仅仅是和中低层收入者有关；微小的增加幅度根本不会影响有钱人。

relief [rɪ'li:f] *n.* 救济；减轻；解除；

Phrase(s): *capital relief; tax relief*

◇ *The Pillar 3 requirements must also be observed for banks to obtain capital relief in respect of any CRM techniques.* 任何风险缓释技术要获得资本减让，必须满足第三支柱所规定的要求。1（18）

◇ *The country agreed to stop its nuclear weapon development program in return for relief from economic sanctions.* 该国同意停止其核武器发展计划，以换取经济制裁的解除。

remaining [rɪ'meɪnɪŋ] *adj.* 剩下的；剩余的

Phrase(s): *remaining sum; remaining income*

◇ *Some fraction of the remaining principal in the mortgage pool is prepaid each month for the remaining term of the collateral.* 抵押债务组合中的一部分剩余本金每个月都在提前还款，这些剩余本金是以那些剩余抵押物为依托的。13（82）

◇ *With the sharp fall in oil price, there is an increasing chance that the country will have a high default risk on its billions of remaining debts.* 随着石油价格急剧下降，该国数十亿美元的剩余债务的违约风险越来越高。

remedy ['remɪdɪ] *vt.* 补救；治疗；纠正；*n.* 补救；治疗；赔偿

Phrase(s): *folk remedy; alternative remedy*

◇ *The only remedy for you to improve your poor credit is to make all kinds of payments on time; otherwise, it will impact you on any of your future loans.* 改善你不良信用的唯一补救办法是及时支付各种款项；否则，它会影响你未来的任何贷款请求。

remit [rɪ'mɪt] *vt.* 宽恕；免除；减轻；传送；使恢复原状；*vi.* 汇款；缓和；*n.* 移交的事物

Phrase(s): *remit money; remit profit*

◇ *Under each swap agreement, only the net amount due by the issuer or by the applicable swap counterparty, will be remitted on each payment date.* 每个互换合约中，只有发行方或者可适用的互换对手方的净金额才能被免除，并且只限于每个支付当期日当天。13（112）

◇ *The brokerage firm was levied heavy fine for not remitting required taxes from trading proceeds gained in overseas accounts.* 经纪公司因为没有为海外账户的交易收益

缴纳必需的税款，被处以高额罚款。

remote [rɪ'məʊt] *adj.* 遥远的；偏僻的；疏远的；*n.* 远程

Phrase(s): ***remote machine; remote indication***

◇ *Challenges to legal structure of the transaction happen only in remote contingencies such as bankruptcy.* 交易过程中法律机构面临的挑战只会在远程突发事件中发生，比如破产。13（143）

remove [rɪ'muːv] *vt.* 消除

Phrase(s): ***remove risk; remove noise***

◇ *Securitization can be used as a corporate risk management tool because it removes the credit risk and the interest rate risk associated with the assets sold to the SPV.* 资产证券化可以作为公司风险管理的一类工具，因为它消除了信用风险，同时也消除了那些卖给特殊目的机构的相关资产的利率风险。13（45）

remuneration [rɪˌmjuːnə'reɪʃ(ə)n] *n.* 报酬；酬劳；赔偿

Phrase(s): ***assessable remuneration; remuneration package***

◇ *On the manager side, hedge funds provide greater remuneration than traditional investment funds.* 从基金经理的角度出发，相较于传统的投资基金，对冲基金能够提供更高的报酬。

◇ *The company sold the drug sales right to another company, however, it received no financial remuneration when the counterparty increased the drug price dramatically.* 公司把该药品的销售权卖给了另一家公司，但是当交易对手大幅增加药品价格时，它却没有得到任何经济补偿。

repayment [riː'peɪm(ə)nt; rɪ'peɪm(ə)nt] *n.* 偿还；［金融］付还

Phrase(s): ***extended repayment; loan repayment***

◇ *A debt instrument is a contract that gives its owner the right to receive periodic interest payments and the repayment of the principal by the maturity date.* 一个债务工具是一种合约，它赋予拥有者获得定期利息以及到期收回本金的权利。5（32）

replacement [rɪ'pleɪsm(ə)nt] *n.* 更换；复位；

Phrase(s): ***replacement ratio; replacement assets***

◇ *Presettlement risk only arises when the contract's replacement cost has a positive value to the institution (i. e. , is in-the money).* 当机构的合同重置成本是正值的时候，交割日前风险才会出现。

◇ *The insurance company hit with heavy penalty because it kept some material risks of replacement variable annuities from its customers and misled them to buy the product for retirement benefit.* 保险公司面临高额罚款，因为欺瞒客户关于可变年金替代产品的一些重大风险，误导他们购买该产品作为退休金。

repo ['riːpəʊ] *n.* 回购债券协议

◇ *Repos play a critical role in the money markets. A repo is a combination of two transactions. In the first transaction, a security dealer sells securities it owns to an investor, agreeing to repurchase the securities at a specified higher price at a future date; in the second transaction, days or months later, the repo is unwound as the dealer buys back the securities from the investor.* 回购债券协议在货币市场上起着关键作用。一个回购债券协议包括两个交易：在第一个交易中，证券交易商将持有的债券卖给投资者，同意在未来的一天以特定的高价将债券购回；在第二个交易中，经过一段时间证券交易商回购债券，回购债券协议结束。10（5）

reprice [rɪ'praɪs] *vt.* 重新定价

◇ *The portfolio manager has access to pricing models that can be used to reprice the securities under various yield environments.* 投资组合经理可以利用价格模型，在多变的收益环境中去重新定价证券。

repurchase [ri'pɜːtʃəs] *n.* 买回；再买；再采购；*vt.* 买回；再买；再采购

Phrase(s): ***repurchase transaction; repurchase price***

◇ *Repurchasing company's own stock shares is only a short-year strategy to boost its value; the long-term measure is to boost sales and introduce more efficient products.* 回购自己公司的股票只是提升其价值的短期策略；长期措施还是促进销售并开发更有效的产品。

reputational risk [repjʊ'teɪʃ(ə)nl rɪsk] *PHR.* 信誉风险

Phrase(s): ***reputational risk assessments***

◇ *Reputational risk can be viewed as the damage, in addition to immediate monetary losses, caused to the ongoing business of an institution from a damaged reputation.* 除了立

即发生的金钱损失之外，信誉风险可以看作因为声誉的受损对正在进行的商业项目带来的破坏性。9（519）

resecuritization [resɪ'kjʊərɪtʌɪ'zeɪʃ(ə)n] *n.* 再证券化；再资产证券化

Phrase(s): ***resecuritization assets; mortgage resecuritization***

◇ *Resecuritization is an activity to package a number of existing securitized debt obligations into a new tradable security.* 再证券化是指将现有的多个证券化债务打包成一个新的可交易证券。

reserve [rɪ'zɜːv] *n.* 储备；储存；［金融］储备金；*vt.* 储备；保留；预约

Phrase(s): ***foreign reserve; reserve carreacy; reserve seats***

◇ *Disclosed reserves correspond to share premiums, retained profits, and general reserves.* 公开储备对应的是股票溢价、留存收益和一般准备。

◇ *Some governments in the world accumulate their foreign-exchange reserves via selling their financial assets.* 世界上的一些政府通过出售它们的金融资产积累它们的外汇储备。

reset [riː'set] *vi.* 重置；清零；*vt.* 重置；重新设定；重新组合

Phrase(s): ***reset time; automatic reset***

◇ *The terms of an interest rate agreement include the frequency of reset.* 利率协议条款应该包括重置的频率。13（116）

◇ *I wish I could hit the reset button so all of my impulsive expenses in the past would disappear.* 我多么希望可以按下重置按钮，过去那些一时冲动花出去的钱可以一笔勾销。

residential [rezɪ'denʃ(ə)l] *adj.* 住宅的；与居住有关的

Phrase(s): ***residential mortgage loans; residential property***

◇ *Income-producing real estate (IPRE) refers to a method of providing funding to real estate (such as, office buildings to let, retail space, multifamily residential buildings, industrial or warehouse space, and hotels) where the prospects for repayment and recovery on the exposure depend primarily on the cash flows generated by the asset.* 产生收入的房地产指的是为房地产（如用于出租的办公室建筑、零售场所、多户的住宅、工业和仓库场所及旅馆）提供资金的方法。这种融资方法下，贷款偿还及清偿的前景主要

依赖于资产创造的现金流。1（40）

residential mortgage [rezɪ'denʃ(ə)l 'mɔːgɪdʒ] *PHR.* 住宅抵押借款

Phrase(s): ***Residential Mortgage Trust***

◇ *Residential mortgage loans are the largest asset class that has been securitized in the United State.* 住房抵押贷款是美国最大的资产证券化类别。13（31）

◇ *In the case of qualifying residential mortgage loans, when such loans are past due for more than 90 days they will be risk weighted at 100%, net of specific provisions.* 对于合格的住房抵押贷款，如果其逾期 90 天以上，在扣减专项准备以后，其风险权重应当为 100%。 1（13）

residual [rɪ'zɪdjʊəl] *n.* 剩余；残渣；*adj.* 剩余的；残留的

Phrase(s): ***residual risk; residual equity; residual value***

◇ *In the early days of the CMO market, floating rate bond classes were sold as part of the residual interest bond class in a structure.* 在早期的抵押担保债券市场中，浮动利率的债券是被当作组合中的剩余利息债券出售的。13（76）

◇ *Nowadays, car lease is getting more and more popular among young people as they know cars don't have as much residual value as houses.* 如今，汽车租赁越来越受年轻人的欢迎，因为他们知道汽车没有像房子那么多的剩余价值。

responsible [rɪ'spɒnsɪb(ə)l] *adj.* 负责的；可靠的；有责任的

Phrase(s): ***responsible investigation; be responsible***

◇ *Governments which are in deep debts need to be fiscally responsible by adhering to spending cut and appropriate tax rise.* 深陷债务危机的政府需要财政上负责任，坚持削减开支和适当增税。

restrict [rɪ'strɪkt] *vt.* 限制；约束；限定

Phrase(s): ***restrict model; informal restrict***

◇ *Last year, people in Greece panicked when the government restricted the cash withdrawals from banks; in front of every bank there was a long line waiting to get their money before the restriction came into effect.* 去年希腊政府限制从银行提款时，民众一阵恐慌；每一个银行前面都排了长队，都是在限制生效前等待取钱的人。

retail ['ri:teɪl] *n.* 零售

Phrase(s): ***retail business; at retail***

◇ *A retail business that provides credit terms on sales of goods to its customers (i. e. , no need to pay immediately) incurs the risk of non-payment by some of those customers.* 给顾客提供信用（不需要立即支付）的零售行业面临它的某些顾客拒绝支付的风险。15（4）

◇ *Retail sales usually grow rapidly in summer as people spend more in hot days to make themselves comfortable.* 零售业销售通常在夏天增长迅速，因为人们在炎热的天气里花更多的钱来让自己舒服。

retail receivables ['ri:teɪl rɪ'si:vəblz] *PHR.* 零售应收账款

◇ *For purchased retail receivables, a bank must meet the risk quantification standards for retail exposures.* 对购入的零售应收账款，银行必须满足零售贷款的风险量化标准。1（65）

◇ *For eligible retail receivables, in common with the retail asset class, there is no distinction between a foundation and advanced approach.* 对合格的零售应收账款和零售资产相同，采用初级法和高级法没有区别。1（47）

retain [rɪ'teɪn] *v.* 留存

Phrase(s): ***retain earnings; retain profits***

◇ *The charity organization retained most of the voting seats in the board to ensure a large proportion of revenues would be used for its philanthropy missions.* 该慈善组织保留了在董事会的大部分投票席位，以确保大部分收入将用于慈善事业。

retention [rɪ'tenʃ(ə)n] *n.* 保留；扣留；滞留；记忆力

Phrase(s): ***retention period; retention index; retention ratio***

◇ *The third form of cash collateral is the retention of the excess spread discussed earlier.* 第三种形式的现金抵押是保留我们之前讨论过的息差的超出部分。13（88）

◇ *Recruiting qualified employees is a challenge to HR department; however, their retention in the company is even more challenging, but rewarding at the same time.* 招聘合格的员工是人力资源部的一个挑战；然而把人才留在在公司更具挑战性，同时也非常值得。

retrieval [rɪ'triːvl] *n.* 检索；恢复；取回；拯救

Phrase(s): ***retrieval data; retrieval system***

◇ *Many transportation tools are equipped with a data retrieval device for investigations if accidents happen.* 很多交通工具都配备了数据检索装置，如果事故发生方便调查。

return [rɪ'tɜːn] *n.* 收益率；退回；*v.* 返回；回报

Phrase(s): ***sales return; annual return***

◇ *The value associated with a 95% confidence level is a return of −15. 5 %.* 在 95% 的置信水平下收益率为－15. 5%。15（3）

◇ *The swimming athlete who was doping in last season can't return to international games until the ban on him is lifted.* 上个赛季服用兴奋剂的运动员直到解禁才能再参加国际比赛。

return on equity [rɪ'tɜːn ɒn 'ekwɪtɪ] *PHR.* 权益收益率

◇ *Return on equity (ROE) is a measure of how the stockholders fared during the year.* 权益收益率测度的是股票持有者这一年的收益。6（55）

revalue [riː'væljuː] *vt.* 再评价；对……重新估价

Phrase(s): ***financial revalue; revalue theory***

◇ *The housing market fluctuation forced the municipal government to revalue all the private properties in the city so undercharge or overcharge of property taxes could be avoided.* 房地产市场的波动迫使市政府对全市所有私人住宅进行重新评估，以避免财产税的过高征收或者征收不足。

revenue ['revənjuː] *n.* 税收；国家的收入；收益

Phrase(s): ***fiscal revenue; enterprise revenue***

◇ *2016 Rio Olympic Games is a great opportunity for Brazilian government to boost revenues through quality services in all aspects.* 2016 里约奥运会是巴西政府通过各方面的优质服务增加收入的好机会。

◇ *Four big state-owned banks took up 70% of the banking industry's domestic revenues.* 四大国有银行占据了 70% 的银行业国内收入。

reverse [rɪ'vɜːs] *n.* 背面；相反；倒退；失败；*vt.* 颠倒；倒转；*adj.* 反面的；颠倒的；反身的；*vi.* 倒退

Phrase(s): ***reverse proxy; reverse mortgage***

◇ *As an ordinary citizen, he is strongly opposed to undocumented immigrants; as a presidential candidate, he totally reversed his stance, promising that he would make immigration reforms as soon as he was elected.* 作为一个普通的公民，他强烈反对非法移民，作为一个总统候选人，他完全扭转了他的立场，承诺他会在他当选后进行移民改革。

◇ *Repo-style transactions include repurchase/reverse repurchase and securities lending/securities borrowing transactions.* 回购交易中的证券借贷包括回购 / 逆回购、证券借出 / 证券借入交易。

reversion [rɪ'vɜːʃ(ə)n] *n.* 回归；逆转

Phrase(s): ***mean reversion***

◇ *You can never depend on a stock's past performance to make your future investment decisions; for reversion theory told us that good return in the past could mean poor return in the future.* 你永远不能依靠一只股票的过去业绩来决定你的未来投资；因为回归理论告诉我们，过去好的回报可能意味着未来差的回报。

◇ *Note that this type of mean reversion does not imply forecast ability as the probability distribution of asset returns at time t + 1 is independent of the distribution at time t.* 请注意，这种向均值回归的形式不意味着可以进行预测，因为资产收益率在 t + 1 时刻的概率分布独立于在 t 时刻的概率分布。5（73）

revocable ['revəkəb(ə)l] *adj.* 可撤销的；可废除的

Phrase(s): ***revocable L/C; revocable offer***

◇ *Revocable: When the institution can still cancel the transfer without the consent of the counterparty.* 可撤销是指机构在没有征得交易对手同意的情况下可以取消交易。

revolving [rɪ'vɒlvɪŋ] *adj.* 循环的；周转的

Phrase(s): ***revolving credits; revolving funds***

◇ *All other securitised revolving exposures (i. e. those that are committed and all non-retail exposures) with controlled early amortisation features will be subject to a CCF of*

90% against the off-balance sheet exposures. 所有其他的具有控制型提前摊还特征的被证券化的循环风险暴露（如，那些承诺的和所有非零售的风险暴露），要对表外风险暴露使用 90% 的信用转换系数。1（111）

reward [rɪ'wɔːd] *n.* 收益

◇ *The HR manager proposed a good reward system which provided incentives to employees in every sector.* 人事经理提出了一个不错的奖励制度，给每个部门的员工提供激励机制。

reweighted ['ri'weɪtɪd] *adj.* 再加权的

Phrase(s): ***reweighted least squares***

◇ *A typical approach is to determine iteratively the weights through an iterative reweighted least squares (RLS) procedure.* 一个典型的确定迭代权重的方法是通过一个迭代的再加权最小二乘（RLS）的过程。5（443）

right [raɪt] *n.* 正确；右边；正义；权利

Phrase(s): ***pre-emptive right; ex-rights***

◇ *A financial asset is any asset that is cash, the right to receive cash or another financial asset; or the contractual right to exchange financial assets on potentially favourable terms, or an equity instrument.* 金融资产包括现金资产、获取现金或另一项金融资产的权利，还包括按照潜在有利条件交换金融资产的合同权利，以及股权工具。1（131）

rise [raɪz] *vi.* 上升；增强；起立；高耸；*vt.* 使……飞起；使……浮上水面

Phrase(s): ***pay rise; peaceful rise***

◇ *A borrower with an existing interest rate liability can protect against a rise in interest rates by purchasing a cap.* 债务人可以通过购买利率顶合约来对抗现有利率上升的责任。13（116）

risk [rɪsk] *n.* 风险

Phrase(s): ***financial risk; credit risk; market risk; risk taking***

◇ *We begin with agency products because it allows us to clearly demonstrate how the risk of the collateral of a pool of assets is redistributed amongst the different bond classes.* 我们从代理产品开始着手，因为代理产品可以让我们更清楚地展示一个资产池的抵

押物的风险是如何重新分配到不同的债权级别中的。13（16）

◇ *Risk taking refers specifically to the active assumption of incremental risk in order to generate incremental gains.* 风险承担指的是愿意承担额外风险来换取超额收益的行为。13（1）

risk appetite [rɪsk 'æpɪtaɪt] *PHR.* 风险偏好

◇ *Financial institutions should conduct regularly comprehensive exercises aimed at estimating risk appetite, using stress tests and a combination of qualitative and quantitative factors.* 金融机构应该定期进行全面的演习，利用压力测试以及定性和定量的组合来评估风险偏好。

risk capital [rɪsk 'kæpɪt(ə)l] *PHR.* 风险资本（指为投机性商业投资提供的资金）

◇ *Risk weighted assets for equity exposures in the trading book are subject to the market risk capital rules.* 交易账户上股权暴露的风险加权资产遵守市场风险资本规则。1（62）

risk exposure [rɪsk ɪk'spəʊʒə] *PHR.* 风险暴露

◇ *The model used must be able to capture adequately all of the material risks embodied in equity returns including both the general market risk and specific risk exposure of the institution's equity portfolio.* 采用的模型必须能充分计算所有体现在股权收益中的重要风险，包括一般的市场风险和银行股权组合的特殊风险。1（95）

risk-free return [rɪskfriː rɪ'tɜːn] *PHR.* 无风险回报

◇ *This difference between risky returns and risk-free returns is often called the excess return on the risky asset.* 风险收益和无风险收益之差常称为风险资产的超额收益。6（317）

◇ *One of the most significant observations of stock market data is this long-term excess of the stock return over the risk-free return.* 对股票市场最显著的观察是股票超过无风险回报的长期超额收益。6（317）

risk premium [rɪsk 'priːmɪəm] *PHR.* 风险溢价

◇ *The Sharpe ratio is calculated as the risk premium of the asset divided by the standard deviation.* 夏普比率等于风险溢价除以标准差。6（320）

risk weight [rɪsk weɪt] *PHR.* 风险加权因子

◇ *Supervisory authorities should increase the standard risk weight for unrated claims where they judge that a higher risk weight is warranted by the overall default experience in their jurisdiction.* 如果监管当局认为，本国公司的总体违约情况严重，应当规定更高的风险权重时，监管当局应当提高对未评级公司债权的标准风险权重。1（41）

risky ['rɪskɪ] *adj.* 有风险的

Phrase(s): ***risky loans; risky move***

◇ *Most illegal immigrants in the world took very risky ways such as long-distance swimming or huddling in an airtight cabin to the other side of the world.* 世界上大部分非法移民都是通过很危险的方式，如长距离游泳或挤在一个密封舱里到达世界的另一边。

RMSE(root mean squared error) [ru:t mi:n skwɛə 'erə] *abbr.* 均方根误差

◇ *To measure forecast errors, we use usual summary statistics based directly on the deviation between forecasts and realizations (actual values) such as the root mean squared error (RMSE), the mean absolute error (MAE) and the mean absolute percentage error (MAPE).* 为了度量预测误差，我们使用普通加和统计量，它们是基于预测值与现实值（实际值）偏差计算得到的，如均方根误差、平均绝对误差以及平均绝对百分比误差。5（332）

ROA(return on assets) [rɪ'tɜ:n ɒn 'æsets] *abbr.* 资产回报

◇ *In the past, performance was measured by yardsticks such as return on assets(ROA), which adjusts profits for the associated book value of assets, or return onequity (ROE), which adjusts profits for the associated book value of equity.* 过去，一般以资本回报率或是股本回报率去衡量投资表现。资本回报率以相关资产账面价值调整利润，股本回报率以相关股本账面价值调整利润。

robust [rə(ʊ)'bʌst] *adj.* 强健的；稳健的

Phrase(s): ***robust estimation; robust identification***

◇ *How can we make our models more robust, reducing model risk?* 我们如何才能使我们的模型更加稳健，减少的模型的风险？ 5（31）

◇ *Only with robust regulations can any investment market expect a sound development.* 任何投资市场只有具有健全的法规才能健康发展。

roll-out period ['rəʊlˌaʊt 'pɪərɪəd] *PHR.* 推广实施期

◇ *During the roll-out period, customers who place an order of more than 5 000 pieces will get a 20% discount.* 在产品推出期间，订购超过5 000件的客户将获得20%的折扣。

royalty ['rɔɪəltɪ] *n.* 专利权费；特许权使用费；版税

◇ *When the bonds matured in 2007, the royalty rights reverted back to David Bowie.* 当债券于2007年到期，特许使用权归还给大卫·鲍伊。13（3）

◇ *Part of the money that online streaming websites subscribers pay will go to songwriters or movie producers as royalties.* 在线流媒体网站用户所支付的钱中，一部分将作为版税付给歌曲作者或电影制作人。

RSI(Relative Strength Index) ['relətɪv streŋθ 'ɪndeks] *abbr.* 相对强弱指数

◇ *Relative strength index (RSI) is an extremely popular momentum oscillator that measures the speed and change of price movements.* 相对强弱指数是衡量价格运动的速度和改变方面应用较广的摆动指标。10（40）

◇ *RSI tends to fluctuate between 10 and 60 in a bear market with the 50–60 zone acting as resistance.* 相对强弱指数在空头市场中，会在10—60间波动，其中50—60的区间作为抵抗力。10（41）

ruin ['ruːɪn] *n.* 损失；崩溃；破产

Phrase(s): ***financial ruin; in ruins***

◇ *In financial applications, it is these tails that provide information about the potential for a financial fiasco or financial ruin.* 在金融领域的应用中，正是这些厚尾提供了有关潜在金融混乱和金融崩溃的信息。5（63）

◇ *Water, electricity and transportation systems have all been ruined in the war.* 水、电、交通系统都在战争中毁了。

run on a bank [rʌn ɒnə bæŋk] *PHR.* 银行挤兑；银行挤提

◇ *The realization that money market funds were at risk in the credit crisis led to a wave of investor redemptions similar to a run on a bank.* 由于认识到货币市场基金正面临着信用风险，导致了一波投资者进行赎回操作，就像银行挤兑一样。7（31）

S

sacrifice ['sækrɪfaɪs] *vt.* 亏本出售；牺牲

◇ *Long-term project quality has been sacrificed in return for an earlier completion.* 为了工程较早地完成，牺牲了项目长期的质量。

salary ['sælərɪ] *vt.* 给……加薪；给……薪水；*n.* 薪水

Phrase(s): ***basic salary; salary deduction; salary adjustment; salary earner; salary rate index***

◇ *This transnational company offers a very competitive employee benefit package, even including children education grant.* 这个跨国的公司提供了一整套非常有竞争力的员工福利，甚至包括子女教育补助。

salvage ['sælvɪdʒ] *n.* 救助；残余

Phrase(s): ***salvage agreement; salvage award; salvage by contract***

◇ *Salvage value is an estimated residual value of an asset when it is sold at the end of its useful life; and depreciation should be taken into consideration.* 残余价值是资产在使用寿命结束后出售时估计的剩余价值；应考虑折旧。

sample ['sɑːmp(ə)l] *vt.* 取样；尝试；抽样检查；*n.* 样品；样本；例子；*adj.* 试样的；样品的；作为例子的

Phrase(s): ***sample period; sample testing***

◇ *The data used to represent return distributions should reflect the longest sample period for which data is available and meaningful in representing the risk profile of the bank's specific equity holdings.* 估计的损失应该可靠，相对银行表示收益分布的数据，应该反映数据最长的样本期，而且数据在代表银行特殊持股风险轮廓方面有意义。1（95）

sanction ['sæŋ(k)ʃ(ə)n] *n.* 制裁

Phrase(s): ***legal sanction; economic sanction***

◇ *Legal sanctions will be imposed on principal shareholders if they intentionally violate the sincere obligation.* 大股东一旦故意违反诚信义务，将受到法律制裁。

Sarbanes-Oxley Act("Sarbox") ['sa:benzɒksli 'ækt] *PHR.* 萨班斯·奥克斯利法案

◇ *In essence, Sarbox makes company management responsible for the accuracy of the company's financial statements.* 本质上，萨班斯·奥克斯利法案促使公司管理对公司的财务状况负责。6（17）

satisfaction [sætɪs'fækʃ(ə)n] *n.* 赔偿；满意度

◇ *Customer satisfaction should be put in the first place in service industries to keep repeating customers and receive new ones.* 顾客满意度应放在服务行业的第一位；这样才能留住老顾客，迎接新顾客。

saving ['seɪvɪŋ] *n.* 节约；挽救；存款；*adj.* 节约的；挽救的；补偿的；保留的；*prep.* 考虑到；除……之外

Phrase(s): ***saving book; saving deposit; savings account***

◇ *Set aside some savings for diversified investments for they will award you more returns than your savings account does.* 留出一些储蓄进行多元化投资，它们会比你的储蓄账户带来更多的回报。

scenario [sɪ'nɑ:rɪəʊ] *n.* 情景

Phrase(s): ***scenario analysis; scenario planning***

◇ *A bank must use scenario analysis of expert opinion in conjunction with external data to evaluate its exposure to high severity events.* 银行必须对外部数据配合采用专家意见的情景分析，求出严重风险事件下的风险暴露。1（128）

schedule ['ʃɛdju:l] *n.* 附表；明细表；*vt.* 安排；给……定时间

Phrase(s): ***schedule of amortization; scheduled payment***

◇ *There is a new regulation that all the airline companies must give customers financial compensation if their flights are delayed based on the fixed schedule.* 新规要求：如果根据固定的时间表航班延误的话，所有的航空公司必须给予顾客经济补偿。

scope [skəʊp] *n.* 范围

Phrase(s): ***business scope; project scope; scope of application; scope of reporting***

◇ *Loans secured by a single or small number of condominium or co-operative residential housing units in a single building or complex also fall within the scope of the residential mortgage category.* 在一栋建筑或单元房中，由单户或几户共管的建筑做抵押或由合住的居民住宅单元房做抵押的贷款也属于住房抵押贷款的范畴。1（42）

scrip [skrɪp] *PHR.* 股息凭证；临时凭证

◇ *Scrip was originally used as a currency issued by a company in some specific industries or by military; and it can only be used in a small scope such as the company stores.* 临时凭证最初是某些特定行业或军方发行的货币；它只能被用在一个小的范围，如公司开的商店里。

◇ *Scrip issue leads to an increase int the number of shares held by existing shareholders, not the value of any shareholding.* 红股发行带来的是现有股东持有股份的增加，并不是股权价值的增加。

second ['sek(ə)nd] *adj.* 第二的；次要的；附加的；num. 第二；ad*v.* 第二；其次；居第二位

Phrase(s): ***second loss credit enhancement; second loss portion; second surplus re-insurance***

◇ *The housing credit mortgage will never be perfect without the second-class mortgage market.* 缺少二级市场的住房贷款抵押市场永远是不完整的市场。

◇ *With regard to banks first-to-default and second-to-default products in the trading book, the basic concepts developed for the banking book will also apply.* 银行账户适用的基本概念同样适用于交易账户的以下两类信用衍生产品：一是一组资产中第一项资产违约即算作整体违约的产品；二是一组资产中第二项资产违约即算作整体违约的产品。1（137）

sector ['sektə] *n.* 机构；行业

◇ *Along with the opening up of China's financial sector, the domestic banks are facing growing pressure of competition.* 伴随着我国金融行业的放开，银行业面临着越来越大的竞争压力。

secured [si'kjuəd] *adj.* 有担保的

Phrase(s): ***secured bonds; secured debenture; secured creditors***

◇ *With declining oil price in the global market, the country whose revenues greatly depend on oil export has to turn to international banks to secure its maturing bonds.* 随着石油价格在全球市场的下降，收入在很大程度上取决于石油出口的国家只能求助于国际上的银行，贷款来偿付到期的债券。

securitization [sɪkjʊərɪtʌɪ'zeɪʃ(ə)n] *n.* 证券化；资产证券化

Phrase(s): ***existing asset securitization; future flow securitization***

◇ *A securitization differs from these traditional forms of financing in several important ways.* 资产证券化（产品）和传统融资形式在许多重要方面存在不同。13（6）

◇ *The securitization of auto loans has an uptrend in the U. S. ; however, the percentage of subprime loans are also increasing at the same time, which will cause risks of delinquency.* 汽车贷款证券化已在美国呈上升趋势；然而次级贷款的比例也同时在增加，这将导致债务拖欠的风险。

security [sɪ'kjʊərətɪ] *n.* 证券；抵押品

◇ *Major TV stations around the world all have a percentage of reports on securities market changes on their hourly news time.* 世界各地的主要电视台在整点新闻时间都有一定比例的报道针对证券市场变化。

◇ *The characteristic line of a security is the regression of the excess returns of that security on the market excess returns.* 证券的特征线即是该证券的超额收益对市场超额收益的回归。

seed capital [siːd 'kæpɪt(ə)l] *PHR.* 原始资本；种子资本

Phrase(s): ***seed capital loans; seed capital fund***

◇ *Typically, those who demand a bigger piece of the pie are the inventor/founders who put up more seed capital, and serial entrepreneurs who bring a track record.* 一般来说，要

求分到更大块蛋糕的是提供较多种子资金的发明者 / 创始人，以及业绩良好的连续创业的企业家。

self [self] *n.* 自我；自身

Phrase(s): ***self financing; self insurance; self retention***

◇ *The town decided to self finance its new gymnasium through a referendum.* 通过全民投票，这个镇决定自筹资金来建造新体育馆。

sell off [sel ɒf] *PHR.* 变现；抛售

◇ *By relying primarily on short-term loans for their funding, these firms needed to constantly refinance their positions, or else face the necessity of quickly selling off their less liquid asset portfolios, which would be difficult in times of financial stress.* 通过主要依赖于短期贷款来筹集资金，这些公司需要经常进行再融资，否则面临将它们流动性差的资产迅速变现的必要性，这个在融资压力下是很困难的。

sequestrate ['siːkwəstreɪt] *vt.* 没收；扣押；*n.* 扣押资产；假扣押

Phrase(s): ***sequestrated account***

◇ *When the union refused to pay its fine, an order was made to sequestrate the union's assets but it was found that they had been transferred abroad.* 当全国矿工工会拒绝支付罚款时，法院命令扣押该工会的资产，但法院发现工会资产已被转移到国外。

service ['sɜːvɪs] *n.* 服务

Phrase(s): ***service debt; service fees; service payment***

◇ *Large state-owned enterprises really should service their huge debts before borrowing more from banks.* 大型国有企业在向银行进一步贷款之前确实应该先偿还之前的巨额债务。

settlement ['set(ə)lm(ə)nt] *n.* 清算；结算

Phrase(s): ***daily settlement; bank for international settlement (BIS)***

◇ *It cost the car manufacturer an arm and a leg to reach a settlement with their customers for the cars with emission defects.* 由于汽车排放设备缺陷，这个汽车制造商耗费大量钱财才和顾客达成和解。

◇ *Banks' activities are basically divided into eight business lines: corporate finance, trading & sales, retail banking, commercial banking, payment & settlement, agency services, asset management, and retail brokerage.* 银行的业务基本分为 8 个产品线：公司金融、交易和销售、零售银行业务、商业银行业务、支付和清算、代理服务、资产管理和零售经纪。

settlor ['setlə] *n.* 财产授予者；信托人

Phrase(s): ***settler settlor; trust settlor***

◇ *A revocable trust is one in which assets are owned by the trustee, but the settlor reserves a power of revocation.* 可撤销信托就是一种受托人拥有财产而委托人保留撤销受托人资格的权利的信托。

share [ʃeə] *n.* 股份

Phrase(s): ***share price; share placement; share purchase***

◇ *Value of stocks in high-tech industry is generally volatile due to fierce competition and short life span of new products; some stocks could drop to $1dollar a share from its original $20 dollars a share.* 由于激烈的竞争和新产品周期短，高科技产业的股票价值波动性很大；一些股票可能从原来的 20 美元每股跌至 1 美元每股。

shell company [ʃel 'kʌmp(ə)nɪ] *PHR.* 空壳公司；控股公司

Phrase(s): ***shell-company stock***

◇ *Shell companies sometimes are used as a tax evasion vehicle or facilitate fund raising in different ways.* 空壳公司有时被用来作为逃税的工具或者促进多渠道筹集资金。

short [ʃɔːt] *v.* 卖出；做空；*adj.* 空方的；空头的；短期的

Phrase(s): ***short hedge; short position***

◇ *A short hedge is appropriate when the hedger already owns an asset and expects to sell it at some time in the futures.* 空头对冲适用于对冲者现在持有资产并期望在未来某时间将其出售的情况。16（48）

◇ *In no event can a short-term rating be used to support a risk weight for an unrated long-term claim.* 在任何情况下，都不能使用短期评级支持未评级长期债权的风险权重。1（16）

sight [saɪt] *adj.* 见票即付的；即席的

Phrase(s): ***sight draft; sight bill; at sight***

◇ *The company wanted to persuade its investors that there was no recession in sight by disclosing the third quarter financial report and good credit rating result.* 公司想要说服投资者近期并没有衰退的迹象；它披露了第三季度财务报告和良好的信用评级结果。

significance [sɪɡ'nɪfɪk(ə)ns] *n.* 显著性

Phrase(s): ***significance test; level of significance***

◇ *The t-statistics of the betas are statistically significant for all levels of significance.* β 的 t 统计值在各（显著性）水平下都显著。5（175）

◇ *The full significance of multinational cooperation in combating tax avoidance worldwide is quite apparent now.* 在打击避税问题上实行跨国合作的充分意义现在已经很明显了。

silver currency ['sɪlvə 'kʌr(ə)nsɪ] *PHR.* 银制流通货币；银本位

◇ *In global monetary market, silver currency is suddenly reverting to its historical role as a hedge against high inflation, just like gold. The increasing demand of silver makes silver mining business boom again.* 在全球货币市场上，银货币突然还原为对冲高通胀的历史角色，就像金子一样。白银需求的增加使银矿业再次繁荣。

skewness ['skjuːnɪs] *n.* 偏态

Phrase(s): ***negative skewness; positive skewness***

◇ *A popular measure for the asymmetry of a distribution is called its skewness.* 对于分布的对称性，一种常用的描述方式称之为偏态分布。5（40）

◇ *A negative skewness measure indicates that the distribution is skewed to the left; that is, compared to the right tail, the left tail is elongated.* 负的偏态值表示这个分布（在图形上）偏向左侧；即，相比（分布图形）右尾，它的左尾更加瘦长。5（40）

small-firm effect [smɔːlf'ɜːm ɪ'fekt] *PHR.* 小公司效应

◇ *Small-firm effect means that in the stock market with firms in all sizes, firms with small market capitalizations could perform better than large corporations due to their growing potential and low stock prices.* 小公司效应指的是在公司规模各异的股票市场中，由于其成长潜力和较低的股票价格，小市值的公司可能比大型企业表现更好。

soft market [sɒft 'mɑːkɪt] *PHR.* 疲软市场

Phrase(s): ***soft (oversupplied) market***

◇ *Steel business has been experiencing soft market conditions for several years in China; overcapacity and capacity dispersion are two main reasons.* 中国钢铁行业已经经历了几年的疲软状况；产能过剩和产能分散是两个主要原因。

sole proprietorship [səʊl prə'praɪətəʃɪp] *PHR.* 独资所有制（公司）

◇ *A sole proprietorship pays no corporate income taxes.* 个人独资公司不需要支付公司所得税。6（4）

◇ *The life of the sole proprietorship is limited by the life of the sole proprietor.* 独资公司的寿命受独资所有人寿命所限制。6（4）

solvency ['sɒlvənsɪ] *n.* 偿付能力；溶解力

Phrase(s): ***solvency ratio; solvency risk***

◇ *The profit rate is fixed in order to make VaR compatible with an almost certain solvency.* 确定利润率以便在险价值与一个可确定的偿付能力相匹配。10（56）

◇ *Most developing countries in the world are facing medical care and social security solvency problems in the long run.* 大多数发展中国家都面临着医疗和社会保障的长期偿付能力问题。

solvent ['sɒlv(ə)nt] *adj.* 有偿付能力的

◇ *It's still hard to say whether the social security would be solvent with the help of the retirement delay policy; for retirement delay would bring other problems if there is no increase in job posts.* 退休延迟政策能否解决社会保障偿付能力的问题仍然很难说；因为如果工作岗位没有增加，退休延迟还会带来其他问题。

specie ['spiːʃiː; 'spiːʃɪ] *n.* 硬币；铸币

Phrase(s): ***specie par; specie reserve; specie shipment***

◇ *Bitcoin specie coin can be used and exchanged as real currency in some markets in the world; no matter how the market will be in the future, these coins at least can keep their value as silver metals.* 比特币硬币在世界上的一些市场可以作为真正的货币来使用和交换；不管这个市场将来如何，这些硬币至少可以保住其银金属的价值。

speculate ['spekjʊleɪt] *vi.* 推测；投机；

Phrase(s): ***speculative bubble; speculate crisis***

◇ *Derivatives also can be used to take highly speculative positions.* 衍生证券也可以

被用来进行高度投机的活动。

speculative ['spekjʊlətɪv] *adj.* 投机的

◇ *The revenues of online streaming networks depend on the increase of subscribers, otherwise, any stock value rise is just a speculative play.* 在线流媒体网络的收入取决于用户的增加，否则，任何股票价值的上升只是一个投机游戏。

split [splɪt] *n.* 拆分；拆股

Phrase(s): ***stock split; expense split***

◇ *The government is currently facing a split economy with retail sales and jobs increasing, while the lower demand in overseas market and a strong domestic currency negatively impact the exports.* 政府目前面临经济分化；零售销售和就业增加，但较低的海外市场需求和强劲的国内货币对出口产生负面影响。

spot [spɒt] *n.* 现货；*adj.* 现时的

Phrase(s): ***spot price; spot rate***

◇ *The spot price should equal the futures price for a very short maturity contract.* 对于一个期限很短的合约来说，现价应该等于期货价格。16（54）

spread [spred] *n.* 利息差价幅度；外汇买卖差价

Phrase(s): ***spread of risk***

◇ *A yield curve depicts yield differences, or yield spreads, that are due solely to differences in maturity.* 收益率曲线描述收益率差异，或仅仅是由于到期期限差异引起的到期收益率价差。10（95）

SPV (special purpose vehicle) ['speʃ(ə)l 'pɜːpəs 'viːɪk(ə)l] *abbr.* 特殊目的载体（资产证券化核心角色）

◇ *The capital structure of the SPV can involve just one bond class or several bond classes with different priorities on the cash flow from the collateral.* SPV 的资本结构可能包含仅仅一个债券级别，或是包含多个拥有不同（抵押贷款）现金流优先级的债券级别。13（12）

stag [stæg] *n.* 非正规证券商；炒买炒卖；新股套利者；投机认股者

◇ *Stags buy newly-issued stock shares at a large quantity, and then sell them quickly to make a profit; they are speculators making money from short-term market movements.* 新

股套利者大量购买新发行的股票，然后迅速卖掉它们以获利；他们是靠市场的短期波动来赚钱的投机者。

stamp duty [stæmp 'dju:tɪ] *PHR.* 印花税

◇ *Stamp duty is tax levied on all kinds of documents required in business activities; in some countries, income from stamp duty all goes to the central government.* 印花税是对经营活动所需的各种文件所征收的税；在一些国家，印花税的收入全部归于中央政府。

stand-by credit ['stændbaɪ 'kredɪt] *PHR.* 备用信用证

Phrase(s): ***stand-by credit line; stand-by credit facilities***

◇ *With opening a stand-by credit, the bank promises to pay the beneficiary if the bank's customer fails to accomplish something previously agreed in the contract with the counterparty.* 开立备用信用证，银行即承诺，如果银行的客户未能完成之前与交易对手在合同中约定的义务，银行将代为付款给受益人。

stock [stɒk] *n.* 股份；股票

Phrase(s): ***common stock; preferred stock; stock exchange***

◇ *An individual might purchase shares of stock anticipating that the future proceeds from the shares will justify both the time that her money is tied up as well as the risk of investment.* 购买股票时，投资者期望该股票的未来收益能够平衡其在投资期间的资金沉淀及其投资风险。

straight line depreciation ['streɪt laɪn ˌdɪpri:ʃɪ'eɪʃ(ə)n] *PHR.* 直线折旧法

Phrase(s): ***straight-line depreciation rate***

◇ *Companies typically use accelerated depreciation for their taxes and straight-line depreciation for their stockholders'books.* 公司通常在《告股东书》中使用加速折旧来计算它们的税收和直线折旧。6（232）

stub [stʌb] *n.* 存根；票根

Phrase(s): ***checkbook stub***

◇ *In securities market, a stub usually refers to the leftover part of stocks in a conversion from the parent security or other undesirable events such as recapitalization and bankruptcy.* 在证券市场上，票根通常是指从母股中转移或其他不良事件如重组和破产发生时股票的剩余部分。

sublease [sʌb'liːs] *n.* 转租；*vt.* 将……转租出去

Phrase(s): ***sublease agreement; sublease underlease; standard sublease***

◇ *While leasing factory buildings to raise fund for other investment, the company also needs to sublease large equipment so the buildings can be of practical use.* 租赁厂房为其他投资筹集资金的同时，该公司还需要将大型设备进行转租才能让厂房发挥实际用处。

◇ *Against the will of the land donor, the city government subleased part of the public park to a private school and transferred the lease right of another part to an entity.* 市政府违背了土地捐赠者的遗嘱，把公共公园的一部分转租给了一个私立学校，把另一部分的租赁权转让给了一家实体。

subprime [ˌsʌb'praɪm] *adj.* 次级的；*n.* 次级贷款

Phrase(s): ***subprime loan; subprime borrower***

◇ *Loans to borrowers of lower credit quality of default are classified as subprime loans and the borrowers are referred to as subprime borrowers.* 那些借给信用水平更低(的借款人）的贷款，可被分为次级贷款，这些借款人则称为次贷借款人。13（21）

◇ *Starting with a down payment as low as nothing and a poor credit history, these subprime borrowers have no ability to cope with the housing market volatility.* 从低到几乎没有的首付和一个不良的信用记录开始，这些次级借款人根本没有能力应付住房市场的波动性。

subrogation [ˌsʌbrə'geɪʃ(ə)n] *n.* 债权移转；权益取代；代位追偿原则（保险业）

Phrase(s): ***subrogation release; loss subrogation***

◇ *In insurance industry, the insurance companies of both parties in an accident are involved in the negotiation of payment and responsibility settlement. This process is called subrogation.* 在保险业中，事故双方的保险公司都参与支付和责任解决的谈判。这个过程被称为代位求偿权。

subscription [səb'skrɪpʃ(ə)n] *n.* 订金；认购；认股；订阅

Phrase(s): ***subscription price; capital subscription; subscription list***

◇ *Some prestigious newspapers and magazines have replaced paper print with digital version; this transformation partly led to a subscription decline since digital versions can easily spread for free.* 一些著名的报纸和杂志都用电子版取代了纸质版；这种转变部

分地导致订阅人数下降，因为数字版本可以很容易地免费传播。

subsidiary [səb'sɪdɪərɪ] *n.* 子公司

Phrase(s): *quoted subsidiary; subsidiary products*

◇ *In order to concentrate on the core businesses, the company decided to sell its several subsidiaries.* 为了集中精力在核心业务上，公司决定出售旗下多家子公司。

substandard [sʌb'stændəd] *adj.* 不合规格的；次级的

◇ *The online retail giant is under investigation for selling fake and substandard products.* 这个网上零售巨头因为销售假冒伪劣产品正在接受调查。

subvention [səb'venʃ(ə)n] *n.* 津贴；补助金；援助

Phrase(s): *discretionary subvention; recurrent subvention; unit subvention*

◇ *Beside salary, all the members in the medical aid team to Africa will be granted a monthly subvention during their service term.* 除了工资，赴非医疗援助队的所有成员在他们的服务期内将获得每月补助。

sum [sʌm] *n.* 总数；金额；总金额

Phrase(s): *sum deductible; sum due; sum in our favour; total sum*

◇ *This means that each point of the yield curve constitutes the sum of the current yield curve value and a relative base point shift of the respective yield curve point.* 这意味着收益率曲线的每一个点构成了当前的收益率曲线值的总和以及相对基础点的变换。

6（221）

summons ['sʌm(ə)nz] *n.* 传票

Phrase(s): *interpleader summons; default summons*

◇ *When a summons came to me from the court saying I had been sued by a payday lender, I panicked! Because I had never heard of it.* 当法院发来传票说我被一个发薪日贷款机构起诉时，我惊慌失措！因为我从来没有听说过这个机构。

sunk cost [sʌŋk kɒst] *PHR.* 沉没成本；已支付成本

Phrase(s): *sunk fixed cost; sunk-cost investment; Sunk-Cost Effect*

◇ *Generally speaking, sunk cost will not change greatly for a period of time in the future, such as six-month rent and new equipment purchase.* 一般来说，沉没成本在未来一段时间内不会发生很大的变化，如 6 个月的租金和新设备的购买等。

superannuation ['sju:pər͵ænju'eiʃən] *n.* 退休金

Phrase(s): ***superannuation fund; superannuation scheme***

◇ *The government got billions of funds from environmental groups and charity organizations for green energy development, including a superannuation fund. These groups are all concerned about the negative impacts caused by carbon emission.* 政府收到了来自环保团体和慈善组织数十亿美元的资金用于绿色能源开发，包括一个养老基金。这些团体都关心碳排放造成的负面影响。

supervise ['su:pəvaɪz] *vt. & vi.* 监督；管理；指导

Phrase(s): ***financial supervise***

◇ *They elect a board of directors that in turn hires and supervises the management of the firm.* 他们选出了执行董事会，执行董事会再去雇佣和监督企业的管理人员。

surcharge ['sɜ:tʃɑ:dʒ] *n.* 额外费；*vt.* 追加罚款

Phrase(s): ***import surcharge; deviation surcharge; capital surcharge***

◇ *Currently in China, if you withdraw money from an ATM machine which belongs to another bank's network, then you need to pay a surcharge fee for each transaction.* 目前在中国，如果你从另一家银行系统网络的 ATM 机上取钱，那么你需要为每次交易支付跨行手续费。

◇ *The bank recently joined Allpoint Network, which provides worldwide customers with surcharge-free ATMs service; many banks had signed agreements to cooperate with this network.* 该银行最近加入了 Allpoint 联盟，为全球客户提供免跨行手续费的 ATM 机服务；许多银行已和 Allpoint 网络签署合作协议。

surety ['ʃʊərɪtɪ] *n.* 担保；保证；保证人

Phrase(s): ***Surety Company; the surety; find surety***

◇ *In a case of a surety promising to pay back the debt for another person under certain circumstances, a written contract is required.* 如果一个担保人承诺在一定情况下替另一个人偿还债务，则必须订立书面合同。

surplus ['sɜ:pləs] *n.* [贸易] 顺差；盈余；过剩

Phrase(s): ***budget surplus; appraisal surplus; earned surplus***

◇ *While red dates from Xinjiang are in great demand, the same products from Shan'xi province are in surplus; this imbalanced economic structure should be improved.* 新疆红枣需求量很大的同时，陕西红枣却出现过剩；这种不平衡的经济结构应该改进。

◇ *Apple growers have to leave their big red apples on the trees to rot due to a marketing agreement in fruit industry.* 由于水果行业的一个营销协议，苹果农们只得让又大又红的苹果烂在树上。

surrender [sə'rendə] *vt.* 解约；屈服

Phrase(s): *surrender charges; surrender option*

◇ *Fragile investors are ready to surrender at the first downturn in the market, but persistent investors will hold stocks in hand as a long-term investment despite ups and downs.* 脆弱的投资者在市场的第一个低迷期就准备投降，但持续的投资者将手中股票作为长期投资，尽管市场跌宕起伏。

surtax ['sɜ:tæks] *n.* 附加税；*vt.* 对……征收附加税

Phrase(s): *Import Surtax; Medicare Surtax; punitive surtax*

◇ *A certain percentage of surtax will be imposed on people whose investments income is exceeding a set threshold; this is an effective measure to balance the distribution of social wealth.* 对投资收入超过设定门槛的人征收一定比例的附加税；这是平衡社会财富分配的有效措施。

suspension [sə'spenʃ(ə)n] *n.* 暂时吊销

Phrase(s): *suspension of trading*

◇ *It was such a pity that she can't take part in the 2016 Rio Olympic Games because of the two-year suspension for doping.* 因为服用兴奋剂被禁赛两年，很遗憾她不能参加2016年在巴西里约热内卢举行的奥运会了。

◇ *He got a three-year suspension of the financial adviser's license for misleading clients to buy subprime bonds.* 由于误导客户购买次级债券，他财务顾问的执照将被吊销三年。

sustain [sə'steɪn] *vt.* 维持；承担；供养

Phrase(s): *sustain losses; sustain development;sustain technique*

◇ *There is no sign of a sustained growth in housing prices in small cities because most young people who were born there choose not to go back after graduating from colleges in big cities.* 小城市的房价没有持续增长的迹象，因为大多数在那里出生的年轻人到大城市上大学，毕业以后就选择不回去了。

◇ *The restructuring of the energy industry will sustain a long-term healthy economic development.* 重组能源行业将保持经济长期健康发展。

swap [swɒp] *n.* 互换掉期；*vt.* 互换交易

Phrase(s): ***swap transaction; rate swap; swap deposit***

◇ *In parallel to the CDO markets, the market in credit default swaps also exploded in this period.* 与 CDO 市场相同，这段时期内信用违约掉期市场也在爆发。

◇ *A swap happens when two parties agree to exchange a fixed-rate payment for a floating rate; compared with treasury bonds, swaps usually have higher yields.* 利率掉期交易发生在双方同意用固定利率支付交换浮动利率；与国债相比，掉期通常具有较高的收益率。

switch trading [swɪtʃ 'treɪdɪŋ] *PHR.* 转手贸易；转口贸易

◇ *Switch trading improves flexibility and efficiency in barter or counter trade, however, since a third party is involved, the procedures are quite complex.* 转手贸易提高了易物交易或对等交易的灵活性和效率，但是由于第三方的参与，程序相当复杂。

syndic ['sɪndɪk] *n.* 经理人；理事

◇ *Syndic, in business world, is quite similar to managers or directors. A syndic is responsible for managing corporate affairs.* 理事，在商业领域，与管理者和董事们的职务很相似。理事负责管理公司事务。

syndicate ['sɪndɪkət] *n.* 辛迪加；企业联合；财团；*vi.* 联合成辛迪加；组成企业联合组织；*vt.* 把……联合成辛迪加；在多家报刊上同时发表

Phrase(s): ***Syndicate Loan; selling syndicate; undertaking syndicate;underwriting syndicate***

◇ *His syndicate of smuggling basic commodities in Africa has been booming for a decade due to higher costs of official route.* 由于官方路线成本较高，其在非洲走私基本商品的集团已经蓬勃发展了十年。

◇ *If an individual can't handle a big transaction, he may form a syndicate with other investors or institutional investors to set up an assets pool.* 如果单个投资者不能应对大的

交易，他可能会与其他投资者或机构投资者联合起来，建立一个资产池。

systematically important financial institution (SIFI) [ˌsɪstə'mætɪklɪ ɪm 'pɔːt(ə)nt faɪ'nænʃ(ə)l ɪnstɪ'tjuːʃ(ə)n] *PHR.* 系统重要性金融机构

◇ *The systematically important financial institutions need a different regulatory system to match with；SIFIs have higher minimum capital requirement for future material failures.* 系统重要性金融机构需要实行特别的监管制度；为了应对未来重大失误，要求系统重要性金融机构具备更高的最低资本要求。

systematic risk [sɪstə'mætɪk rɪsk] *PHR.* 系统性风险

◇ *This new financial model was brimming with systemic risk, a potential breakdown of the financial system when problems in one market spill over and disrupt others.* 这个新的金融系统充满了系统性风险，当一个市场的问题溢出并且影响其他市场时，这就造成金融系统潜在的崩溃。

T

Tag-Along Rights [tægə'lɒg raɪts] *PHR.* 跟随权

◇ *Tag-Along Rights are intended to protect minority shareholders' interests in capital deals; with the rights, they are allowed to follow the majority's practice and enjoy better prices which can only be achieved by major stockholders.* 跟随权的目的是在资本交易中保护小股东的利益；他们被允许追随大股东的做法，并享受只能由大股东来实现的更好的交易价格。

takeover ['teɪkəʊvə] *n.* （通过购买或交换股票等方式实现对企业的）吞并；收买；接收；吞并垄断

Phrase(s): ***hostile takeover; takeover bid; takeover offer***

◇ *Facing the stock value declining, the company could have competitive rivals in the coming takeover business.* 面对股票价值下跌，该公司可能在未来收购业务中遇到有力的竞争对手。

tangible asset ['tæn(d)dʒɪb(ə)l 'æset] *PHR.* 有形资产

Phrase(s): ***tangible current asset; tangible movable asset; tangible fixed asset***

◇ *A tangible asset is an object you can see, feel or touch; it can either be a fixed asset like land or a current asset like inventory.* 有形资产是您能够看到、感觉到或触摸到的对象。它可以是一个固定资产如土地或流动资产如存货。

target ['tɑːgɪt] *n.* 目标；靶子

Phrase(s): ***target language; target market***

◇ *The CEO resigned because he didn't reach the company's target to achieve a 10% annual revenue growth.* 因为没有达到公司制定的 10% 的年收入增长目标，首席执行官辞职了。

tariff ['tærɪf] *n.* 关税表；收费表；*vt.* 定税率；征收关税

Phrase(s): ***import tariff; tariff barrier; tariff rate; export tariff; tariff policy***

◇ *Governments in weak economies may use political power to impose protectionist tariffs on imported goods; in the global market, this will have negative impacts as a whole.* 政府在经济疲软时，可能利用政治权力对进口商品征收保护性关税；在全球市场上，这将带来整体性的负面影响。

tax [tæks] *n.* 税金；重负

Phrase(s): ***tax avoidance; tax revenue; tax heaven***

◇ *Other examples of availability criteria include: restrictions on transferability due to regulatory constraints, to tax implications and to adverse impacts on external credit assessment institutions' ratings.* 其他可用性标准包括：监管规定、税收政策以及外部信用评级机构的评级的不利影响对可转换性产生限制。1（3）

taxable ['tæksəbl] *adj.* 应纳税的；可征税的

Phrase(s): ***taxable income***

◇ *Fifteen percent will be charged on your taxable income.* 在你的应征税的收入中将征收 15% 的所得税。6（64）

◇ *The Federal Reserve has set ranges for family incomes and individual incomes; if your income has exceeded this range, then the interest earned from other investments is taxable.* 美联储对家庭收入和个人收入设置了范围；如果你的收入已经超过了这个范围，其他投资所得的利息必须纳税。

taxable gain ['tæksəbl geɪn] *PHR.* 应课税收益

Phrase(s): ***taxable gain or loss***

◇ *Taxable gains for assets are taxed at different rates according to the length of holding time; usually you need to pay the tax when you sell the assets.* 对资产应税收益征税，根据资产持有时间的长短税率不等；通常在你出售资产时才需要缴纳收益税。

tax haven [tæks 'heɪv(ə)n] *PHR.* 避税天堂（税率很低的国家或地区）

Phrase(s): ***tax-haven; tax haven jurisdiction***

◇ *Avoiding taxes by setting up subsidiaries in tax heaven countries has posed serious threat to government authority and caused disorderly and unfair competition in global market.* 在避税天堂国家设立子公司来逃税，严重威胁政府的权威，造成全球市场无序的、不公平的竞争。

T-bill ['tiːbil] *n.* 短期国库债券

Phrase(s): ***T-bill rate; T-Bill Futures; T-bill Futures Contract***

◇ *Treasury bills or T-bills are quite attractive to investors pursuing for short-term return; besides, the interest has been prepaid to you as the difference between your purchase price and the face value of the bills.* 国库券或国债对追求短期回报的投资者很有吸引力；此外，你的购买价格和债券面值的差额就等于提前支付给你的利息。

technical ['teknɪk(ə)l] *adj.* 工艺的；科技的；技术上的；专门的

Phrase(s): ***technical parameters; technical information***

◇ *Since release of the QIS 3 Technical Guidance, the Committee has spent considerable time refining its proposals for the New Accord.* 在公布了 QIS 3 技术指导文件后，委员会花了大量的时间对新协议的规定进行修改。1（12）

telecommunication [ˌtelɪkəmjuːnɪ'keɪʃ(ə)n] *n.* 电讯

Phrase(s): ***telecommunication network; telecommunication satellite***

◇ *Project finance is usually for large, complex and expensive installations that might include, for example, power plants, chemical processing plants, mines, transportation infrastructure, environment, and telecommunications infrastructure.* 项目融资通常针对大型、复杂且昂贵的设备，比如它可能包括电厂、化学品加工厂、矿山、交通基础设施、环境和电讯基础设施。1（40）

temporarily ['temp(ə)r(ər)ɪlɪ] adv. 临时地，临时

Phrase(s): ***extinguished temporarily; temporarily relieves***

◇ *The economic measures make things temporarily worse, yet, they will stimulate exports and lower inflation rate in the long run.* 经济措施让事情暂时恶化，然而长远来看，将会刺激出口并降低通胀率。

tender ['tendə] *vi.* 投标

Phrase(s): ***tender for; open tender; tender offer; legal tender***

◇ *Firstly, a tender notice is released to public; then any interested bidder are supposed to submit their tenders; next step will be evaluations of all the tenders; finally, a contract will be signed between the tenderer and the tenderee.* 首先，招标公告公开发布；然后有兴趣的投标人应提交标书；下一步将评估所有标书；最后，被招标人和招标人签订合同。

term [tɜːm] *n.* 术语；学期；期限；条款

Phrase(s): ***short term; long term; financial terms***

◇ *African countries need long term investments from developed countries or emerging markets for infrastructure construction.* 非洲国家需要来自发达国家或者新兴市场的长期投资进行基础设施建设。

terminable ['tɜːmɪnəb(ə)l] *adj.* 可终止的；有期限的

Phrase(s): ***terminable contract; terminable interest***

◇ *The transaction is governed by documentation specifying that if the counterparty fails to satisfy an obligation to deliver cash or securities or to deliver margin or otherwise defaults, then the transaction is immediately terminable.* 交易由文件具体说明，如交易对象不能按规定给付现金、证券、保证金或违约，则交易立即终止。1（28）

terminal value ['tɜːmɪn(ə)l 'væljuː] *PHR.* 终值

Phrase(s): ***terminal stabilized value; terminal salvage value; terminal value control***

◇ *Terminal value of securities can be influenced by many factors such as term of maturity, interest rate and market volatility.* 证券的终值受到期期限、利率和市场波动性等因素的影响。

term sheet [tɜːm ʃiːt] *PHR.* 条款清单；条款说明书

Phrase(s): ***term sheet; revenue sharing term sheet; credit approved term sheet***

◇ *Before sign on the contract, please read the term sheet carefully, especially the tax rules.* 在合同上签字前，请仔细阅读条款，特别是税收规定。

threshold ['θreʃəʊld] *n.* 入口；门槛；开始；极限；临界值

Phrase(s): ***academic threshold; threshold amount***

◇ *Subject to national discretion, supervisors may allow banks, as a failsafe, to substitute total assets of the consolidated group for total sales in calculating the SME threshold and the firm-size adjustment.* 按照各国自己的决定，监管当局允许银行在计算中小企业标准和进行企业规模调整时，用并表的集团总资产代替总销售。1（50）

◇ *The maximum aggregated retail exposure to one counterpart cannot exceed an absolute threshold of € 1 million.* 对单一客户总的零售风险暴露的绝对金额最大不能超过 100 万欧元。1（11）

timeliness ['taimlinis] *n.* 及时；时间性；好时机

Phrase(s): ***strong timeliness; timeliness principle***

◇ *The overall risk management process at a regular basis should address the verification of the consistency, timeliness and reliability of data sources used to run internal models, including the independence of such data sources.* 定期开展的综合风险管理程序评估应确认数据资源的一致性、时效性、应用数据库运行内部模型的可靠程度以及这些数据来源的独立程度。1（26）

timely ['taɪmlɪ] *adj.* 及时的；适时的

Phrase(s): ***timely adjustment; timely help***

◇ *Supervisors will monitor actions taken by the subsidiary to correct any capital shortfall and, if it is not corrected in a timely manner, the shortfall will also be deducted from the parent bank's capital.* 监管当局还应当监测子公司是否采取措施弥补资本的不足，如果措施不及时，则不足部分就应从银行的资本中扣除。1（2）

timetable ['taɪmteɪb(ə)l] *n.* 时间表；时刻表；课程表

Phrase(s): ***school timetable; travel timetable***

◇ *The timetable of this open tender is not under the tenderee's control; for the tender proposals' evaluation totally depends on the government supervision.* 这个公开招标的时间表不在招标人的控制之下；因为对投标方案的评估完全取决于政府监管。

title ['taɪt(ə)l] *n.* 冠军；标题；头衔；权利；字幕

Phrase(s): ***professional title; title tag***

◇ *The CEO of the famous footwear company gave up his title last week due to health problems; and his contributions to the company in the past two decades won him delicious retirement benefit*. 著名鞋业公司的首席执行官上周因健康问题放弃了他的头衔；在过去的二十年里对公司的贡献为他赢得了丰厚的退休福利。

tool [tuːl] *n.* 工具；用具

Phrase(s): *machine tool; tool storage*

◇ *In the case where a bank has multiple CRM covering a single exposure (e. g. a bank has both collateral and guarantee partially covering an exposure), the bank will be required to subdivide the exposure into portions covered by each type of CRM tool (e. g. portion covered by collateral, portion covered by guarantee) and the risk weighted assets of each portion must be calculated separately*. 如对单独一项风险暴露存在多项信用风险缓释技术（如果银行的风险暴露分别被部分抵押品和部分担保所抵补），则银行须将风险暴露再细分为每一信用风险缓释技术对应的部分（如抵押品部分、担保部分），每一部分的加权风险资产分别计算。1（37）

traded [treɪdɪd] *v.* 交易；贸易（trade 的过去分词形式）

Phrase(s): *publicly traded; amount traded*

◇ *If you are going to buy gold as a hedge against financial risks, you'd better choose some exchange-traded funds connected with gold because they are in lockstep with the gold price changes*. 如果你要买黄金作为防范金融风险的对冲，你最好选择一些与黄金挂钩的交易所交易基金，因为它们与黄金价格的变化同步。

trade finance [treɪd 'faɪnæns] *PHR.* 贸易融资

Phrase(s): *International Trade and Finance; Asian Trade and Finance*

◇ *International trade relies heavily on trade finance; many global banks provide multi-currency trade finance services to their customers including letters of credit issuance*. 国际贸易在很大程度上依赖于贸易融资；全球许多银行为它们的客户提供多种货币的贸易融资服务包括开立信用证。

tranches [trɑːnʃs] *n.* 部分；一份

Phrase(s): *senior tranches; equity tranches*

◇ *Securitisation tranches that are rated between BB+ and BB− will be risk weighted at 350%*. 评级在 BB ＋至 BB －之间的证券化头寸，其风险权重为 350%。1（13）

transaction [træn'zækʃ(ə)n] *n.* 交易；事务；办理；会报；学报

Phrase(s): ***securitisation transaction; transaction cost; accounting transaction***

◇ *The transaction fee of money transferring service in some African countries is extremely high; a10% charge of the total transferred value for international money transfer is not unusual.* 在一些非洲国家转账汇款的交易费用是非常高的，国际汇款收取汇款总额 10% 的手续费是正常的。

◇ *For some transactions, depending on the nature and frequency of the revaluation and remargining provisions, different holding periods are appropriate.* 对一些交易，考虑到特性、评估的频率和保证金调整情况，不同的持有期是恰当的。1（26）

transfer [træns'fɜː] *n.* 转让；转移；传递；过户；*vt.* 使转移；调任；*vi.* 转让；转学；换车

Phrase(s): ***data transfer; transfer function***

◇ *While the use of CRM techniques reduces or transfers credit risk, it simultaneously may increase other risks to the bank, such as legal, operational, liquidity and market risks.* 尽管使用风险缓释技术可降低或转移信用风险，但同时它可使银行承担其他的风险，如法律风险、操作风险、流动性风险和市场风险。1（18）

transferability [ˌtrænsfərə'bɪlətɪ] *n.* 可转移性；可转让性

Phrase(s): ***transferability detection; transferability coefficients***

◇ *National regulatory practices will determine the parameters and criteria, such as legal transferability, for assessing the amount and availability of surplus capital that could be recognised in bank capital.* 至于评估可计入银行资本的超额资本的数量及其可用性标准和参数，比如法律的可转换性，取决于各国的监管规定。1（3）

transferring ['trænsfərɪŋ] *v.* 移动；［计］转移

Phrase(s): ***transferring calls; transferring information***

◇ *During the roll-out period, supervisors will ensure that no capital relief is granted for intra-group transactions which are designed to reduce a banking group's aggregate capital charge by transferring credit risk among entities on the standardised approach, foundation and advanced IRB approaches.* 推广实施期内，监管当局要确保在使用标准法、IRB 初级法和 IRB 高级法时，集团内部通过在各个实体中转移信用风险来降低

集团总资本要求的内部交易不会起到减少资本要求的作用。1（48）

transformed [træns'fɔ:md] *adj.* transform 的变形

Phrase(s): *transformed ability; transformed section*

◇ *Risk weight functions are the means by which risk components are transformed into risk weighted assets and therefore capital requirements.* 风险权重函数是风险要素转换成风险加权资产及资本要求的方法。1（46）

transient ['trænzɪənt] *adj.* 短暂的；路过的

Phrase(s): *transient current; transient vibration*

◇ *This target is not expected to be used as a hard limit that would lead to ineligibility in the case of small or transient deviations.* 这样做的目的不是用这个比率作为硬性限额，硬性限额将导致在发生小的或短暂偏离限额情况下，循环零售贷款无法循环。1（43）

transition [træn'zɪʃən] *n.* 过渡；转变

Phrase(s): *transition economy; transition matrix*

◇ *The transition from the planned economy to the market economy takes many years; it is a process of trial and error.* 从计划经济向市场经济的转型需要很多年；这是一个反复试验的过程。

transitional [træn'zɪʃ(ə)n(ə)l] *adj.* 变迁的；过渡期的

Phrase(s): *transitional words; transitional economy*

◇ *The church-sponsored charity organization provides transitional homes for individuals and families who are temporarily stuck in financial difficulties; applications need to be submitted two weeks in advance.* 教会资助的慈善机构为暂时陷入经济困难的个人和家庭提供过渡住所；申请需要提前两个星期提交。

transparency [træn'spær(ə)nsɪ] *n.* 透明；透明度；幻灯片；有图案的玻璃

Phrase(s): *transparency management; transparency falloff*

◇ *An independent ratings process, internal review and transparency are control concepts addressed in the minimum IRB standards.* 独立的评级过程、内部审核和透明度是 IRB 法最低标准强调的内控概念。1（6）

transportation [trænspɔ:'teɪʃ(ə)n] *n.* 运输；运输系统；运输工具；流放

Phrase(s): *transportation business; urban transportation*

◇ *Before asking citizens to protect the environment by reducing car driving, governments around the world should make the public transportation network as convenient as possible.* 在要求市民减少开车以保护环境之前，世界各国政府应该尽可能方便地建设公共交通网络。

treasury stock ['treʒ(ə)rɪ stɒk] *PHR.* 库存股份

Phrase(s): ***treasury stock; treasury stock surplus; profit on treasury stock***

◇ *Treasury stock could either be stock which a corporation has issued and later reacquired from shareholders or be stock that has never been issued before.* 库存股票可以是一个公司发行后又从股东那里购回的股票；也可以是从未发行过的股票。

trend [trend] *n.* 趋势；倾向；走向

Phrase(s): ***trend analysis; economic trend***

◇ *Due to health concerns, there is a consumer trend that middle-class families reduce their coke drinking and sweet food eating greatly.* 鉴于对健康的关注，减少可乐和甜食摄入量已经成为中产阶级家庭的一种消费趋势。

treatment ['triːtm(ə)nt] *n.* 治疗；疗法；处理；对待

Phrase(s): ***preferential treatment; accounting treatment; IRB treatments***

◇ *The treatment of each asset class begins with presentation of the relevant risk weight function(s) followed by the risk components and other relevant factors, such as the treatment of credit risk mitigants.* 每一类资产的处理都讨论风险要素和其他相关因素构成的风险权重函数，例如对信用风险缓释工具的处理。1（38）

◇ *Medical treatment for incurable diseases requires a large amount of money; yet, it can only extend life in a miserable way.* 治疗疑难杂症需要大量的资金；然而，它只能以痛苦的方式延长寿命。

trigger ['trɪgə] *n.* 触发器；扳机；*v.* 触发；引起

Phrase(s): ***triggering factor; triggering element***

◇ *Banks estimates of EAD should reflect the possibility of additional drawings by the borrower up to and after the time a default event is triggered.* 银行对违约风险暴露的估计，应该反映在促发违约事件之时或之后借款人另外提款的可能性。1（84）

troubled ['trʌb(ə)ld] *adj.* 动乱的；不安的；混乱的；困惑的

Phrase(s): ***troubled industries; troubled economy***

◇ *Some economists hold the view that delayed retirement is a reflection as well as a reason of a troubled economy; what's worse, it cannot help improve the situation either.* 一些经济学家认为，延迟退休既是经济陷入困境的一种反应也是其原因；更糟糕的是，延迟退休不能帮助改善状况。

◇ *Recalling the troubled teenage years, the famous rock star expressed immense gratitude to his parents for tolerance and guidance.* 回顾坎坷的青少年时代，这位著名的摇滚明星对父母的宽容和指导表达了无限感激。

trustee [trʌs'tiː] *n.* 受托人；托管人；*vt.* 移交（财产或管理权）给受托人

◇ *A trustee is legally trusted by a beneficiary to manager his/her assets, thus the beneficiary's interest should always be the first concern.* 受托人由受益人委托依法管理他 / 她的资产，因此受益人的利益应该是首先要关注的。

trustor ['trʌstə] *n.* 委托人；信托人

Phrase(s): ***trustor system; audit trustor; trustor name***

◇ *The person who creates and funds a trust is called a trustor; only a trustor has the right to name a beneficiary or beneficiaries.* 建立一个信托基金并为之注入资金或资产的人被称为委托人；只有委托人有权利指定信托基金的受益人。

turnover ['tɜːnəʊvə] *n.* 翻覆；［贸易］周转率；成交量；营业额；流通量；半圆卷饼；失误

Phrase(s): ***inventory turnover; stock turnover***

◇ *An increase in the firm's total asset turnover increases the sales generated for each dollar in assets. This decreases the firm's need for new assets as sales grow and thereby increases the sustainable growth rate.* 企业总资产周转率的提高促进了销售的增加进而提高了资产价值。因为销售增长，降低了公司对新资产的需求，从而增加了可持续增长率。6（128）

typically ['tɪpɪkəlɪ] adv. 代表性地；作为特色地

Phrase(s): ***share typically; typically used***

◇ *In recognition that securitisations typically involve longer dated unsecured receivables, the one-year requirement has been relaxed on an exceptional basis.* 考虑到证券化涉及期限较长的无担保应收款，一年的期限要求在个别情况可以放宽。1（16）

U

unbundling [ˌʌn'bʌndliŋ] *v.* 把……分开；分拆收购；*n.* 分类计价

Phrase(s): ***unbundling strategy; unbundling bank***

◇*Many passengers believe that the unbundling airfare is actually an excuse for airline companies to compensate for their loss in discounted prices.* 许多乘客认为，机票解绑（乘客在付基本费用的基础上自选其他服务）实际上是航空公司补偿折扣机票损失的一个借口。

uncovered [ʌn'kʌvəd] *adj.* 未保险的；未覆盖的；被揭露的

Phrase(s): ***uncovered option***

◇*The secret of this investor's long time success has been uncovered by some statistical analysis; yet, many people still think they don't have as much luck as he has.* 这个投资者长期成功的秘密已被一些统计分析揭开；然而，许多人仍然认为自己没有和他一样的运气。

undercapitalized [ʌndə'kæpɪtəlaɪzd] *adj.* 资本不足的

Phrase(s): ***undercapitalized firm***

◇*Undercapitalized enterprises are the real culprits of financial crisis; thus, setting the minimum capital requirement is the most important regulatory task.* 资金不足的企业是金融危机的罪魁祸首；因此，设置最低资本要求是最重要的监管任务。

underlying [ʌndə'laɪɪŋ] *adj.* 潜在的；根本的；基础的

Phrase(s): ***underlying assets; underlying risks***

◇ *The term specialized lending is associated with the financing of individual projects where the repayment is highly dependent on the performance of the underlying pool or collateral.* 专业贷款是指单个项目提供的融资，其还款与对应的资产池或抵押品的营运情况紧密相关。1（14）

underperform [ˌʌndəpə'fɔːm] *vt.* 弱于大盘；表现不佳

Phrase(s): ***underperform the market***

◇ *Please be careful when choosing a managed fund for your pension investment, because most so-called actively managed fund underperformed their benchmarks.* 请小心选择你的养老金投资管理基金，因为大多数所谓的积极管理型基金运作都比基准差。

underprice [ʌndə'praɪs] *v.* 低估；折价

Phrase(s): ***stock underpricing; bond underpricing***

◇ *The big increase of stock value in IPO doesn't guarantee a blue chip, for some companies will underprice their stock at the beginning to trade for a good sales.* 首次公开募股时股票价值大幅增加不能保证这只股票就是蓝筹，一些公司为了开局好的销售，会把股票价格压低。

undersubscribed [ʌndəsəbsk'raɪd] *adj.* 认购不足的

◇ *Undersubscribed situation is often caused by inappropriate pricing; and future security price will also be influenced by the situation.* 认购不足的情况往往是由不恰当的定价引起的；而未来的证券价格也会受到认购不足的影响。

undervalue [ʌndə'væljuː] *v.* 低估；价值被低估

Phrase(s): ***undervalue invoice; undervalue price***

◇ *Some companies choose to repurchase their stock when it is undervalued; if they can time the repurchase effectively, they probably will gain higher returns.* 有些公司在自己的股票被低估时，选择回购自己的股票；如果回购的时机有效，它们可能会获得更高的回报。

underwriting ['ʌndəˌraɪtɪŋ] *n.* 保险业；证券包销；授信；*v.* 给……保险；承保

Phrase(s): ***underwriting account; underwriting fee; securities underwriting***

◇ *In general, the risk bucketing process will reflect the seller's underwriting practices and the heterogeneity of its customers.* 通常，划分风险栏的过程反映了销售方授信做法

及客户的异质性。1（87）

◇ *Insurance is a typical example of underwriting; underwriters of an insurance company will help it when lots of people file claims at the same time after a big natural disaster.* 保险是一个典型的承保例子，一次大的自然灾害发生时，会有很多人同时申请索赔，承保人将有助于保险公司及时赔付。

undistributed [ʌndɪ'strɪbjuːtɪd] *adj.* 未分配的

◇ *Remaining undistributed money from this donation will be kept for next charity project.* 本次捐款中未分配的余款将用于下一个慈善项目。

unemployment [ʌnɪm'plɒɪm(ə)nt] *n.* 失业；失业状况

Phrase(s): ***unemployment rate; unemployment benefit***

◇ *Unemployment rate varies from one country to another in the world and it is one of the most important indexes to judge economic performance.* 各个国家的失业率不一样，它是衡量经济表现的重要指标之一。

◇ *In some European countries, jobless people can apply for unemployment insurance to support families and their own daily lives.* 在一些欧洲国家，失业者可以申请失业保险，以支持家庭和他们自己的日常生活。

unlisted [ʌn'lɪstɪd] *adj.* 未上市的；未编入册的

Phrase(s): ***unlisted securities market; publicly unlisted company***

◇ *Real estate investment trusts have an upward trend in the U. S. stock market in recent years, however, there are also unlisted REITs; both are greatly influenced by commercial property market.* 最近几年房地产投资信托基金在美国股票市场有上升趋势，但也有非上市的房地产投资信托基金；商业房地产市场对两者的影响较大。

unquoted [ˌʌn'kwəʊtid] *adj.* 未上市的

Phrase(s): ***unquoted issue; unquoted securities***

◇ *It is difficult to value the unquoted securities, since they stopped trading on an exchange either due to failure to meet the listing requirements or other internal reasons of the issuing companies.* 很难给非上市证券估值，因为它们已经不在交易所交易了，可能由于不符合上市条件或发行公司其他的内部原因。

unrealized [ʌn'rɪəlaɪzd] *adj.* 未实现的

Phrase(s): ***unrealized revenue; unrealized exchange reserve***

◇*Revenue is recognized on an income statement when the earnings process is virtually completed and an exchange of goods or services has occurred. Therefore, the unrealized appreciation from owning property will not be recognized as income.* 盈利过程事实上已完成，商品或服务的交换已经发生的情况下，收益才体现在损益表上。因此，拥有财产中未实现增值的部分将不被确认为收入。6（79）

unsecured ['ʌnsɪ'kjʊəd] *adj.* 无担保的；未固定的

Phrase(s): ***unsecured creditors; unsecured loan; unsecured accounts***

◇ *Banks must estimate the volatility of the collateral instrument or foreign exchange mismatch individually: estimated volatilities must not take into account the correlations between unsecured exposure, collateral and exchange rates.* 银行必须逐一地估计抵押品或外汇错配的折扣系数。估计出的折扣系数一定不可考虑未保护的风险暴露、抵押品和汇率的联系。1（25）

upside ['ʌpsaɪd] *n.* 上部；上面；好处

◇ *Most Chinese parents pay for their children's college tuitions; while most American college students find their own way out, one surprising upside is that they learn to take financial responsibilities on their own and become very cautious in their financial planning.* 大多数中国父母为孩子支付大学学费；而大多数美国大学生自己寻找出路，一个令人惊讶的好处是他们学会了独自承担经济责任，而且在财务规划时变得非常谨慎。

U. S. Treasury [juːɛs'treʒ(ə)rɪ] *PHR.* 美国财政部

◇ *Generally speaking, if economies go down and political situation is not stable in other countries, people would buy more of their own governments' bonds, such as U. S. Treasury bills, though the yield is quite low.* 一般来说，如果经济往下走，而且其他国家的政治形势不稳定的情况下，人们会更多地购买本国政府的债券，如美国国债，尽管收益率很低。

usufruct ['juːzjʊfrʌkt] *n.* 使用权；用益权

Phrase(s): ***usufruct loans; mutual usufruct***

◇ *As a professor, he has the usufruct in this house which was built by his university;*

yet, his children have no right to inherit it from their father. 作为一名教授，他享有这所房子的用益权，房子是他所在的大学造的；然而，他的孩子们没有权利从父亲那里继承它。

utilization [ˌjuːtɪlaɪˈzeɪʃən] *n.* 利用；使用

◇ *Another utilization of cash flow analysis is setting the bid price on a project.* 现金流分析的另一个应用是在一个项目上设定投标价格。6（252）

◇ *When using credit card, always be careful with your utilization ratio; only spend an amount which you can guarantee to repay within the interest-free period.* 使用信用卡的时候，注意你的信用卡利用率；只花能保证在免息期内偿还的数额。

V

valid ['vælɪd] *adj.* 有效的；有根据的；合法的；正当的

Phrase(s): ***valid bilateral netting arrangement; valid endorsement***

◇ *Valid bilateral netting arrangement increased the efficiency of financial system overwhelmingly.* 有效双边净额结算协议极大地提高了金融系统的运行效率。

◇ *Many big shopping malls offer back-to-school promotions to students, as long as you present your valid student ID, you will enjoy discounts when buying stationeries.* 许多大商场在学术返校季提供促销，只要你出示有效学生证，您在购买文具时将享受优惠折扣。

value ['vælju:] *n.* 风险；*vt.* 估价

Phrase(s): ***value at risk; option value***

◇ *The appropriateness of the market inputs for the particular position being valued should be reviewed regularly by banks.* 银行应该对在计算特定头寸价值时所采用的市场参数进行定期审查。1（132）

◇ *Many snack shops in China conduct loyalty program; customers' spending each time can be converted into points and points can be used to offset part of the future spending; these shops find extra value in this strategy.* 在中国许多零食店开展忠诚顾客反馈活动；客户每次消费的金额可以转化为积分，积分可以用来抵消未来消费的一部分；这些商店从这个策略里找到了额外价值。

value-added tax(abbr. VAT) ['vælju:ædɪd ˌtæks] *n.* 增值税

◇ *The calculation of value-added tax varies from country to country, however, the tax burden will finally be shifted to consumers.* 增值税计算因国而异，但是税收负担最终都会转移到消费者身上。

value at risk ['vælju: æt rɪsk] *PHR.* 在险价值

Phrase(s): ***conditional value at risk***

◇ *The value at risk is the amount of capital required to ensure, with a high degree of certainty that the company will remain solvent.* 风险值的定义是一定数量的资金量，它可以极大地确保一个公司有偿还债务的能力。

variance ['veərɪəns] *n.* 变异；变化；方差

Phrase(s): ***variance-covariance matrix; variance rate; variance swap***

◇ *In the U. S. , if some private property owners want to renovate their houses or construct more houses on their land, they must apply for a zoning variance to the government; this process usually takes lots of money and time before you finally get the permission.* 在美国如果一些私人业主想装修自己的房子或在他们的土地上建更多的房子，他们必须向政府提出土地使用变更申请；在你得到最后许可前，这个过程通常需要很多的时间和金钱。

◇ *In a date set, variance is used to measure how far each number is away from the mean; variance and standard deviation of the distribution of the returns are the two most important ways to measure investment risks.* 在一个数据集上，方差是用来衡量每个数和均值之间的距离；方差和收益分配的标准偏差是衡量投资风险的最重要的两种方式。

variation [veərɪ'eɪʃ(ə)n] *n.* 变量；变化；变动

Phrase(s): ***variation margin; variation coefficient***

◇ *Internal models must adequately explain historical price variation, capture both the magnitude and changes in the composition of potential concentrations, and be robust to adverse market environments.* 内部模型必须完全解释历史价格变化，捕捉潜在的集中性风险构成范围及变化，充分反映不利的市场环境。1（95）

vega ['veɪgə] *n.* 期权或其他衍生品价格变化同波动率变化的比率

Phrase(s): ***Vega-Neutral Portfolio***

◇ *Vega is the derivative of the option value with respect to the volatility of the underlying asset.* Vega 是期权价值的衍生品对于标的资产波动率的比率。

vendor ['vendə] *n.* 卖方

Phrase(s): ***vendor market***

◇ *One business relationship is the vendor's pricing model, which may influence the selection of a particular product.* 业务关系的一个方面就是卖主的价格模型，它可能会影响到某个特定产品的选择。

venture ['ventʃə] *n.* 冒险事业；商业冒险

Phrase(s): ***venture capital; venture company; joint venture***

◇ *A joint venture will benefit from two parties to make promising investments which a single company can never afford.* 合资公司将从双方获得资本进行有前途的投资，这样的投资往往是单个公司承受不起的。

venture capital ['ventʃə 'kæpɪt(ə)l] *PHR.* 风险投资

◇ *One characteristic of venture capital is high risk; thus financing through banks or ordinary financial institutions is less possible.* 风险投资的一个特点是高风险，因此，通过银行或普通金融机构的融资是不太可能的。

◇ *Venture capital is often pursued by small, start-up companies who specialize in new high-tech products.* 小规模初创的高新技术公司往往需要风险投资。

vesting ['vestɪŋ] *n.* （雇工）保留退休金的权利；兑现条款

Phrase(s): ***vesting period; proper vesting***

◇ *After working in the same company for more than 30 years, he finally reached the moment to accrue all his benefits, rights and money listed in the vesting contract.* 在同一家公司工作了30年多后，他终于等到了这一时刻：获得所有退休兑现条款上列出的福利、权利和金钱。

◇ *It is a pity that the share vesting period is longer than your working period in this company, so you can't own these shares when leaving unless you buy them at a much higher price than the original price.* 可惜的是股权归属期比你在这家公司工作的时间长，所以

你离职时不能拥有这些股票，除非你用比原来价格高得多的价格买下来。

viability [ˌvaɪəˈbɪlətɪ] *n.* 健全性；稳健性；合法性

Phrase(s): ***viability of currency policy***

◇ *Where some issuers of the receivables are reliant on the borrower for their viability or the borrower and the issuers belong to a common industry, the attendant risks should be taken into account in the setting of margins for the collateral pool as a whole.* 应收账款的发行人依赖于左右其生存的借款人或借款人和发行人都属于同一行业，在设定抵押品整体收益时，应该考虑两者伴生的风险。1（93）

◇ *Many people are skeptical about the viability of big department stores and shopping malls since so many families do shopping just in front of their computers now.* 很多人对大百货公司和购物中心的生存能力持怀疑态度，因为很多家庭现在都在电脑前购物。

virement [ˈvirimənt] *n.* 转账；票据交换；剩余基金挪用

Phrase(s): ***virement translation***

◇ *Virement has anorigin in French, meaning transfer in English.* Virement 起源于法语，在英语中是转账的意思。

VIX (Volatility Index) [viːaɪɛks] *abbr.* 波动率指数

Phrase(s): ***options VIX; stock market VIX***

◇ *VIX is a key measure of near-term market volatility expectations. The higher the VIX index is, the more worried investors are about the short-term market performance.* VIX 是衡量市场近期波动预期的关键指数。波动率指数越高，投资者对短期市场表现就越担心。

◇ *As the bull market continues to extend, investors begin to be more cautious about their long-term investments, which can be seen from the VIX index, or so-called "fear index".* 随着牛市继续延续，投资者开始对他们的长期投资更为谨慎，这可以从 VIX 指数（或所谓的“恐慌指数”）中看出来。

volatility [ˌvɒləˈtɪlətɪ] *n.* 波动率

Phrase(s): ***volatility skew; volatility smile; volatility surface; volatility swap; volatility term structure***

◇ *Estimates of the return volatility of equity investments must incorporate relevant and available data, information, and methods.* 对股权投资收益波动性的估计必须体现相关的、可得到的数据、信息和方法。1（96）

◇ *To my surprise, according to a study on stock price volatility in the past 90 years, there are actually no significant changes in return volatility on a monthly basis.* 出乎我意料的是，根据对过去90年的股票价格波动的研究，如果按月计算收益波动率的变化并不明显。

Volcker Rule ['vəʊlkə 'ruːl] *PHR.* 沃克尔法则（以禁止银行业自营交易为主，将自营交易与商业银行业务分离，即禁止银行利用参加联邦存款保险的存款，进行自营交易、投资对冲基金或者私募基金）

◇ *"Volcker rule" is a financial regulation in the U. S. , which prohibits banks to use customer's deposits or government insured money for risky investment; this is especially useful to maintain the country's financial stability.* "沃克尔法则"是美国的一个金融监管法规，禁止银行动用客户存款和政府保险存款进行高风险投资。

◇ *"Volcker rule"strengthened the government regulation on financial system; it is a heavy blow to big banks which make huge profit for their own accounts, not customers' accounts.* "沃克尔法则"加强了政府对金融系统的监管；它给那些靠自营交易带来巨大利益的大银行造成沉重的打击，客户并没有从中受益。

volume ['vɒljuːm] *n.* 量；体量

Phrase(s): ***volume of business; volume of trade***

◇ *Bonds are bought and sold in enormous quantities every day. You may be surprised to learn that the trading volume in bonds on a typical day is many, many times larger than the trading volume in stocks.* 债券每天大量买进和卖出。你可能会惊讶地得知，正常情况下，每天的债券交易量比股票交易量大很多、很多倍。6（302）

voluntary [ˌvɒləntri] *adj.* 无偿的；自律的；志愿的

Phrase(s): ***voluntary agreement; voluntary code***

◇ *Voluntary liquidation is a measure to protect investors in stock market in high risk.* 自动清盘机制是一种在高风险市场中保护投资者的措施。

vote [vəʊt] *v.* 投票表决；投票； *n.* 投票权；投票；表决；投票数；决议

Phrase(s): ***voting share; vote of confidence; voting seats***

◇ *Generally speaking, directors of a corporation board will be elected once a year at the shareholders' meeting; votes are closely related to shares in hand.* 一般来说，公司的董事会每年在股东大会上选举一次；投票与持有的股票数量密切相关。

voucher [ˈvaʊtʃə(r)] *n.* 代金券；收据；凭证

Phrase(s): ***gift voucher; hotel voucher; voucher program***

◇ *There is significant difference between a voucher and a coupon; you pay no extra money with a voucher since the money needed has been prepaid, but you pay at a discount with a coupon.* 代金券和优惠券之间有显著不同；使用代金券时你不用再付额外的钱，因为所需要的钱已预付，但使用优惠券你只是享受折扣价格。

W

WACC (Weighted Average Cost of Capital) ['weɪtɪd 'æv(ə)rɪdʒ kɒst (ə)v 'kæpɪt(ə)l] *abbr.* 加权平均资金成本

◇ *The precise calculation of WACC will measure whether a project is worth investing or not; it is worth investing only when the return is higher than the weighted average cost of capital.* WACC 的精确计算可以来衡量一个项目是否值得投资；只有当回报高于加权平均资金成本时，项目才能获利，即值得投资。

wage [weɪdʒ] *n.* 工资；代价；报偿

Phrase(s): ***wage freeze; wage base; minimum wage***

◇ *Some governments force employers to raise their employees' pay by setting higher minimum wage.* 一些政府通过设定更高的最低工资水平来迫使雇主提高员工的薪酬。

waiting period ['weɪtɪŋ 'pɪərɪəd] *PHR.* 等待期间（指向美国证券交易委员会进行新证券登记注册至证券获准在公开市场出售的一段时间，一般是 20 天。）

◇ *One of the important reasons for this company to list on the New York Stock Exchangeis the long waiting period and great difficulty in operation before being listed on domestic stock market.* 选择到纽交所挂牌上市的其中一个重要原因是在国内证券市场上市要经过很长的等待期，并且操作难度大。

Wall Street [wɔːl striːt] *PHR.* 华尔街（美国纽约市曼哈顿南区的一条街道，集中了美国大财团和金融机构）；美国的金融市场；美国金融界

◇ *Wall Street is not only good at making rich people richer, but also excels in making movies to tell people these legends; Wall Street itself is a wise investor.* 华尔街善于把富人变得更富，而且擅长制作电影告诉人们这些传说；华尔街本身就是一个明智的投资者。

Wanted For Cash ['wɒntɪd f(ə)r kæʃ] *PHR.* 当日交割购股

◇ *Wanted For Cash is a piece of notice that requires a bidder to cash for same day settlement of a block of a specified security.* 当日交割购股是一则书面通知，要求买方投标者必须在结算日当天为一批指定的证券支付现金。

warehouse ['weəhaʊs] *n.* 仓库；货栈；*v.* 把……存入仓库

◇ *In some crowded cities, urban planners wanted to reconstruct large public warehouse roofs to be parking lots, swimming pools or botanic garden in the air.* 在拥挤的城市，城市规划者想要把大型公共仓库的屋顶改造成停车场、游泳池或者空中植物园。

warrant ['wɒr(ə)nt] *n.* 权证；认购权证；保证；认股权证；*v.* 授权；批准；担保

Phrase(s): ***equity warrant; search warrant; warrant product***

◇ *If an issuer has a short-term facility with an assessment that warrants a risk weight of 150%, all unrated claims, whether long-term or short-term, should also receive a 150% risk weight, unless the bank uses recognised credit risk mitigation techniques for such claims.* 如果根据发行人短期便利的评级，应当给予 150% 的风险权重，所有的未评级债权，不管是长期的还是短期的，也应当给予 150% 的风险权重，除非银行对这些债权采用了经认定的信用风险缓释技术。1（17）

wash sale [wɒʃ seɪl] *PHR.* 虚卖；虚抛；虚假交易

◇ *Wash sale is a tax deduction strategy which enables investors to sell their stock at a loss and then repurchase it very quickly, so tax payment will be deducted or deferred.* 虚抛是寻求减税的一个策略，即投资者亏本卖出股票然后迅速回购，以此获得减税或延期缴纳的便利。

wasting asset ['weɪstɪŋ 'æset] *PHR.* 减耗资产；递耗资产

◇ *The value of wasting assets keep declining as time goes on; cars, machinery and equipment are common wasting assets.* 消耗性资产的价值随着时间的推移不断下降；汽车、机械、设备是常见的消耗性资产。

watch list [wɒtʃ lɪst] *PHR.* 在查证券；监视清单

◇ *The company has be included in the regulators' watch list due to selling and repurchasing large quantities of identical stock within very short period of time.* 该公司已被列入监管人员的监查名单，由于在很短的时间内出售和回购大量相同的股票。

wealth [welθ] *n.* 财富；财产；资源

Phrase(s): *Stealth Wealth; wealth management*

◇ *Wealth management service generates nice profit for banks for the target group of this service consists of high-income people.* 财富管理服务为银行带来了不错的利润，因为它的目标群体主要是是高收入人群。

Weak Form Efficiency [wiːk fɔːm ɪ'fɪʃ(ə)nsɪ] *PHR.* 弱式有效

◇ *Weak Form Efficiency indicates that the performance of a stock in the past doesn't have relations with its current and future performance; technical analysis using models is not reliable either.* 弱式效率表明股票过去的表现与当前和未来的表现没有关系；利用模型的技术分析也是不可靠的。

weekend effect [wiːk'ɛnd ɪ'fect] *PHR.* 周末效应

◇ *It is necessary to figure out whether the stock price drop on Monday resulted from the weekend effect or was due to the release of a poor financial report.* 有必要搞清楚周一股票价格的下跌是因为周末效应，还是由于公布了一份糟糕的财务报告。

weight [weɪt] *n.* 加权

Phrase(s): *risk weight*

◇ *The exposure amount after risk mitigation will be multiplied by the risk weight of the counterparty to obtain the risk weighted asset amount for the collate ralised transaction.* 风险缓释后的风险暴露乘以交易对象的风险权重，则为抵押后的风险加权资产。1（23）

weighted average coupon ['weɪtɪd 'æv(ə)rɪdʒ 'kuːpɒn] *PHR.* 加权平均利息

◇ *The duration of the fixed-rate coupon bond is the weighed average of the duration of the floater and inverse floater.* 固定息票率债券的存续期是浮动利率证券的存续期和逆向浮动利率证券的存续期的加权平均数。

weighted average life (WAL) ['weɪtɪd 'æv(ə)rɪdʒ laɪf] *PHR.* 加权平均回收期

◇ *Weighted average life measures how long your bonds will be paid back including principal and interest on average.* 加权平均期限衡量的是平均意义上，你的债券（包括本金和利息）多久能偿清。

weighted average maturity (WAM) ['weɪtɪd 'æv(ə)rɪdʒ mə'tʃʊərətɪ] *PHR.* 加权平均期限

◇ *The weighted average maturity can be used to measure whether a mortgage-backed security has high risk or not.* 加权平均期限可以用来衡量一种住房抵押贷款支持证券是否具有高风险。

well diversified portfolio [wel daɪ'vɜːsɪfaɪd pɔːt'fəʊlɪəʊ] *PHR.* 已分散风险之投资组合

◇ *A well diversified portfolio is the same as putting fragile eggs in different baskets; investing in different kinds of securities will generally have higher yield and lower risk.* 一个多元化的投资组合就如同把易碎的鸡蛋放在不同的篮子里一样；投资于不同种类的证券通常会有更高的回报和更低的风险。

whole life insurance [həʊl laɪf ɪn'ʃʊər(ə)ns] *PHR.* 终身寿险

Phrase(s): ***limited payment whole life insurance***

◇ *Whole life insurance is a good choice for those who don't want their deaths to impact their family members financially since this type of insurance covers funeral and other final expenses.* 终身保险对那些不希望他们的死亡影响他们家庭成员财务支出的人是一个很好的选择，因为这种类型的保险包括葬礼和其他最终费用。

wholesale ['həʊlseɪl] *n.* 批发；大规模买卖；*adj.* 批发的；adv. 大量地；大规模地

Phrase(s): ***wholesale price; wholesale trade; wholesale supplier***

◇ *Walking through some big wholesale markets in African continent, you will surely know that business is flourishing and money is flowing.* 穿行在非洲大陆一些大的批发市场，你一定会发现那里生意红火，资金流动。

◇ *Nowadays, many big cities in the world have wholesale clubs open to ordinary consumers such as Sam's Club and Metro; they mainly sell goods at bulks.* 目前在世界上许多大城市都有对普通消费者开放的批发俱乐部如山姆会员店和麦德龙；它们主要出售量贩商品。

wholesale mortgage ['həʊlseɪl 'mɔːgɪdʒ] *PHR.* 批发抵押

Phrase(s): ***wholesale mortgage banking; wholesale mortgage lending***

◇ *Applying for a wholesale mortgage, you are hopeful to get a lower rate and more lender options; wholesale mortgage is one of the triggers of subprime crisis.* 申请批发抵押贷款，你有希望得到较低的利率和更多的贷款人选择；批发抵押贷款是次贷危机的诱因之一。

Wiener ['wiːnə] *n.* 维纳

Phrase(s): ***Wiener process***

◇ *The Wiener process describes a variable whose change is measured to t.* 维纳过程描述了一个依赖 *t* 的变量。

winding up ['waɪndɪŋ ʌp] *PHR.* 清算；停业清理

◇ *The company is now in the process of winding up; all the remaining assets will be sold to pay off all the creditors.* 公司现在处于清盘的过程中；所有剩余的资产将被出售以偿还所有债权人。

with dividend [wɪð 'dɪvdɪend] *PHR.* 附有红利；附有股利

◇ *Stocks with dividend are very attractive to investors because dividends provide them with financial security to some extend, especially in low-interest rate period.* 附有股利的股票对投资者非常有吸引力，因为股息为他们提供了一定程度上的金融安全，特别是在低利率时期。

◇ *Companies which have issued stocks with dividend will put up "Dividend Initiation" notice on their official websites as well as other media channels to inform their investors that they begin to serve dessert.* 发行附股息股票的公司会通过其官方网站以及其他媒体渠道发布“首次发放股利”通知，告知投资者投资的甜头开始了。

withholding tax [wɪð'həʊldɪŋ tæks] *PHR.* 代扣所得税（指企事业雇主代替政府从雇员薪金中扣除的所得税）

◇ *Governments usually have different income taxes withheld from residents and nonresidents of a country; the withholding tax system improves governments'efficiency in collecting income taxes.* 政府通常对居民和非居民有不同的所得税扣缴税率；代扣税制度提高了政府征收所得税的效率。

without recourse [wɪ'ðaʊt rɪ'kɔːs] *PHR.* 无追索权

Phrase(s): ***without recourse to drawer; an endorsement without recourse; discounted bills without recourse; credit without recourse***

◇ *If the bank considers that the obligor is unlikely to pay its credit obligations to the banking group in full, without recourse by the bank to actions such as realising security (if held), then a default could probably happen.* 如果银行认定，除非采取追索措施，如变现抵押品（如果存在的话），借款人可能无法全额偿还对银行集团的债务，则认为违约发生。1（80）

with rights [wɪð raɪts] *PHR.* 有追索权；附认股权；有优惠认股权

◇ *Existing shareholders are granted with rights to buy new shares at a lower price in seasoned equity offerings.* 现有股东有权以较低的价格购买新股。

working capital ['wɜ: kɪŋ 'kæpɪt(ə)l] *PHR.* 营运资本；运用资本

Phrase(s): ***net working capital***

◇ *Working capital is defined as current assets minus current liabilities; if the result is in a declining tread, it sends out a warning to stakeholders that the company is in poor performance.* 营运资本是指流动资产减去流动负债；如果结果呈下降的趋势，则是对利益相关者发出公司业绩不佳的警告。

World Bank [wɜ:ld bæŋk] *PHR.* 世界银行

◇ *The World Bank and the International Monetary Fund keep cutting their forecasts towards global growth recently due to sluggish economy in both developed and emerging countries.* 世界银行和国际货币基金组织最近由于发达国家和新兴国家的经济不景气，继续调低对全球经济增长速度的预测。

World Trade Organization (WTO) ['wɜ:ld 'treɪdˌɔ:gənaɪˈzeɪʃn] *PHR.* 世界贸易组织

◇ *After Brexit, the trade between Britain and European countries will be governed under the World Trade Organization terms rather than the internal terms of the European Union.* 英国脱欧后，英国和欧洲国家之间的贸易属于世界贸易组织条款管辖下，而不是欧盟的内部贸易条款。

worth [wɜ:θ] *n.* 价值；*adj.* 值得的；有价值的

Phrase(s): ***risk-worth; be worth doing***

◇ *Please note Bitcoin has not been recognized by any government and bank in the world as a legal currency; in real world legal transactions, it is worth nothing.* 请注意比特

币并没有被世界上任何政府和银行承认为法定货币；在现实世界的合法交易中，它是没有价值的。

write-down ['raɪtdaʊn] *n.* 账面价值的故意降低；债务减记

Phrase(s): ***inventory write-down; write-down bonds***

◇ *The book value of the stockshares in this company had a write-down when they recalled their products in the market and caused a fall of their stock.* 公司召回市场上的产品造成了股票下跌，引起股票账面价值减记。

◇ *The percentage of the write-down on Greek holdings has long been a controversial topic among big creditors of Greece, such as Germany and France.* 希腊债务减记的百分比问题一直以来都是希腊各大债权人（如德国、法国）之间一个有争议的话题。

write-off ['raitɔf] *n.* （债务的）取消；注销；冲销；减计

Phrase(s): ***tax write-off; receipt write-off***

◇ *All exposures are measured as the amount legally owed to the bank, i. e. gross of specific provisions or partial write-offs.* 风险暴露的总额都以法律意义上借款人欠银行的数量来计量，不考虑专项准备或部分冲销。1（56）

wrong-way risk [rɒŋweɪ rɪsk] *PHR.* 错向风险

Phrase(s): ***specific wrong-way risk***

◇ *There is a high potential of wrong-way risk when the counterparty and the underling issuer are one and the same.* 交易对手和标的证券发行人合二为一时，错向风险的发生率极高。

X

XEROX ['zɪərɒks] *v.* 复印；印制；*n.* 施乐公司；复印印制品

◇ *XEROX is a leading supplier of digital and information products in the world; they produce both office digital devices and large printers for production process.* 施乐公司是一家世界领先的数字信息产品供应商；它们既生产办公数码设备也制造生产过程中使用的大型打印机。

Y

Yankee bond ['jæŋki bɒnd] *PHR.* 扬基债券

◇ *A Yankee bond is a dollar denominated bond sold in the U. S. by a non-U. S. issuer.* 扬基债券是指以美元为计值货币由非美国发行者在美国发售的债券。7（33）

yardstick ['jɑːdstɪk] *n.* 衡量；评价的标准；尺度

Phrase(s): ***economic yardstick; weighted yardstick***

◇ *Performance used to be measured by yardsticks such as return on assets (ROA).* 绩效过去是由一些指标来衡量的，例如资产回报率（ROA）。

◇ *For some experienced investors, the increase rate in book value per share is a very important yardstick to measure a company's investment success.* 对于一些有经验的投资者来说，每股账面价值的增长率是衡量一个公司投资是否成功的非常重要的尺度。

yen [jen] *n.* 日元（日本货币单位）

◇ *One-year subscription to the Economist magazine will cost you 41 000 in Japanese yen or 2 000 in Chinese rmb approximately.* 订阅一年期的《经济学人》杂志大概需要花费 41 000 日元或 2 000 元人民币。

yield [jiːld] *n.* 产量；收益

Phrase(s): ***yield curve; high-yield bond***

◇ *If the government's treasury bills have a declining trend in yield, it shows that investors see a slowdown or even worse situation in economy and seek security by shifting from high-risk investments.* 如果政府国债收益率有下降的趋势，这表明投资者看到经

济增长放缓甚至恶化的局面，从高风险投资转向寻求安全保护。

YTM(yield to maturity) [jiːld tə mə'tʃʊərətɪ] *abbr.* 到期收益率

◇ *Please do not confuse a bond's yield to maturity with its current yield; the former will only be realized when the bond mature, yet the latter is the bond's annual coupon divided by its price.* 请不要将债券的到期收益率和本期收益率混为一谈，前者只会在债券到期时才实现，而后者则是债券的年息除以其价格得到的比率。

Z

zero H ['zɪərəʊ eɪtʃ] *PHR.* 零折扣系数

Phrase(s): ***zero haircutting***

◇ *For repo-style transactions where the following conditions are satisfied, and the counterparty is a core market participant, supervisors may choose not to apply the haircuts specified in the comprehensive approach and may instead apply a zero H.* 对满足以下条件的回购交易，并且交易对象为核心市场参与者，监管当局可不使用综合法所规定的折扣系数，而使用零折扣系数。1（27）

zero-probability ['zɪərəʊprɒbə'bɪlɪtɪ] *n.* 零概率

Phrase(s): ***zero-probability events; zero-probability estimate***

◇ *To avoid this problem, we condition on σ-algebras and not on single zero-probability events.* 为了避免这个问题，我们将条件基于 σ 代数而不是基于单独的零概率时间。5（60）

zero-sum game ['zɪərəʊ'sʌm geɪm] *PHR.* 零和游戏；零和博弈

◇ *The IPO process is actually a zero-sum game between the listing company and its public investors; insider investors already get profit when they buy stock at a cheaper price.* 首次公开募股实际上是上市公司与公众投资者之间的零和博弈，公司内部投资者以低价购买股票时已经开始获利了。

List of Reference Books

（参考文献）

[1] Basel Committee on Banking Supervision. (2003). *Overview of The New Basel Capital Accord*. Basel, Switzerland: Bank for International Settlements.

[2] Garp, P. J. (2009). *Financial Risk Manager Handbook*(5th ed.). Hoboken, New Jersey: John Wiley & Sons, Inc.

[3] Marks, J. (2007). *Check Your English Vocabulary For Banking And Finance* (2nd ed.). Great Britain: A & C Black London.

[4] Meulbroek, L.& Barnett, J. (2000). *Honeywell, Inc. and Integrated Risk Management*. Retrieved November 2nd, 2016 from Harvard Business School official website: https: //cb.hbsp.harvard.edu/cbmp/product/200036-PDF-ENG.

[5] Rachev, S. T. , Mittnik, S. , Fabozzi, F. J. , Focardi, S. M. & Jasic, T. (2007). *Financial Econometrics: From Basis to Advanced Modeling Techniques*. Hoboken, New Jersey: John Wiley & Sons, Inc.

[6] Ross, S. A. , Westerfield, R. W. & Jaffe, J. (2012). *Corporate Finance*(9th ed). New York, NY: McGraw-Hill/Irwin.

[7] Bodie, Z. , Kane,A. & Marcus, A. J. (2012). *Investments*(9th ed). Jointly published by McGraw - Hill Education (Asia) and China Machine Press.

[8] Coogan-Pushner, D. & Bouteille, S. (2013). *The Handbook of Credit Risk Management: Originating, Assessing, and Managing Credit Exposures*. Hoboken, New

Jersy: John Wiley & Sons, Inc.

[9] Jorion, P. (2007). *Value at Risk: The Benchmark for Controlling Market Risk* (3rd ed). New York, NY: McGraw- Hill Professional.

[10] Szylar, C. (2014). *Handbook of Market Risk*. Hoboken, New Jersy: John Wiley & Sons Inc.

[11] Benjamin, J. (2007). *Financial Law*. Oxford: Oxford University Press.

[12] Girling, P. X. (2013). *Operational Risk Management: A Complete Guide to a Successful Operational Risk Framework*. Hoboken, New Jersey: John Wiley & Sons Inc.

[13] Fabozzi, F. J. & Kothari, V. (2008). *Introduction to Securitization*. Hoboken, New Jersey: John Wiley & Sons Inc.

[14] Paulson, H. M. (JR) (2010). *On the Brink: Inside the Race to Stop the Collapse of the Global Financial System*. New York, NY: Hachette Book Group.

[15] Scheweser. (2015). Schweser Notes for the FRM Exam. Kaplan University School of Professional and Continuing Education.

[16] Jones , D. (1972). *English Pronouncing Dictionary*. London: J. M. Dent & Sons Ltd/New.

[17] The official website of Financial Times:

https://www.ft.com/

http: //www.investopedia.com/

[18] The online dictionary website of youdao:

http://dict.youdao.com/

[19] The online dictionary website of baidu:

http://dict.baidu.com/

http: //xueshu.baidu.com/